Secrets of the Carolina Coast

100 Secrets of the Carolina Coast

A Guide to the Best Undiscovered Places Along the North and South Carolina Coastline

Randall H. Duckett
AND
Maryellen Kennedy Duckett

Rutledge Hill Press®
Nashville, Tennessee
A Thomas Nelson Company

To our parents—Donald J. Duckett and Elizabeth Duckett and John and Mary Kennedy—who raised us to go the extra mile and not be afraid to explore what's around the next bend in the road.

Published in Nashville, Tennessee, by Rutledge Hill Press, a Thomas Nelson Company, P.O. Box 141000, Nashville, Tennessee 37214.

Cover design by Harriette Bateman

Typography by Brecca Beauchamp

Map and icon designs by Mendenhall-Mitchell Design, Knoxville, Tennessee.

Library of Congress Cataloging-in-Publication Data

Duckett, Randall H., 1958–

100 secrets of the Carolina coast : a guide to the best undiscovered places along the Carolina coastal area / Randall H. Duckett and Maryellen K. Duckett.

p. cm.

Includes index.

ISBN 1-55853-813-5 (pbk. : alk. paper)

1. Atlantic Coast (N.C.)—Guidebooks. 2. Atlantic Coast (S.C.)—Guidebooks. I. Title: One hundred secrets of the Carolina coast. II. Duckett, Maryellen Kennedy, 1961- III. Title.

F262.A84.D83 2000

917.56'10444—dc21 99-08658

Printed in the United States of America

1 2 3 4 5 6 7 8 9 QPV 05 04 03 02 01 00

Acknowledgements

Contributing Editor: Elizabeth Duckett
Contributor: Kim Cressell

We'd also like to thank the following people who helped us with the editing, research, writing, and design of this book: Brad Duckett, Gordon Fee, Susan Hamilton, Chuck Laine, Cindy Prince, Sharon Pound, and Anne Ward.

Thanks as well to the always welcoming citizens of North Carolina and South Carolina, especially those who generously provided information, ideas, and photographs.

Special thanks to Geoff Stone, Larry Stone, and the rest of the staff at Rutledge Hill Press.

Contents

Introduction

It had been one of those years. We were in our thirties and trying to cope with all the pressures of supporting a young family. Work seemed a constant series of deadlines and demands to do more and more in less and less time. We had young daughters, born within forty-four months of one another, whom we adored with all our hearts, but who required our constant care. Stress and sleep deprivation were the normal state of our lives. There was only one ray of hope—the time for our annual week-long vacation at the beach had finally come.

A few years earlier, we'd started spending our vacations on Hilton Head Island, South Carolina, about eight hours from our home in East Tennessee. We'd fallen in love with its broad beaches, warm waters, and safe, family feel. We planned a trip to start on the traditional kick off to the summer travel season—Memorial Day weekend. When that Saturday finally arrived, we feverishly stuffed the van with a portable play pen, a beach umbrella, beach chairs, beach toys, beach towels, swimsuits, shorts, sunscreens, and a closetful of clothes. We hit the road, speeding hundreds of miles over the mountains of western North Carolina and down into the South Carolina Lowcountry. Hours passed before we finally saw the sign for the Hilton Head exit off I-95. Almost out of gas because we were so anxious to get to the beach that we refused to make more than one refueling and bathroom stop, we pulled off the highway and into a gas station about thirty minutes from our final destination.

Then it hit us, with all the excitement of packing and anticipation of the beach, we forgot to double check the date of our reservations. *When were our reservations for? Wasn't there something different about this trip as compared to the one the year before when we stayed at the same place? What exactly is today's date anyway?*

We pulled out our reservations confirmation. There in black-and-white was the terrible truth. We were a day early. Our week at the beach was scheduled to run from Sunday to Sunday, not Saturday to Saturday. If we showed up at our condo now, there would likely be some other family staying there, enjoying the last day of their holiday. We had no place to stay for the night during one of the most heavily booked travel weekends of the year.

Now we look back on it and laugh at how we could have been so absent minded. We only relate it to you now to show you how much the beach means to our family. It goes beyond mere sand, sun, and sea. It is a state of mind. The beach represents a complete escape from all the problems and pressures of real life. It is an excuse to wear nothing but t-shirts, shorts, and flip flops; to let your beard grow to a scraggly stubble; to gorge yourself on fried clams or fresh oysters; to waste time bobbing in the water doing absolutely nothing productive; to prove to your kids that Mom and Dad aren't always right on the verge of cracking up.

There are, of course, great beaches everywhere around the country. When we want to get away to the beach, though, we most often choose the Carolina coast. The stretch of shore running from the Outer Banks in the north to the Lowcountry in the south offers an amazing array of travel experiences, not just spots to sun on the sand, but wonderful places to stay, places to eat, adventures, and attractions.

As you travel the coast, you see the contrast between the two states. The North Carolina shore has more of a nautical feel, a slightly rawer quality exemplified by locals representing seafaring families that have lived on the edge of America for generations. To us, South Carolina has a more steamy South atmosphere, a sometimes tropical "it-can-wait-until-tomorrow" attitude. Lying just off the most heavily traveled interstate in the country, I-95, both areas are magnets for millions of vacationers annually. The high season tends to shift by geography and climate—the Outer Banks crowds concentrate between the fourth of July and Labor Day, whereas South Carolina has pleasant "shoulder seasons" in the spring and fall. We've even been to the Hilton Head area at Christmas time and been able to ride bikes in 60-degree temperatures.

There are many well-known vacation spots along the Carolina shore, but there are also more than a few relatively undiscovered destinations that you don't want to miss. That's why we wrote *100 Secrets of the Carolina Coast,* the second book in the *100 Secrets* series, along with *100 Secrets of the Smokies*. (Thanks to all of you who bought it and made it such a success.) We've scoured the North and South Carolina shores looking for the best lesser-known, off-the-beaten-path travel experiences. We've tried to include something for everyone by featuring a wide variety of secrets—from down-home shrimp shacks to gourmet bistros; from primitive campgrounds to luxury bed-and-breakfasts; from spectacularly scenic wilderness areas to fascinating historic towns. While there are plenty of places featured that are within view of the water, we've also headed inland to show off spots an hour or two away from the shore. These make great day trips when you're sunburned or want to broaden your vacation beyond the beach—not even water dogs like our kids can spend every day in the surf.

What makes something a secret? It's true that none of the places in this book are completely unknown, and some are already featured elsewhere. Our definition of a secret, though, is summed up in our motto: "It's a secret if it's new to you." If you look through the book and find something to do on your vacation that you might not have done otherwise, then we've done our job. And even if you've heard about a place already, we've tried to tell the story behind it and give inside information that should help you decide whether it's worth your time and money to go there.

To help you better navigate *100 Secrets to the Carolina Coast,* we've designated each suggestion as falling into one of the following six categories:

- Places to eat
- Places to stay
- Adventures
- Attractions
- Getting around
- FYI

Each secret is identified with an icon for its category so you can easily find the perfect place to take a hike or have dinner. Under the heading Secret Information for each item, we give the appropriate details about the secret (location, address, phone, hours, and so on). For each secret, we've also included a Top Secret, which is an extra bit of inside information that will help you get even more out of the recommended place or activity.

In researching and writing *100 Secrets of the Carolina Coast*, we've attempted to include only high-quality travel suggestions. We've picked experiences that we think pass the "Fussy Friend or Family Member Test." We feel comfortable guiding a close friend or relative— someone from whom we'd never hear the end of it if he or she had a rotten time—to the places in this book.

No travel guide can be perfect in describing an experience and, between the time we wrote this book and the time you are reading it, circumstances can change. Places may go out of business; change products, services, or prices; or simply not measure up to your expectations. Despite our best efforts to be accurate, mistakes may have crept their way into the book as well. Therefore, before you take off to a place we recommend, always call first to confirm location, hours, prices, and other information (this is particularly true outside prime tourist season).

If a recommendation we've made turns out to be disappointing—say, the fried clams give you food poisoning—please remember that the people who run and own the places are responsibile for the quality of their products and services, not us. By featuring these secrets, we are not guaranteeing them. We do, though, apologize in advance if something doesn't live up to our description or your expectations. We urge you to e-mail us at *Carolinas@100Secrets.com* with any corrections or comments, so that we can update information on our Web site (*www.100Secrets.com*) and in any future editions of the book.

Just to tie up the story of our mistaken vacation, after going from hotel to hotel we finally found a place to stay on Hilton Head during the Memorial Day weekend. In fact, the error we made got us an extra day of beach time, so it all worked out in the end. We had a great family getaway, let the stress melt away, and returned home with a whole new attitude about life. We hope this book will help you enjoy your vacation and bring back great memories from the beach.

—RANDALL H. DUCKETT AND MARYELLEN KENNEDY DUCKETT

To help you better navigate *100 Secrets of the Carolina Coast*, we've organized our suggestions into the following categories (the icons identify into which category each secret falls). See the maps for North Carolina on pages 2 thru 5 and the maps for South Carolina on pages 158 thru 161 to find the approximate location of each secret along the Carolina coast.

PLACES TO EAT—great spots for everything from a quick snack to a gourmet dinner.

PLACES TO STAY—the best places to find not only a bed (or campsite) but also to have a special experience.

ADVENTURES—outdoor recreation and other activities that answer the age-old vacation question, "What do you want to do today?"

ATTRACTIONS—sights, shops, and amusements that answer the next question, "I dunno, what do you want to do?"

LAY OF THE LAND—overviews of selected areas that give you a sense of where you are and where you.

FYI—bits of background and other information to help you get the most out of your vacation on the Carolina coast.

North Carolina Secrets

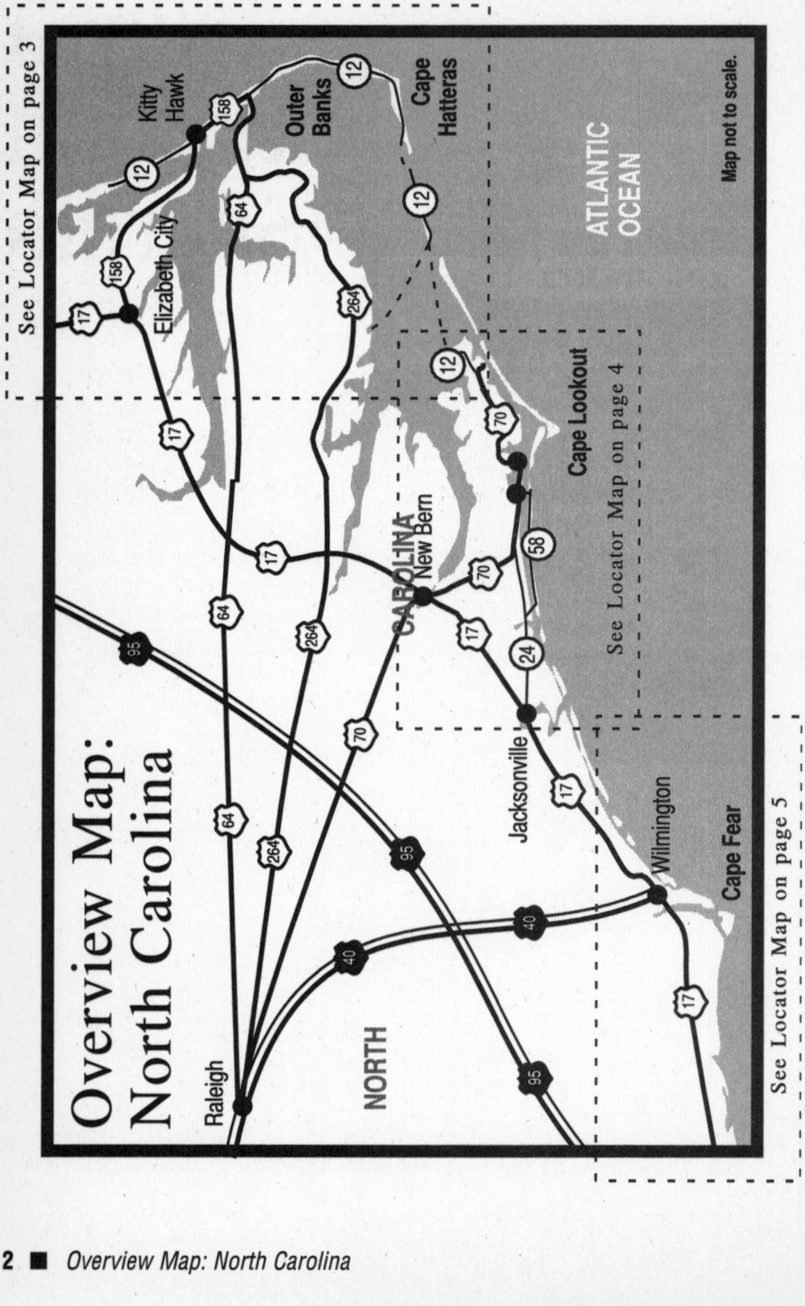
Overview Map:
North Carolina
See Locator Map on page 3
See Locator Map on page 4
See Locator Map on page 5
Raleigh
NORTH
CAROLINA
Elizabeth City
Kitty
Hawk
Outer
Banks
Cape
Hatteras
New Bern
Cape Lookout
Jacksonville
Wilmington
Cape Fear
ATLANTIC
OCEAN
Map not to scale.
17
158
12
64
264
70
58
24
95
40

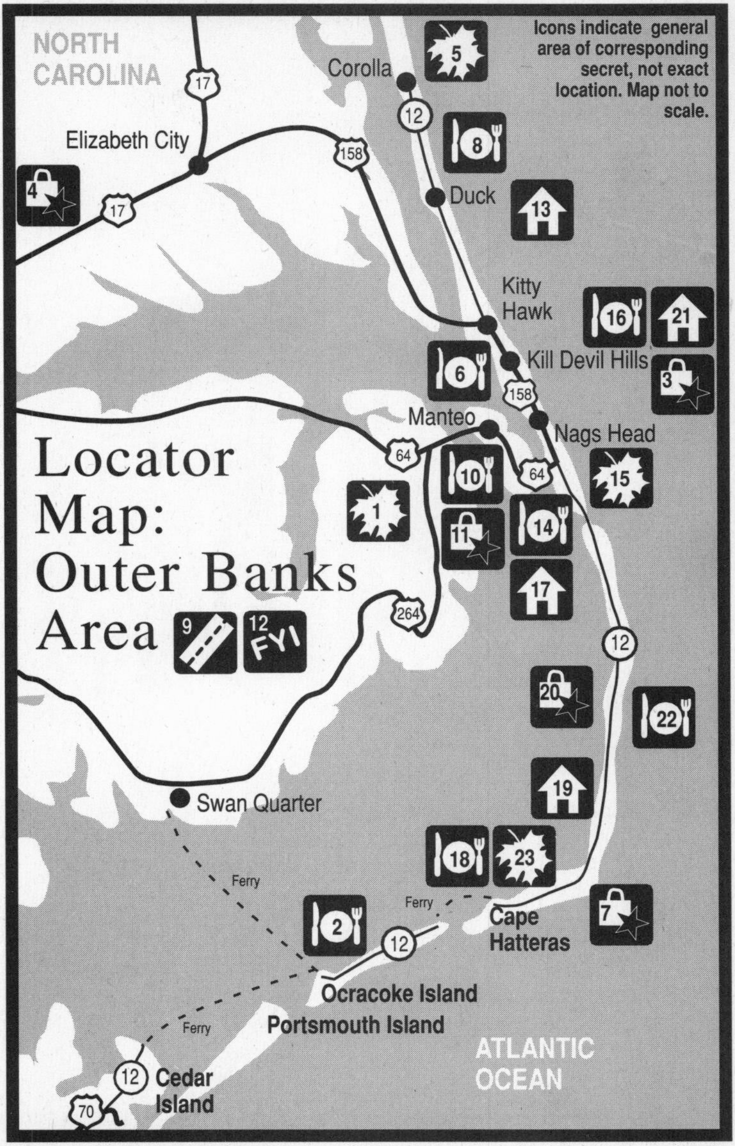
Locator Map: Outer Banks Area
NORTH CAROLINA
Icons indicate general area of corresponding secret, not exact location. Map not to scale.
Corolla
Elizabeth City
Duck
Kitty Hawk
Kill Devil Hills
Manteo
Nags Head
Swan Quarter
Ferry
Ferry
Cape Hatteras
Ocracoke Island
Portsmouth Island
Ferry
Cedar Island
ATLANTIC OCEAN
17
158
12
64
264
70
FYI

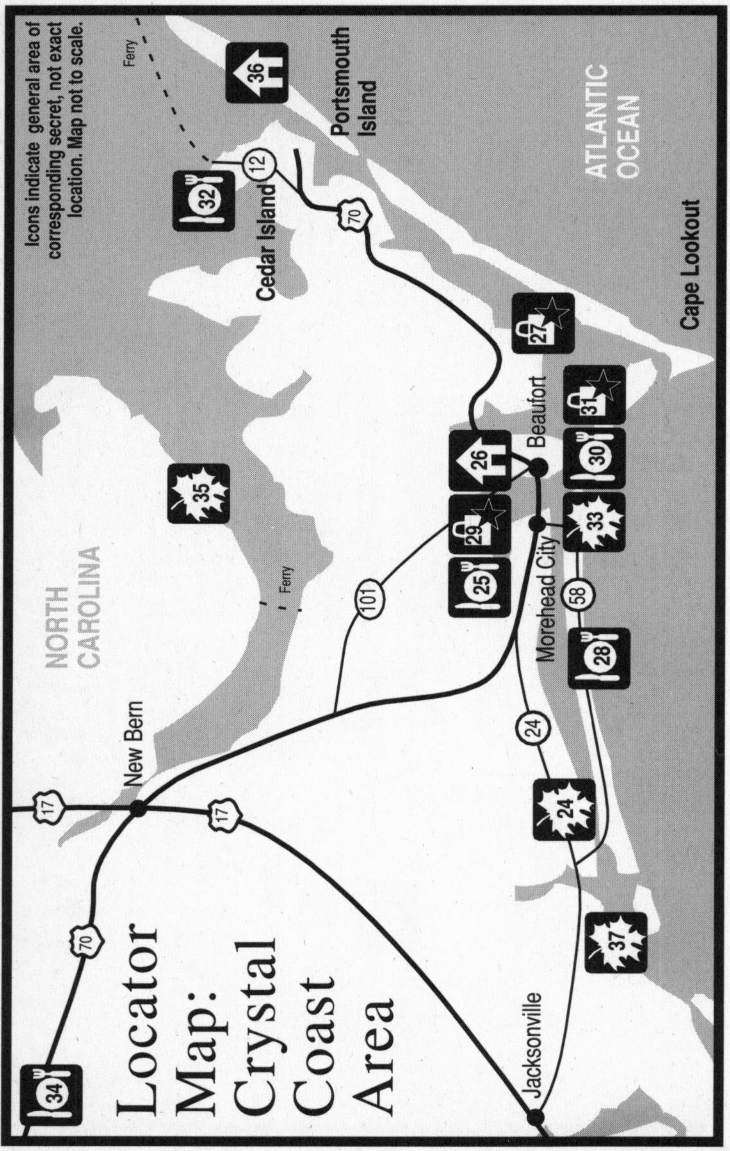
Locator Map: Crystal Coast Area
Icons indicate general area of corresponding secret, not exact location. Map not to scale.
Ferry
36
Portsmouth Island
ATLANTIC OCEAN
32
12
Cedar Island
70
Cape Lookout
27
31
Beaufort
26
30
35
29
33
NORTH CAROLINA
Ferry
25
101
Morehead City
58
28
New Bern
24
17
17
24
70
37
Jacksonville
34

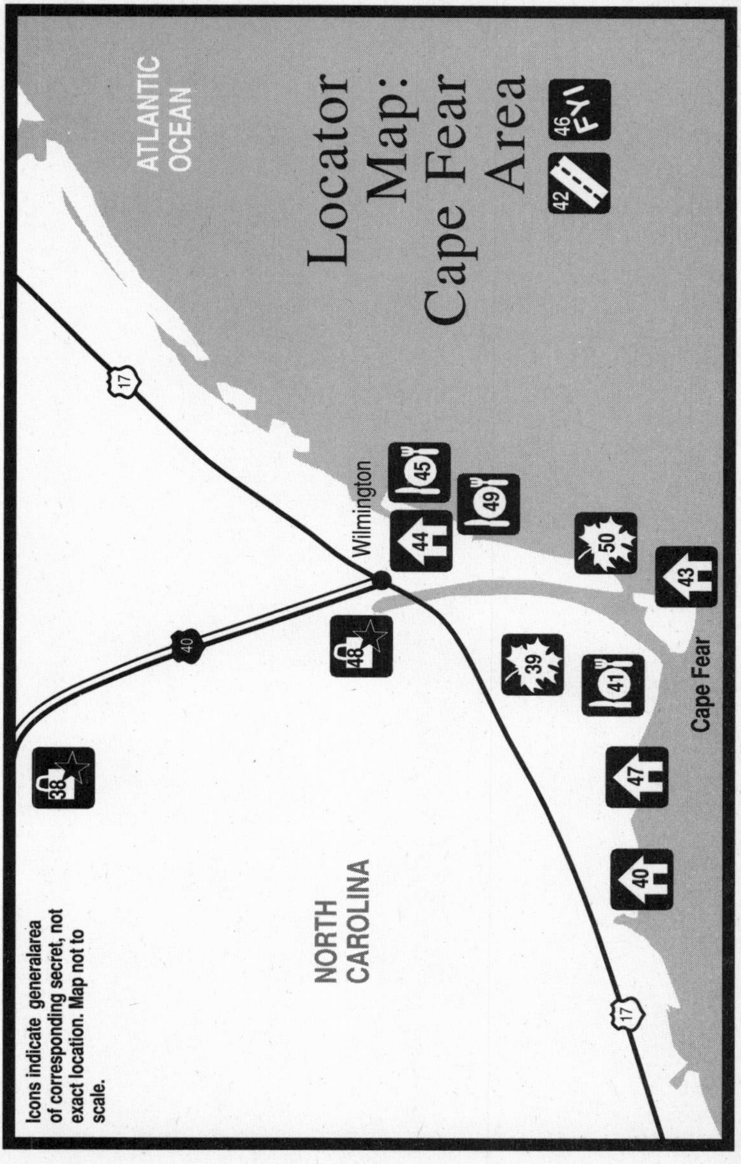
Locator Map: Cape Fear Area
Icons indicate generalarea of corresponding secret, not exact location. Map not to scale.
ATLANTIC OCEAN
NORTH CAROLINA
Wilmington
Cape Fear
17
40
17
38
40
39
41
42
43
44
45
46
FYI
47
48
49
50

1

On the Refuge Road

Every profession has its heroes. Basketball players emulate Michael Jordan, computer programmers Bill Gates, salespeople Zig Ziglar. Even travel writers such as ourselves have our heroes. At the top of our list is Charles Kuralt—the bald, rotund television journalist who spent decades discovering out-of-the-way places and unsung people and telling their stories with charm and wit. His *On the Road* reports that aired on CBS, for which he traveled to all fifty states in a motor home and logged more than a million miles, in no small way inspired our search for secret spots and things to do to reveal to readers like you.

It's fitting, then, to kick off this book with a secret that celebrates the memory of America's most famous roving reporter. He passed away at age sixty-two on the Fourth of July, 1997, after a forty-year career as a correspondent covering everything from wars to the world's largest ball of string. Among his passions, Kuralt loved the outdoors and during the years he hosted *CBS Sunday Morning*, he always closed the show with an unnarrated video of the sights and sounds of nature. In particular, he treasured the wild places of his home state of North Carolina, where he grew up and started his reporting career.

To celebrate its native son, several of the state's wildlife refuges dedicated the Charles Kuralt Trail: On the Refuge Road in the fall of 1999. A driving tour of natural wonders stretching along the coast, it includes eleven refuges and a fish hatchery, offering the public the chance to take a fantastic journey through the flora and fauna of the Tar Heel State. The idea came about when Kuralt's brother, Wallace, went to a ceremony to accept a posthumous award for Charles from the U.S. Fish and Wildlife Service. Some awardees Wallace met were Marvin and Lee Cook, who had been creating signs and exhibits for wildlife areas for years. Because of the meeting the Cooks came up with a way to memorialize the *On the Road* reporter. They began working with Bonnie Strawser of the Alligator

The Charles Kuralt Trail of wildlife refuges was dedicated in late 1999. (COURTESY OF ALLIGATOR RIVER NATIONAL WILDLIFE REFUGE)

River Wildlife Refuge and, within two years, the Charles Kuralt Trail was a reality.

Each site along the way has designated Charles Kuralt Trail areas, with wilderness to explore and scenery to soak up. The refuges have been previously open to travelers but haven't been well known because their primary purpose is to be a safe haven for everything from endangered red wolves to migrating Canada geese. Collecting them into a driving tour is, in part, a way to showcase the attractions each has to offer and to invite visitors to stop by. As part of the project, the organizers have produced a colorful guide that tells about the trail, as well as an extremely helpful companion audio documentary. The seventy-four-minute program (available on both cassette and CD) is not a site-by-site description of what you'll see but a collection of information, stories, and music that serves as a sort of soundtrack for car trips to each site. Wallace Kuralt, who sounds a lot like Charles, provides the narration, but the recording also includes snippets from his famous brother. There is no set route between sites and no set amount of time to spend at each location.

We think Charles Kuralt would gaze graciously over his bifocals and flash that familiar knowing grin in pleasure at the news of this beautiful tribute to him. We greatly admired his spirit of exploration and appreciation for natural beauty and would like to thank him for inspiring us to go on the road, too.

Secret Information

Location: The Charles Kuralt Trail includes National Wildlife Refuges at Mackey Island, Poconsin Lakes, Alligator River, Pea Island, Mattamuskeet, Roanoke River, and the Edenton National Fish Hatchery in North Carolina and the Great Dismal Swamp and Back Bay refuges just north of the Virginia border. Three other North Carolina refuges—Currituck, Swan River, and Cedar Island—are developing Charles Kuralt Trail areas to be opened in the future.

Address: For information about the Kuralt Trail, write to the Coastal Wildlife Refuge Society, P.O. Box 1808, Manteo, NC 27954.

Phone: Alligator River National Wildlife Refuge: 252-473-1131 ext. 19.

Fax: Alligator River National Wildlife Refuge: 252-473-1668.

E-mail: pea-island@outer-banks.com.

Web site: www.fws.gov/r4all.

Price: FREE.

Details: Charles Kuralt Trail Guides and admission to sites are free; cassette tapes are $5.95 and CDs are $6.95; guides and brochures are available at refuges, some visitor's centers, by phone, or by Internet.

TOP SECRET

Among the areas that make up the Charles Kuralt Trail, the Edenton National Fish Hatchery is unique. While the others are undeveloped habitats set aside to protect plants and animals, the hatchery is in the business of raising millions of striped bass and American shad each year to restock the coastal areas of the mid-Atlantic. The site was first used as a hatchery in 1899; the current hatchery was started in 1957. The public is welcome to walk the hatchery's boardwalk trail, which is especially beautiful during the fall foliage season, and to roam among its thirty-six ponds, covering twenty-five acres. Spring is the best time to see the fish since there's lots of activity cleaning the ponds and doing other work. There's also a newly renovated visitor's center featuring three aquariums of native fish, a display of live alligators, and other exhibits. Call ahead (252-482-4118) if you want a tour led by the park ranger. Large groups may also arrange fishing lessons and other educational activities.

2

Howard's Pub and Raw Bar

Always Open

Buffy Warner doesn't scare easily. In the ten-plus years that he and his wife Ann have owned Howard's Pub and Raw Bar Restaurant on Ocracoke Island, North Carolina, no hurricane or power outage has ever caused him to close his doors.

"Howard's Pub is the only restaurant on the entire Outer Banks that can honestly boast to being open 365 days a year for more than nine years," says Warner, a former West Virginia state senator who proposed to Ann and suggested moving to Ocracoke in the same sentence. (She accepted both offers; Warner adds, however, that her friends claim she never heard the marriage proposal, only the invitation to move to the island.) "People have come to know that no matter what is going on and no matter what time of the year, Howard's Pub is going to be here and open for business. We have a 125-kilowatt generator to provide power during the many power outages, and, in fact, we sell power back to the electric company when they need it. Next storm, we're going to order an evacuation of the mainland and bring 'em out to the Pub where they'll be safe."

On the few days Warner can't be at the Pub, his staff takes charge and ensures that Buffy and Ann's original vision is maintained. "Our staff is the best anywhere and they are the reason we have been able to live up to our original goal of providing for locals and tourists alike through whatever obstacles life on the Outer Banks might include. We couldn't do it without them," Warner praises.

Life on Ocracoke—"if the world came to an end, we wouldn't find out for three days" says the sign at Howard's—operates at a pace one step above a nap. Cars are allowed on the island, but once people pull off the ferry, it's safer and smarter to find a parking spot and forget how to drive. People stroll, ride bikes, and roller blade in the street as well as on the sidewalks. The most popular pastime is sitting in a rocker on a front porch enjoying being cut off from the world on this quirky little

Howard's Pub prides itself on staying open on remote Ocracoke no matter what the weather.

island. There are also sixteen miles of undeveloped beach, and anyone looking for a little more action goes to Buffy and Ann Warner's place.

The restaurant (which has been through seven major construction projects since 1989) is the first place after disembarking from the ferry from Hatteras where you can grab a brew and a burger. Don't worry about trying to find the place. The cars parked on the grass along NC Highway 12 offer a telltale clue that this is *the* place to be on Ocracoke.

If you're having a bad day or are grumpy about the long ferry ride, Howard's Pub is the kind of place that can induce an immediate attitude adjustment. There are more than two hundred domestic, imported, and microbrewed beers available; live music on many nights; games and coloring books for the kids; and someone is always up for a good game of darts. It has the island's only pool table and seven televisions to meet the viewing needs of its eclectic customer base—seniors, families, boaters, fishermen, locals, college kids, couples, and anyone else who knows a good time when they see it. The roof-top porch is the island's only ocean-view "skydeck" and provides the perfect vantage point for people-watching, stargazing, sunbathing, or "if you're lucky," adds Warner, "to slip into the total bliss of an 'Ocracoma.'"

Along with all the noise and friendly atmosphere there's actually some pretty fine food being served at Howard's Pub. The menu includes the island's only raw bar, fresh local seafood, pizzas, soups, salads, and juicy burgers. The French fries are hand cut and the salsa, chili, and chowder (from the Pub's secret recipes) are made several times each day to ensure freshness and an ample supply. All this homemade food means it takes a bit longer to get your order than the place with the golden arches, but take our word for it, it's worth the wait. Besides, you're sitting on an island forty minutes by ferry from civilization. What's your hurry?

Secret information:

Location:	On U.S. Highway 12 on Ocracoke Island, North Carolina.
Address:	P.O. Box 670, Ocracoke Island, NC 27960.
Phone:	252-928-4441.
Fax:	252-928-6003.
E-mail:	info@howardspub.com.
Web site:	www.howardspub.com.
Hours:	11 A.M. to 2 A.M.
Price:	Lunch $6 to $12, Dinner $8 to $14, lobster $12.95 per pound.
Reservations:	Not required except for special events or a very large group.
Credit cards:	Diners Club, Discover, MasterCard, Visa.

TOP SECRET

In the summer of 1999, the owners of Howard's Pub added Ocracoke's Blackbeard's Lodge, which Buffy Warner calls the island's "oldest and most famous, if not infamous, hotel," to their real estate holdings. The lodge, originally The Wahab Village Inn, was built in 1936 by a well-known developer named Stanley Wahab. According to Warner, it offered "rooms for hire" at least twenty years before any other building on the island. In the early years, the hotel housed Ocracoke's only movie theater and roller skating rink, and affluent guests were known to taxi their planes right up to the front door to unload their luggage. Lifelong Ocracoke residents all have tales to tell about the place, including legends of ghosts, and now the Warners are ready to write their own chapter of the Blackbeard's Lodge story. Dr. Bob Martin, a retired dentist from Virginia Beach who owned the hotel since 1983, gave the Warners the first crack at buying the place when he was ready to sell. Apparently he liked what the couple had done with Howard's Pub and knew his hotel would be in good hands. When the Warners got the call from Martin in January 1999, Buffy says, "it was a foregone conclusion that we had to take it." The Warners plan an eight- to ten-year, section-by-section renovation project to restore the hotel to its original prominence. The lodge is just down the road from Howard's Pub, so stop by when you're on the island to see how construction is going or call 252-928-3421 for information or 800-892-5314 to book a room.

Rogallo Kite Flying Festival

Go Fly a Kite

3

And the category is: Stuff You Learned in School That's Completely Wrong. The question: Where did Orville and Wilbur Wright fly the first airplane? Kitty Hawk, North Carolina, you say? Wrong. The Wright Brothers did indeed live and conduct experiments in Kitty Hawk while working to take wing. However, boundaries between towns were less defined back then than they are today. It turns out, the actual first foray into the air occurred just down the road in Kill Devil Hills.

The Outer Banks was the perfect place for the Wright Brothers to try to violate the laws of nature because of the combination of stories-high sand dunes from which to launch and the whipping winds that helped keep their invention aloft. Today, the brothers are honored by a monument on the spot of their first flight, yes, in Kill Devil Hills. They aren't the only high-flying inventors who are celebrated on the Outer Banks, however. Though less famous than Orville and Wilbur, Francis Rogallo also made aviation history. In 1948 he flew a craft with the first flexible wing. He and his wife, Gertrude, developed the flexible flyer using a homemade wind tunnel in their house in Kitty Hawk, and they made it from their kitchen curtains. That technological leap led to hang gliding, ultralight airplanes, modern parachutes, and high-tech stunt kites. Though the NASA scientist and his wife don't have a huge stone monument on the Outer Banks like the Wright Brothers, they are recognized every year with a colorful celebration: the Rogallo Kite Festival.

The high-flying fete is held the first weekend of June at Jockey's Ridge State Park, home to the largest natural living sand dune on the East Coast. The 420 square-acre sand box rises up to 140 feet high, but it's always reshaping itself with the near-constant winds, making it the ideal place for you to go fly a kite.

The festival includes colorful competitions and demonstrations of kites from around the world as well as a range of activities for kids and adults, including a kite auction. Now in his nineties, Rogallo attends the

Anytime of year, families flock to fly kites and savor the spectacular scenery at Jockey's Ridge State Park, site of the largest living sand dune on the East Coast. (COURTESY OF JOCKEY'S RIDGE)

awards ceremony on the afternoon of the second day (if his health permits), and hang-gliding groupies and kite-flying fanatics line up to meet their hero. The event is sponsored by Kitty Hawk Kites, which has one of its several Outer Banks stores across the street from Jockey's Ridge, and is worth a visit anytime. It is the place to go to buy a kite of your own—as essential to an Outer Banks vacation as a beach chair and Nerf football. The Rogallo festival is just one of several kite-flying events that Kitty Hawk Kites organizes, so check with them about other events if you're visiting the area at other times of the year.

If you are interested in taking wing yourself, Kitty Hawk Kites also operates the largest hang gliding school in the world. Most lessons are held at Jockey's Ridge, where the easy takeoffs and soft sand make it safe for nervous beginners to get a taste of the sport. The flight school offers everything from an inexpensive, three-flight introduction to multi-day packages that prepare students to earn United States Hang Gliding Association ratings. Some individuals or families spend their whole vacations mastering the ups and downs of working the wind.

For that opportunity, and the spectacle of seeing a sky full of kites at the Rogallo Kite Flying Festival each year, we have "The Father of Hang Gliding" to thank. The Wright Brothers may have invented the airplane, but Francis Rogallo's lifework to "give everyone the opportunity to experience flight first hand" took flying to new heights.

Francis Rogallo invented the flexible wing and inspired the cool kites flown at the festival honoring him. (COURTESY OF JOCKEY'S RIDGE)

Secret Information

Location: Jockey's Ridge State Park in Nags Head, North Carolina.
Address: Jockey's Ridge State Park, P.O. Box 592, Nags Head, NC 27959.
Phone: Jockey's Ridge State Park: 252-441-7132; Kitty Hawk Kites: 800-334-4777 or 252-441-4124.
Fax: Jockey's Ridge State Park: 252-441-8416; Kitty Hawk Kites: 252-441-7597.
E-mail: Jockey's Ridge State Park: ncs1180@interpath.com; Kitty Hawk Kites: mail@kittyhawk.com.
Web site: www.kittyhawk.com.
Dates: First weekend in June.
Price: Admission free, but there may be a charge for some activities and events.

TOP SECRET

December 17, 2003, marks a century since the Wright Brothers took their twelve-second, 120-foot flight into history. To commemorate the occasion, First Flight Centennial is organizing celebrations around North Carolina, the U.S., and the world over the next few years, culminating with a big bash at the Wright Brothers National Memorial in Kill Devil Hills on the day of the hundredth anniversary of the high-flying feat. For information about events celebrating a century of aviation, contact the First Flight Centennial Commission at 919-715-8958 or visit www.firstflight.com.

4

Historic Edenton

Past Perfect

When most of us imagine the first European settlers coming to America, we picture the pilgrims of New England, who arrived on the Mayflower in 1620 and gave us such traditions as Thanksgiving and witch-hunts. In reality the first pilgrims to America settled further south in the mid-Atlantic area. Coastal North Carolina, in fact, was home to the first English settlement in the New World. A group of brave souls arrived on Roanoke Island, between Pamlico and Albemarle sounds in 1585, then, perhaps thinking better of the whole idea, turned around and left in 1586. A second set of settlers showed up in the same spot a year later, and shortly after, the first European baby, Virginia Dare, was born in America. This history would probably be more familiar had the settlers remained. However, by the time the next ships arrived in 1591, it was found that the entire colony was missing. In a sixteenth-century version of *Unsolved Mysteries*, Virginia and her neighbors were never heard from again and became known as the Lost Colony.

Those early explorers began four centuries of rich history that can be found throughout the Albemarle Sound region. It's most concentrated in the small town of Edenton, North Carolina, which was founded in 1712, making it the state's third oldest community. "History is evident everywhere," says Linda Jordan Eure, manager of Historic Edenton, which is a state historic site. "We've got a lot to offer for a little town. We are known for our historic district being compressed into a small area so a person can walk through it and see a variety of architectural styles—Georgian, Federal, Greek Revival, Victorian, and so on. Historic Edenton is the name of the specific site where we operate and where our organization is located, but history is so much a part of the community that people tend to call the whole town Historic Edenton. It's like using 'Xerox' to refer to photocopying. We're losing our identity."

The name Edenton aptly captures the idyllic, small-town atmosphere that permeates the place. With so many tiny communities being swallowed up by urban sprawl, it's nice to know that outposts of simpler times, like this community of about six thousand people, still exist. The town's several eighteenth- and nineteenth-century buildings were largely spared from the destruction the Civil War caused elsewhere. The streets of Edenton are particularly pleasant to stroll in the late summer when trees shade the narrow streets and crepe myrtle bloom everywhere.

The best way to see the town is through the Historic Edenton Visitor Center's walking tours, which vary from one-tenth of a mile to 1.2 miles. There are also forty-five-minute trolley tours for those with tender feet. The walking tours show off such sites as the 1767 Chowan County Courthouse, the oldest courthouse in the state (it's been undergoing renovation, so check on whether it's open to tour), and the 1758 Cupola House, so named for the hat-like room topping its Jacobean architecture. You'll hear stories about the town's history, such as the Edenton Tea Party. In 1774, about fifty women got together to protest English rule of the colonies by pledging to boycott "East India tea"—a year after the more famous Boston Tea Party.

If you want to stay overnight in Edenton, call the Beechtree Inn (252-426-7815). It shares a site with fourteen buildings built before 1840, three of which have been restored as guest houses. Or call the Trestle House Inn (252-482-2282), which lies on six acres next to a wildlife refuge and is surrounded on the other three sides by water. For a bite to eat, check out Waterman's Grille (252-482-7733) for seafood and the Lovin' Onion (252-482-7465), a bakery specializing in gingerbread.

"Edenton offers a blend of scenic beauty and history," says Eure, summarizing the appeal of her hometown. "Our little town has a lot to offer—the waterfront park, playgrounds, piers, relaxing bed-and-breakfasts, antique stores. It's a place for people who want to get away from it all."

Secret Information

Location: Edenton, North Carolina, about two hours west of the northern Outer Banks.
Address: Visitor center, 108 N. Broad Street, Edenton, NC 27932.
Phone: 252-482-2637.
Fax: 252-482-3499.
E-mail: edentonshs@inteliport.com.
Web site: www.edenton.com.
Hours: 9 A.M. to 5 P.M. Monday through Saturday and 1 P.M. to 5 P.M. Sunday April through October; 10 A.M. to 4 P.M. Tuesday through Saturday and 1 P.M. to 4 P.M. Sunday November through March.
Price: Walking tours range from $3 to $7, and the trolley tour is $5.
Reservations: Not required, except for groups of ten or more.
Credit cards: Cash and checks only for tours; the visitor's center accepts MasterCard and Visa for merchandise purchases.
Details: Call or stop by to check tour times.

TOP SECRET

Edenton is part of the Historic Albemarle Tour—a group of nineteen sites and attractions that form a terrific trek for history lovers. The self-guided tour includes such spots as Somerset Place, one of the few slave-supported plantations in upper North Carolina and now a center of African-American history; the Aurora Fossil Museum, which features bones, teeth, shells, and coral from millions of years ago; and the Museum of the Albemarle, which documents the region's history starting with the time of the Native Americans. For a brochure and map of all the sites, contact Historic Albemarle Tour, Inc., P.O. Box 1604, Washington, NC 27889, 888-TRAVL NC (888-872-8562).

Corolla Outback Adventures

5

Outback in the Outer Banks

When Jay Bender's family moved to the Outer Banks forty years ago or so, you could still get directly from Virginia to North Carolina via the beach. "People would pack up supplies and drive along the sand from Virginia Beach to places like Corolla, Duck, and Nags Head," he says. "It was a day-long journey and if you got caught at high tide, a real ordeal. As people started building homes at the end of Virginia Beach, they figured development would continue southward and they started buying up land just over the border in North Carolina. In the '70s, though, the Department of the Interior decided to create an estuary reserve and the Currituck Wildlife Refuge, which cut off access from Virginia and meant basically that all those people who had bought lots couldn't get to them. It was a blessing in disguise because it kept the area from being developed. Our family was one of only fifteen who were given permits to continue to travel across the border at the coast."

Although just in his thirties, Bender has built a business showing tourists how the primitive Outer Banks looked. As the owner of Corolla Outback Adventures in Corolla, North Carolina, he prides himself on learning from the old timers the history of the area in which he grew up. During guided All Terrain Vehicle (ATV) excursions into the area at the northernmost end of the Outer Banks, which is gated at the end of NC Highway 12 and off limits to the public, he passes along the stories of old.

He says he fell into the business naturally. In the '60s his father was an avid outdoorsman and owner of Bender's Beach Service that offered guided sightseeing and fishing excursions in the area. After graduating from college with a degree in environmental science, the younger Bender tried his hand at real estate, hated it, and got involved with local water sports outfitters. In the early '90s, his father came up with the idea of offering ATV trips, and Jay says he "took the ball and ran with it."

The excursions start at Corolla Outback Adventures headquarters in the heart of Corolla, which Bender points out is pronounced Care-o-la, not Core-o-la like the Toyota. Adventurers are shuttled to the beach where up to two people per vehicle get on the big-tired cycles and start caravaning along the beach. The trip is not for wild four-wheeling in the water or dune jumping. It is for those who want to soak up the scenery and speeds are kept to fifteen to twenty miles an hour. Up the beach a few miles, the tour turns inland toward the area roamed by the famous Corolla wild horses. The population has dwindled, so you're likely to see only a couple at a time. Along the way, Bender will make three or more stops to point out landmarks, such as houses swallowed by the shifting sand, and tell stories about his home area, including his having to travel fifty-two miles to and from school when he was a kid. The whole adventure covers about twenty miles and takes about two hours.

"More than anything else, people are taken by being able to see the Outer Banks still relatively the same as it was a hundred years ago," says Bender of the appeal of the tour. "In essence you are kind of stepping back in time."

Bender also started a business offering ATV excursions to Portsmouth Island (Secret 36), but sold it to a friend who met his wife while guiding her on a trip in Corolla. Though his business is successful and draws raves from visitors, Bender says he has little interest in expansion because it might cut down on the quality of what he has created on his home turf. "We're not trying to grow," he says. "Even though we get busier each season, we have had the same number of vehicles—eight or nine—for five years. We are the oldest guide service in the area because over the last decade as eco-tourism has taken off, we've decided to stay with our niche. We are confident we give our customers the best possible tour and experience because it's our own backyard."

Secret Information

Location: Corolla, North Carolina, on the northern end of the Outer Banks.
Address: P.O. Box 244, Corolla, NC 27927.
Phone: 252-453-4484.
Fax: 252-261-2262.
E-mail: jay@corollaoutback.com.
Web site: www.corollaoutback.com.
Hours: 9 A.M. to 5 P.M. daily during season.
Season: Memorial Day to Labor Day; call for hours at other times of the year.
Price: $95 per ATV, which can hold two people; off-season rates lower.
Reservations: Recommended.
Credit cards: Discover, MasterCard, Visa.
Details: ATV driver must have a driver's license; children may ride as passengers.

TOP SECRET

Besides their basic two-hour ATV tours, Corolla Outback Adventures offers some special trips. Early morning shelling treks take ATV riders along deserted beaches to hunt for conch, angel wings, razor clams, and scallops. Kayaking trips combine exploring on an ATV with about an hour and a half of peacefully paddling out-of-the-way tidal waters. And for folks who don't want to ride an ATV, there's also a "Wild Horse Safari," which covers the same ground as the ATV trip in a Chevy Suburban but includes more time to tell stories about the Outer Banks back country.

6

Colington Cafe

Pursuing Perfection

"I'm like a Jewish mother, I love to feed people, and when people come to my house I'm not happy unless they eat something," says Carlen Pearl, who with her husband, Kenneth, owns the Colington Cafe in Kill Devil Hills, North Carolina. "It's a pleasure feeding them and giving them a good time. It's a matter of personal pride. It's what I want on vacation."

Pearl's pursuit of perfection has a downside. Though she does nothing to advertise the cafe, which is housed in a French Victorian home amid the woods on the Outer Banks, word has gotten out, and she's forced to turn away about two hundred diners a day for lack of space—the cafe seats just sixty-four people in four little rooms. She feels terrible about not being able to serve everyone, but she's unwilling to sacrifice the quality of the food and level of service for more business. "Everyone always mentions when they come to the restaurant that they feel like they are in Carlen and Ken's home," she reports. "Nothing ever goes out of the kitchen that I wouldn't put out at a dinner party. In ten years in business we've only had two people who weren't happy with their meals—one person said the steak was overdone and the other didn't really like salmon."

Pearl started honing her culinary craft as a child under the guidance of her mother, who was French. "We didn't like it, but every Christmas we would have to miss school for two to three days and bake," she recalls. "We would make twenty-five different pastries for people who would stop by to visit. Now I'm glad, because from age nine or ten we would bake and bake."

Perhaps not surprisingly, Pearl went to work in the restaurant industry when she was fourteen, became a teacher for awhile, but eventually returned to her first love—cooking. Part of the reason she started a restaurant on the coast was because of all the great local ingredients. "I went to Paris and thought I would be so intimidated by

The Colington Cafe is in a Victorian house in an out-of-the-way spot on the Outer Banks. (COURTESY OF CARLEN PEARL)

the quality of the food," she says. "But I came back with an appreciation of the Outer Banks. We get the best crab meat, the best shrimp, the best scallops, the best tuna, the best soft-shell crabs—all caught right here. All of our wonderful produce is right from Currituck—beautiful corn and fresh tomatoes. I drive about an hour and forty-five minutes each direction to pick up crab meat because it's the best way to get what I want. 'I am not picky,' I tell the salesmen, 'just give me the best you have,' and they laugh."

After a couple of years at another location in the early '90s, she and her husband moved the Colington Cafe to its current home. The out-of-the-way spot was owned by the previous family for 150 years; it includes one of the oldest oaks on the island. The twenty-two-year-old house is a beautiful Victorian replica. "It is different for the Outer Banks because it's on a hill amid oak trees. People love the upstairs room because it was a little girl's bedroom before the renovations. It still has white lace curtains and about twenty windows."

Recently the Pearls hired a chef, Jeff Lane, to help with the cooking because a few years ago Carlen broke her back and now can't endure ten hour days at the stove. She still keeps a keen eye on each and every dish served. She describes the menu as having a "Continental flair with local ingredients." One of the most popular dishes is "the Tuna with Shrimp in a Mediterranean sauce with olives and artichokes, tomatoes, fresh garlic, and sweet peppers. That's always a big one for us," exclaims Pearl. They also feature award-winning crab cakes that are so acclaimed because of all the crabmeat. Need we add that all the desserts—white truffle key lime pie, white and dark chocolate cheesecake with raspberry sauce, and sundried cherry bread pudding, for example—are homemade?

Given all the attention to quality, prices at the Colington Cafe are surprisingly affordable. But that just further reflects the Pearls' dedication to pleasing their guests. "My heart and soul is in the restaurant," says Carlen. "Our philosophy is to give people really good food at a really good price. When it rains here, in fact, I tell the staff to give the guests extra big portions so at least their stomachs will be happy."

Secret Information

Location: On Colington Road, west of Kill Devil Hills, North Carolina.
Address: 1029 Colington Road, Kill Devil Hills, NC 27948.
Phone: 252-480-1123.
Hours: 5 P.M. to 10 P.M.
Season: Dinner only; open every day from April through Thanksgiving; open Thursday through Sunday from mid-February through April.
Price: Around $15 per entree.
Reservations: Recommended; accepted up to three days in advance.
Credit cards: Diners Club, MasterCard, Visa.

TOP SECRET

Spring is the season when the crabs that populate the Carolina shore shed their old shells and are temporarily soft enough to clean and cook in a variety of ways from Calabash- to Cajun-style, and to eat legs, claws, shells, and all. There's no better spot to get them than the small island town of Colington, up the road from the Colington Cafe. "It is a beautiful little community and is the soft-shell crab capital of the world," says the cafe's co-owner Carlen Pearl, who's sure to have them on the menu in season.

Hatteras Lighthouse

Moving Motif

7

The Cape Hatteras Lighthouse—the most recognizable symbol of the Outer Banks—is gone from the site upon which it stood since 1870. The United States' tallest lighthouse, at 208 feet, was built primarily to warn boaters about Diamond Shoals—a treacherous stretch of sandbars where many a sailor, pirate, and pleasure boater have run aground over the centuries. But its secondary role as a monumental magnet for tourists is what made the lighthouse beloved by locals and visitors alike.

All that history and the "ca-ching" of cash registers from tourist interest was about to come crashing into the sea. The lighthouse stood strong, but the beach around it had receded. By 1999, the mighty tower, which was built sixteen hundred feet from the ocean in the 1800s, was a mere 120 feet from being swallowed by the sea. For most of the twentieth century, the government and concerned locals threw millions of dollars and thousands of sandbags into the effort to stop the beach erosion and save the lighthouse. But by the '80s it was apparent that the sea was winning and would soon claim the tower. In response, Congress approved $9.8 million to move the Cape Hatteras Lighthouse to higher ground.

In the summer of 1999, in an unbelievable engineering feat, the forty-eight hundred-ton structure was picked up and moved more than half a mile from its original home. It was relit the following November and scheduled to open again to visitors on Memorial Day 2000. The monumental task of painstakingly relocating the lighthouse inland along a twenty-nine hundred-foot path fell to International Chimney Corp. (ICC) of Buffalo, New York, and Expert House Movers of Maryland. Although Buffalo is on a lake, not an ocean, the ICC is considered the national expert on lighthouse moves. Before Hatteras, there were three lighthouse relocations in the U.S., all successfully completed by International Chimney Corp.

First, workers separated the tower from the granite foundation,

The Cape Hatteras Lighthouse was lifted off its old foundation and moved 1,600 feet to save it from being swallowed by the sea.

which turned out to be a lot more sturdy than they'd anticipated. Then, a grid of beams, hydraulic jacks, and steel rollers were constructed under the lighthouse to form its new, temporary base. While crews worked on the lighthouse excavation and new base, other workers cleared and graded the path through the dunes that the tower would follow. Fifteen-ton vibrating rollers compacted the sand, which was covered with twenty-four inches of gravel topped by ten-inch steel-beam mats.

One hundred jacks cushioned the lighthouse's ride while hydraulic rams slowly rolled it over the top of a track of forty-foot beams. There were three lengths of track in all, totaling 120 feet, so when the lighthouse moved off of one section, crews picked the track up and moved it around to the front. The twelve-hour days seemed even longer because the hydraulic jacking system, which was custom built to elevate and push the lighthouse, operated on a biodegradable vegetable-based oil, which attracted swarms of pesky gnats. The move took twenty-three days—from June 17 to July 9, 1999—at a pace of about 1.5 inches a minute. Not one of the nearly 1.2 million bricks used to build the Cape Hatteras Lighthouse was lost.

Why go to all this trouble? Park service spokesperson Bob Woody, who led efforts to keep the public updated on the move, notes the historic and architectural value of the Cape Hatteras Lighthouse but says the reason for preventing it from being swallowed by the sea runs deeper. "It serves as an icon for what's best about the American character," he observes. "It represents all the positive traits of the light keepers who kept it going—commitment, concern, caring. They took care of people they didn't even know, people over the horizon whom they couldn't see but who could see them in the dark from out in the ocean. They didn't get anything out of it, but they did their duty and made sure people had a safe trip. The Cape Hatteras Lighthouse represents the light in the American character."

Secret Information

Location: Hatteras, North Carolina.
Address: Cape Hatteras National Seashore, Route 1, P.O. Box 675, Manteo, North Carolina 27954.
Phone: 252-995-4474.
Fax: 252-473-2595.
Web site: www.nps.gov/caha/capehatteras.htm.
Hours: Hours vary by season; call ahead.
Price: At the time of publication, they hadn't decided whether to charge a minimal fee or not.

TOP SECRET

The coast of North Carolina has seven lighthouses, positioned in such a way as to always be in view of ships traveling fifteen to twenty miles offshore through what came to be called the Graveyard of the Atlantic. The unique paint job for each tower allowed sailors to identify them from miles away in the daylight, telling them where they were in the days before Global Positioning Systems. The Cape Hatteras Lighthouse boasts two black and two white spiral stripes, each of which circles the tower one time—a tough paint job that no one's quite sure how the original designers got right. If you'd like to get an in-depth view of how the massive lighthouse was moved, order the video documentary *The Cape Light: Away from the Edge*, or the companion CD-ROM. Both were produced by television station WRAL in Raleigh, North Carolina, which had cameras and reporters on site during the entire time it took to lift the lighthouse up and haul it to its new home. The video is $15 and the CD-ROM is $12 plus $3.95 shipping and handling; to order visit the station's Web site at www.wral-television.com or call 800-217-6161.

8

Sanderling Restaurant and Bar

Lifesaving Lunch

Everyone has places that they've heard about, read about, and would love to see one day—even if they can't afford to actually stay there. For many coastal Carolina visitors, the elegant, oceanfront Sanderling Inn Resort, just north of downtown Duck, North Carolina, tops that list. With the soundside first floor rooms in the North Inn starting at $214 a night (okay, so a complimentary newspaper and continental breakfast are included), the Sanderling would bust the vacation budget of most mainstream American minivan families. But there is a way to experience the Sanderling without mortgaging your house if you're willing to swap some beach time for a sumptuous lunch.

Although the Sanderling Inn itself only sprang from the dunes in the early 1980s, the building housing the resort's restaurant is listed on the National Register of Historic Places. It's the original Caffey's Inlet Life-Saving Station (located just north of the Currituck County Line), which was built in 1899 as part of a chain of life-saving stations plopped down on the sand every seven miles along the coasts of North Carolina and Virginia. Many of the stations remain; a few have been turned into restaurants, and the jewel of them all (thanks to extensive historical renovation and reconstruction by the Sanderling folks back in 1985) is the Sanderling Restaurant and Bar.

When you drive up NC Highway 12 from Kitty Hawk the road starts to narrow down to practically nothing as you approach the village of Sanderling. Actually, Sanderling isn't even a village; it's a resort development located five miles north of the once sleepy fishing village of Duck. The inn and its accompanying facilities encompass enough land on this sliver of sand, however, that most folks staying there feel like they're in a village all their own. The first building you see on your right, all white and bright with an American flag flapping in the breeze out front, is the life-saving station turned restaurant, and your ticket to the Sanderling experience.

Step inside the restored life-saving station that houses the Sanderling Inn Restaurant for a taste of coastal history and some of the best crab cakes and chowder on the Outer Banks.

The Sanderling Restaurant is open for breakfast, dinner, and Sunday brunch all year round ("as long as we have power," says the concierge), but the best time to go is for lunch. Although there isn't a posted dress code, the Sanderling Restaurant is not a board shorts and flip-flops kind of place. You should take a shower, put on the least rumpled of your vacation clothes, and comb the kids' hair before you go there. Requiring this minimal amount of sophistication keeps the dedicated beach bums and water dogs away during the day, making lunch at the Sanderling less crowded. It also happens to be less expensive than the more popular dinner hour, which is the main reason for sampling the Sanderling at midday.

They have a kid's menu featuring the ever-popular chicken fingers and burgers, plus plenty of grown-up fare for Mom and Dad: Plump crab cake sandwiches; rich homemade chowder with shrimp, corn, and crabmeat; risotto with seared scallops; and Caesar salad with chicken, to name a few. Whatever was caught that morning appears on the menu, and the restaurant's pastry chef specializes in everything chocolate.

Although the food is superb, it's the setting that makes the meal. Massive windows—filling the space where the station's doors once stood—let in the sun, blue sky, and views of the resort. The gleaming wood-paneled walls and floors preserve the authenticity of the lifesaving station and make you feel like you're on a grand sailing ship. There are priceless nautical antiques everywhere—high enough to escape the clutches of curious fingers. Some of the more unusual items include a lyle gun used to fire a line across the bow of ship to rescue travelers and an odd-looking contraption called a breeches buoy that was also used for rescue. The restaurant staff is most proud of the original gold U.S. Lifesaving Medal of Honor awarded to local hero Rasmus Midgett in 1899 for lifesaving service beyond the call of duty. In a hurricane in August 1899, the barquentine *Priscilla* broke up on the shoal. Rasmus swam out ten times to bring the ten men to safety. Only about twenty-six of these medals were awarded along the North Carolina coast. There are also signal lamps, lantern buoys, and dozens of other little pieces of equipment related to lifesaving and the sea.

But that's not the total Sanderling lunch experience. Since you've driven all the way up there and maybe even taken a shower, you owe it to yourself to stroll over to the main inn and look around. The Sanderling bills itself as "A Far From Ordinary Place Not Far Off The Carolina Mainland." Not a bad line and right on the mark from what we've seen. The resort is bordered on the west by Currituck Sound and on the east by the Atlantic Ocean. In between are light gray and white buildings of traditional Outer Banks design elegantly aged by the salt air, sun, and fierce winds. Everything from the simple wooden Sanderling sign to the white picket fences is classically understated and charming. Walk up the stairs to the main inn and step inside where antiques and artwork fill the gathering rooms and hallways. Audubon prints, Boehm birds, and intricate bird carvings by world-renowned artist Grainger McCoy create a peaceful, natural, and yes, pricey air (you'll be glad you didn't wear those flip-flops) but the staff is welcoming and helpful to the curious day-trippers.

Secret Information

Location: North of Duck, North Carolina.
Address: 1461 Duck Road, Duck, North Carolina 27949.
Phone: 800-701-4111 or 252-261-4111.
Fax: 252-261-1638.
Web site: www.hotelroom.com/ncarolina/ngsander/sandeco.html.
Hours: 8 A.M. to 10:30 A.M. for breakfast; 11:30 A.M. to 4 P.M. for lunch; 4 P.M. to 9:30 P.M. for dinner.
Price: Around $10 a plate.
Reservations: Accepted.
Credit cards: American Express, Discover, MasterCard, Visa.

TOP SECRET

The Sanderling Inn Restaurant and Bar is only one slice of the huge Sanderling Inn pie you can sample without actually staying at the resort. Another adventure is the Sanderling Inn Eco-Center, which is located on the soundside of the resort. The Eco-Center is a North Beach sailing watersport facility that offers Kayak Eco-Tours. These two-and-a-half-hour, guided paddling tours of the Pine Island Audubon Nature Preserve and the islands of the Currituck Sound focus on the unique flora and fauna of the area. They cost $39 per person and spaces fill up quickly in season, so call to make a reservation when you arrive on the Outer Banks. The Eco-Center also has kayak, canoe, bike, and paddleboat rentals. The emphasis at the center is on sharing and preserving the fragile historic, and cultural characteristics of the Currituck Sound while having a bunch of fun, of course. The Eco-Center is open 8 A.M. until 8 P.M. May 24 through September 12. For information on current programs and to make reservations, call the Sanderling Inn Resort and Fitness Center at 252-449-6656.

9 Outer Limits

When you're soaking up the sun on the beach or munching on a crab cake sandwich at a picnic table overlooking a marina, it's easy to forget how remote the islands that make up the Outer Banks really are. This mere sliver of sand stretching from north of Corolla (pronounced Care-o-la, not like the Toyota car) south to Ocracoke Island is roughly twenty miles from the mainland at the furthest point. Buffeted by wind and water, the Outer Banks are constantly reshaping in small and, when a hurricane hits (Secret 12), not so small ways. In a rainstorm on the two-lane stretches of NC Highway 12 lined by sand dunes when the water is streaming across the fragile-looking pavement, you feel as though you're traveling on the edge of nowhere.

Access to the mainland has determined how the Outer Banks have developed. The most densely populated and most visited communities—Nags Head, Kitty Hawk, Kill Devil Hills, and Roanoke Island—lie between two bridges—the Wright Memorial Bridge to the north and the combination of the Umstead Memorial Bridge and the Washington Baum Bridge to the south. This stretch is where there are most tourist activities—seafood restaurants, sights such as the Wright Brothers Memorial, large hotels, souvenir shops, and a slew of spots to fish or enjoy watersports. Because it's away from the water, Manteo on Roanoke Island has a more village-like feel and is home to the live performance of the legend of the Lost Colony—the story of the strange disappearance of the island's first settlers—and the Elizabethan Gardens. The North Carolina Aquarium is scheduled to reopen in May 2000; you should drop by and see what improvements \$10 million buys.

To the north of the bridges are the towns of Southern Shores, Duck, and Corolla, which are comparatively harder to get to and therefore comparatively less crowded, though the road to them can get choked with traffic on summer weekends. Corolla is famous for

Miles of windblown beach along the Outer Banks are protected from development as part of wilderness preserves.

its Currituck Lighthouse and wild horses, although the dwindling population of ponies has been fenced in, away from town, despite the equines' efforts to roam where they want. Duck is our favorite place on the upper Outer Banks, an upscale village community that reminds us of a small, artsy enclave where everyone seems to know everyone else.

South of the main vacation communities, where Highway 158 turns inland and Highway 12 continues down the Outer Banks, the scenery starts to get more natural (less developed) as you pass through Bodie Island and into the Pea Island Wildlife Refuge, which offers some of the best birdwatching on the coast. Eventually you hit civilization in the form of communities stringing from Rodanthe south to Hatteras, at the end of the island. Though they draw plenty of tourists, these villages feel far more remote than their northern neighbors and appeal more to people who want to feel the wind in their face as they fly a kite or fish on the beach. The area experienced a boom in visitors when the Cape Hatteras Lighthouse was moved to prevent it from being swallowed by the sea (Secret 7). We like this area because of its genuineness—it still feels wild, and people still have weather-beaten faces, looking like they'd ride out any storm. There are lots of big-wheeled trucks with holders on the front grill for multiple fishing rods. There are still small motor hotels like the Falcon Hotel in Buxton that give you a key with your room number printed on a big plastic tag rather than a card for an electronic lock.

Further down the coast, the opposite of the inhabited upper Outer Banks is Ocracoke Island, which is accessible only by ferry from Hatteras to the north or Cedar Island to the south. Most of the island is part of the Cape Hatteras National Seashore and is undeveloped, save for the village of Ocracoke, which was once pretty much an insider's secret but has become a bit more trendy. It has a full range of upscale condos and cottages for those folks who fancy fishing village life, without much else to do but eat, drink, and explore.

Most maps of the Outer Banks end with Ocracoke, and there is some dispute about exactly what's the Outer Banks and what's not, but we include the areas around Cape Lookout. The Northern Core Banks and the Southern Core Banks parallel the coast from Cedar Island south to Beaufort, North Carolina. They are undeveloped but open to campers and fishermen (Secret 36). The area west of Beaufort, as the North Carolina coast takes an abrupt jag at Cape Lookout, is often called the Crystal Coast, although, in a blatant attempt at marketing spin, we've seen it called the Southern Outer Banks. Along the so-called southern Outer Banks are highly developed hotel-and-condo-packed places to sun and surf, such as Atlantic Beach and Emerald Isle, which are separated from the mainland by Bogue Sound. These beaches are less windy than those of the upper Outer Banks because they have the advantage of facing south rather than east.

We think the Outer Banks—excluding the more touristy Crystal Coast—tend to bring out one's true nature. Some people go there and find them too remote—even raw—for their tastes and never return. Others immediately fall in love with the lighthouses along the coast, the windswept dunes, and seafaring feel of the area, returning year after year. It would be a great mistake, though, never to see the edge of nowhere for yourself.

Secret Information

For more information about the Outer Banks, contact the following organizations:

- Outer Banks Chamber of Commerce, P.O. Box 1757, 101 Town Hall Drive, Kill Devil Hills, NC 27948; 252-441-8144; chamber@outer-banks.com; outerbankschamber.com.
- Crystal Coast Tourism Development Bureau, P.O. Box 1406 Morehead City, NC 28557; 800-SUNNY-NC (786-6962); www.sunnync.com.

TOP SECRET

The Outer Banks, and the rest of the North Carolina coast are dominated by water, water everywhere. To save time trying to find a land route around the endless sounds, streams, inlets, estuaries, and bays, take advantage of the state's excellent ferry system. North Carolina operates twenty-one technologically up-to-date ferries, which carry up to three hundred passengers and fifty-three vehicles at a time. Seven routes make up the system, and the ferries operate in five bodies of water: Pamlico Sound, Currituck Sound, the Neuse River, the Pamlico River, and the Cape Fear River. The average speed of the ferries is ten knots, and their design allows them to operate in as little as five feet of water. The shortest crossing is Cherry Branch to Minnesott Beach, a quick 2.3 mile, twenty-minute sail. The longest is a twenty-seven mile, two-and-a-half-hour cruise between Swan Quarter and Ocracoke. Some ferries are free and all you need do is drive up to the landing; others require reservations and cost up to $30 per vehicle. For information about state-operated ferries, call 800-BY FERRY or visit www.dot.state.nc.us/transit/ferry. There are also several private ferry services throughout the state, so keep your eyes open for spots where you can quickly cross the water and save time and trouble.

10

Weeping Radish Brewery and Bavarian Restaurant

A Taste of Bavaria

As much as we love Carolina seafood, four days of restaurants featuring taxidermied game fish mounted on the walls; heaping platters of battered and fried shrimp, oysters, and clams (with fries, coleslaw, and hush puppies as sides); and "I Got Crabs at FILL IN THE BLANK" t-shirts, can get a little monotonous, not to mention expensive. When we've had our fill of the cast of *The Little Mermaid*, we like to look for a place that bucks the conventions of local cuisine and offers a different flavor, which perfectly describes the Weeping Radish Brewery and Bavarian Restaurant in Manteo, North Carolina.

You may be a bit startled to be driving along U.S. Highway 64 and suddenly catch sight of what looks like a tiny Bavarian village on the side of the road. Upon closer examination, you'll find a family-friendly compound featuring a beer garden and restaurant; a playground perfect for keeping the kids amused; a gingerbread house that serves ice cream and cookies; a candy store; a toy and train store; and a duck pond in which you can sail remote-control boats.

This Teutonic fantasyland is the creation of Uli Bennewitz, who says his life is the classic immigrant story: A Bavarian farmer comes to North Carolina to manage thousands of acres of farmland. While still on a non-immigrant visa he starts the only Bavarian restaurant brewery in the South. Now after opening three restaurants his company is actively pursuing franchise options and is planning to build a larger brewery on a farm in a neighboring county. Though he started with rags, he is still waiting for the riches.

The Weeping Radish was on the forefront of the restaurant-microbrewery trend that swept the country. It had been illegal for breweries to retail beer in North Carolina before 1985, but Bennewitz successfully lobbied for a law to lift the ban and began competing with Miller and Budweiser in 1986. The name Weeping Radish comes from the way beer is served in Bavaria—with a radish cut in a spiral and sprinkled

It's Oktoberfest all year round at the Weeping Radish Brewery and Bavarian Restaurant.

with salt, causing the moisture to seep out of the vegetable, making it look like it's crying.

Bennewitz emphasizes, though, that the Weeping Radish is not just for guys who like to guzzle exotic alcoholic beverages. "We even make our own root beer for the children," he says. "We are one of the few breweries catering to families, which is in keeping with Bavarian tradition. Over there beer is food and the entire family can celebrate around beer. It is ideal for parents to enjoy a quiet beer while the children are happily occupied in the beer garden."

The main restaurant in Manteo and its sister restaurants in Corolla and Kitty Hawk feature awarding-winning brews made without preservatives or pasteurization, entirely in accordance with the *Reinheitsgebot* —German purity law of 1516. Varieties include Black Radish Dark Lager, Winter Wheat, and Christmas Double Bock. If you want to see how the beers are made, you can take a brewery tour April through October.

Even if you can't stand the taste of beer, there are plenty of other flavors to sample at the Weeping Radish. The menu features both hearty German fare such as sauerbraten, jagerschnitzel, and potato pancakes, as well as lighter dishes like the fruit and cheese platter, which consists of homemade Obazta cheese spread, cubes of Swiss and Muenster, fresh fruit, and beer bread. American items are also available, including buffalo chicken wings served as spicy hot as you can stand. Although any of the three Weeping Radish locations are worth a visit anytime, the annual Members Club Weekend (see Top Secret) in April, Microbrew Festival in June, and Oktoberfest in September are especially fun.

Secret Information

Location: Main location in Manteo, North Carolina; other locations in Corolla and Kitty Hawk.
Address: P.O. Box 1471, Manteo, NC 27954.
Phone: Manteo: 252-473-1157; Corolla: 252-453-6638; Kitty Hawk: 252-261-0488.
Fax: 252-473-5147.
E-mail: info@weepingradish.com.
Web site: www.weepingradish.com.
Hours: 11:30 A.M. to 10 P.M. daily; hours and days open may change in the off-season.
Season: Corolla location closed December to March.
Price: From $6 sandwiches to $10 to $15 entrees.
Reservations: Recommended.
Credit cards: Discover, MasterCard, Visa.

TOP SECRET

As a special treat for beer lovers, you can have brews bottled by the Weeping Radish Brewery delivered right to your door by joining its beer of the Month Club that will do just that. For $35 a month (plus shipping and handling) for a three-month membership or $30 a month (plus shipping and handling) for a six-month membership, they'll send you a case of 12 twenty-two-ounce brews close to every thirty days. (You can also buy single cases of beer rather than commit to the club.) As a member, though, you'll be invited to attend the annual Members Weekend in the Outer Banks, which in 1999 had a Hawaiian theme and featured a luau, volleyball, beach music, and, oh yes, BEER! (Non members also may attend.) To sign up for the club or order beer by the case call 800-896-5403, or for more information visit the Weeping Radish Web site (see Secret Information).

A Halley's Comet Production and Lighthouse Memorabilia

11

Nautical Collectibles

"All my friends call me The Clock Man," says Craig Robb who, with his wife Becky, owns A Halley's Comet Productions and Lighthouse Memorabilia. The mail-order business, with a showroom open to the public in Manteo, North Carolina, specializes in creating clocks of all shapes and sizes adorned with artwork of area lighthouses. "We named the business after our daughter Halley and our Umbrella Cockatoo bird, Comet," reports Craig. If you love to collect nautical memorabilia, stop in at the showroom to see all manner of knick-knacks adorned with lighthouses.

The Robbs got into the printing business in 1994 by doing business cards, menus, and personal greeting cards for friends, then decided to build a business showing off the most recognizable symbols of their home area in the Outer Banks—the beacons that for hundreds of years have kept sailors on course in treacherous waters. But why clocks? "I started with clocks because I was tired of plain clocks. Why not look at something you enjoy?" Craig explains matter-of-factly.

The Robbs design and assemble all the timepieces they sell, using original photographs and local artwork. They create everything from common plastic wall clocks to wood-and-brass pendulum clocks, all featuring famous lighthouses from North and South Carolina. They also produce lighthouse t-shirts, mouse pads, banners, candles, and, new as of 1999, neckties.

If you're not into nautical designs, though, don't dismiss the idea of contacting A Halley's Comet Production and Lighthouse Memorabilia. The Robbs are more than willing to customize a clock or other item with a photograph or drawing of your choice. "Nothing is impossible," boasts Craig. "I can put any photo or logo art on anything."

Craig Robb creates collectibles by putting pictures of lighthouses on almost anything that keeps time. (COURTESY OF CRAIG ROBB, OWNER OF A HALLEY'S COMET PRODUCTION & LIGHTHOUSE MEMORABILIA)

Secret Information

Location: Manteo, North Carolina.
Address: 412 Highway 64 S., Manteo, NC 27954.
Phone: 252-473-2562.
Fax: Same as phone number.
E-mail: info@hcomet.com or hcomet@interpath.com.
Web site: www.hcomet.com.
Hours: 10 A.M. to 6 P.M. Monday to Friday.
Price: See catalog.
Credit cards: American Express, MasterCard, Visa.
Details: A catalog of clocks is on The Halley's Comet Web site (see above), or you may call or write for a printed catalog.

TOP SECRET

If you love lighthouses as much as the folks at A Halley's Comet Production and Lighthouse Memorabilia and want to help preserve them, consider joining the Outer Banks Lighthouse Society. It was founded in 1994 to help protect these historic sentinels of the seashore. Membership is $15 per person, $25 per family, or $40 per business and includes three issues of the organization's newsletter, *The Lighthouse News*. For more information about the group or lighthouses in general, write to Outer Banks Lighthouse Society, P.O. Box 1005, Morehead City, NC 28557, send e-mail to society@ncnets.net, or visit www.outerbanks.com/lighthouse-society.

Blow Hards

12

They have names that sound like the doting great aunts and uncles your folks use to make you kiss as a kid—Hugo, Hazel, Fran, Floyd. Their names belie their power: hundred plus-mile-an-hour winds, rain that beats you into submission, waves that swell stories high, then surge onto the shore, inundating everything and leaving tons of sand everywhere. Perhaps it's just the cosmic cost of being an ocean-front paradise the rest of the time, but the mighty hurricanes that have hit the North Carolina and South Carolina shores over the past few decades have exacted a huge toll on the environment, property, and, often, human life.

Hurricane season lasts from June 1 to November 30, which also, unfortunately, happens to be the heart of the tourist season. Chances are slim that you'll have your beach vacation washed out by a big blow, although most of the Carolina coast has about a 40 percent chance of being affected by a hurricane sometime during the season. Cape Hatteras, in fact, shares with Miami and San Juan, Puerto Rico the dubious distinction of being one of the three spots with about a 50/50 chance of being hit by a big storm. Although a dangerous storm can come at any time, the season tends to peak in mid-September, after the kids are back in school and beach visitation starts to fall off.

As you're driving what seems like endless hours to get to the beach, think about the long trip the typical hurricane takes to get to the Carolinas. It starts out forming in the warm tropical waters near Africa and slowly makes its way across the Atlantic. As it travels over the open ocean, it picks up energy, and when its winds reach more than thirty-nine miles an hour, it's declared a Tropical Storm and given a name. The list of storm names is set years in advance; for example, the first four storms in the year 2002 will be Arthur, Bertha, Cristobal, and Dolly. The names of particularly terrible storms, like 1989's Hugo, which hammered the South Carolina coast around Charleston, are retired and never used again.

When the storm's winds top seventy-four miles an hour, it officially becomes a hurricane and starts to be measured on the Saffir-Simpson Scale. Hurricanes are ranked from category one to five. The top three categories, which start at winds of 111 miles an hour, are the kind of storms that can level houses and cause storm surges—the wall of water that comes ashore when a hurricane hits land—that flood streets. A category five storm's winds are greater than 155 miles per hour—compare that to the 20 mph winds that sometimes come with thunderstorms and are enough to send your trash cans flying down the street. Once a hurricane hits shore, it tends to die out due to the lack of energy from the water that fuels it.

Unlike some other natural disasters such as earthquakes and tornadoes, hurricanes generally give plenty of notice allowing time to prepare. If you're at the beach in the Carolinas when a hurricane is forecasted, follow the instructions of authorities, including orders to evacuate along marked routes leading inland. If you've planned ahead, you may be able to get back some of the money you've invested if your trip is cut short (see Top Secret).

The only upside to a hurricane we can think of is for serious shell collectors. Even storms less powerful than official hurricanes stir up the surf and sand on the bottom of the sea. The morning after a big blow is the perfect time to walk the beach with a bucket and collect a windfall: beautiful fanned, spiral, and cylindrical treasures.

Secret Information

For everything you ever wanted to know about hurricanes and to keep up with the latest news about storms that may threaten your vacation, check out the National Oceanic and Atmospheric Administration (NOAA) Web site at www.noaa.gov.

TOP SECRET

If your vacation gets blown away by a hurricane, you can't be sure you won't lose the money laid out for lodging, transportation, tour packages, or other services. To prevent problems, first check the cancellation and trip interruption policies of the people you are dealing with before you make a decision to buy. If they won't guarantee you'll get your money back if the weather, for example, forces you to flee your two thousand dollars-a-week beach-front rental house, you may want to buy travel insurance. It compensates you when a trip is canceled or interrupted by something out of your control. It makes the most sense when you've laid out a lot of cash in advance, and it doesn't duplicate insurance you already have, such as your automobile insurance or special insurance provided by a credit card company. The cost of such insurance tops out at about $80 per thousand dollars of coverage. Shop around for the best deal and carefully check out what's covered and what's not—the company's not likely to pay, for example, if you have a big fight with your spouse and have to call off that romantic beach getaway. For more information, check out these travel insurance providers: Access America (800-284-8300; www.accessamerica.com/accessamerica/consumer), Travel Guard International (800-826-1300; www.travel-guard.com) or Travelex Insurance Services (888-457-4602; www.travelex-insurance.com).

13

Advice 5¢

Simple Pleasure

According to Nancy Caviness, operating a bed-and-breakfast involves more than just cleaning rooms and making meals. "We'd originally taken the name Advice 5¢ from Lucy in Charles Schulz's *Peanuts* comic strip," she says. "After we opened, we realized how much advice an innkeeper really gives guests—how to maximize a short stay, where to go, and what to do. Some people are skeptical of the name; for others it fits into their adventurous spirit, but it's turned out to fit what we do." With partner Donna Black, Caviness built Advice 5¢ in 1995 in the upper Outer Banks community of Duck, North Carolina. The place's laid-back attitude is summed up in its slogan: "Life is too short to wear tight shoes."

The pair had become friends through their shared interest in marathon running. Caviness was a health educator and Black an exercise physiologist. Neither had any experience in the hospitality industry. "We are from upstate New York—the Finger Lakes area," Caviness explains. "Part of the reason we came to the Outer Banks originally was to run free of ice and snow. We wanted to stay in a bed-and-breakfast in Duck, but there wasn't one, so we decided to open our own."

Their bed-and-breakfast is tucked away in the residential neighborhood of Sea Pines, just a short walk from what could be generously called "downtown" Duck. "The village has a charm and quaintness unlike other Outer Banks communities," says Caviness, "but there are no hotels here. People who stayed here before we opened had to either rent a cottage that sleeps ten to twelve or stay at the Sanderling Inn (Secret 8), which is upscale and elegant. We fill a niche."

Simplicity is the guiding principle at Advice 5¢. "The decor is cottage style with traditional seaside cottage furnishings," says Caviness, describing the feeling she and Black tried to create for not only their bed-and-breakfast, but the home in which they live. "It's not antique and not modern; our decorating style is minimalist. We maximize the

The Great Room at Advice 5¢ sets a tone of casual comfort for the only bed-and-breakfast on the northernmost Outer Banks. (COURTESY OF ADVICE 5¢)

sunlight, using minimal window treatments. There are ceiling fans used for ambience—though the place is centrally air-conditioned. There is nothing in trendy seaside style. We decorated it to be our home."

Advice 5¢ is set up as a place for adult rest and relaxation; they'll take children over age sixteen when staying with a parent but not younger boarders. There are just five guest rooms (one is a suite with a day room, cable television, and whirlpool), all with private baths and a private deck or porch. A continental breakfast includes the bed-and-breakfast's own blend of coffee, muffins, scones, breads, fresh fruits, juices, smoothies, and cereals. Guests also get treated to an afternoon "tea" with goodies such as lemonade served with homemade ginger snaps or brownies served on the porch. "Guests say they appreciate the baked-from-scratch, homemade, not ostentatious foods," says Caviness.

A private walkway from the bed-and-breakfast takes you right to the beach where there are towels and chairs to borrow and an outdoor shower to wash the sand from between your toes. A swimming pool and tennis courts lie nearby. In cooler weather, the pair of proprietors light the fireplace, protecting guests against the chill that sometimes travels between the Atlantic Ocean and Currituck Sound. If you really want to tell your stress to scram, have them schedule a therapeutic massage for you.

"People at the beach are looking for a casual, simple ambience," says Caviness summing up Advice 5¢'s appeal, "You can come in from the beach, take a big glass of lemonade out on deck, and hang out or go upstairs and play a game. It is not formal or stuffy."

Our nickel's worth of advice: check into Advice 5¢.

Secret Information

Location: Duck, North Carolina.
Address: 111 Scarborough Lane, PO Box 8278, Duck, NC 27949.
Phone: 800-238-4235 or 252-255-1050.
E-mail: advice5@theouterbanks.com.
Web site: www.theouterbanks.com/advice5
Season: From the President's Day/Valentine's Day weekend in February through Thanksgiving Day.
Rates: Off-season $95 to $120 per night. In-season $140 to $175 per night.
Reservations: Recommended.
Credit cards: MasterCard, Visa.
Details: Two-night minimum stay; three nights minimum during holidays; one-night stays may be booked within seven days, if available, for an additional charge.

TOP SECRET

Nancy Caviness and Donna Black, owners of Advice 5¢, are proud of their adopted home of Duck—a (forgive the cliché, but it applies) cozy village unlike any other on the Outer Banks. Even if you don't stay at their bed-and-breakfast, head up North Carolina Highway 12 for a day trip to engage in water sports, shop for antiques, visit galleries, or eat at local favorite restaurants like the Blue Point Bar and Grill (252-261-8090) and Elizabeth's Cafe and Winery (252-261-6145). The community completed the "Duck Trail," a pedestrian/bicycling path a couple of years ago making it easy to explore the tiny town.

Fisherman's Wharf Restaurant

14

Down by the Docks

Most people who travel over Roanoke Sound on the Washington Baum Bridge from Whalebone Junction take a right when they hit Roanoke Island, North Carolina. That's where the county seat of Manteo is located, and there's a lot worth looking at up there. But if you're out around lunch or dinner time, don't be like most people. Instead, take a left just after the bridge at the little sign that says WANCHESE.

Wanchese was named for the Native American who accompanied Chief Manteo to England on the 1584 return voyage of the original English explorers. It is not a squeaky clean tourist version of a fishing village with gift shops and lots of windsocks, but a real down-and-dirty working fishing village where the locals actually fish to put, well, fish on the table. Generations of fishermen have grown up, married, raised families, and died here. In fact local real estate transaction records show that less than ten Wanchese properties come up for sale each year. Roots run deep in Wanchese, and they all stretch deep into the ocean.

If you follow Route 345 south into Wanchese you'll run smack into the heart of this fishing Mecca. There are huge fishing boats, refrigerated trucks backing in and pulling away with loads of fresh seafood, marine repair and supply stores, shipbuilding outfits, and in the middle of it all, the best place on the Outer Banks for a fresh seafood lunch or supper, The Fisherman's Wharf Restaurant.

The restaurant and docks and boats that surround it belong to the Daniels family—proud owners of the Wanchese Fish Company. What began in 1936 as a small commercial fishing company by Malcolm Daniel's father-in-law, W. R. Etheridge, has grown into an international operation, which includes modern packing and processing facilities in Hampton, Virginia, and New Bedford, Massachusetts. Malcolm, who died in 1986, is survived by his wife Maude and eleven sons and four daughters. Although some have chosen non-fishing careers, they all

Catch seafood fresh from the working docks of Wanchese at the Fisherman's Wharf Restaurant.

have played a role in building the Daniels family seafaring tradition, which includes the Wanchese restaurant that opened in 1974.

Back then, the Daniels served fifty to sixty customers a day. Now five hundred to six hundred lunches and dinners are served in the simple, dockside restaurant with views of the fishing boats and marsh. During the summer, many of the trawlers visible through the huge dining room windows are ones in the Daniels' fleet. Each boat bears a family name like *Capt. Malc.* and *Miss Maude*, both of which were constructed in Wanchese by the Roanoke Island Steel and Boat Works. While the Daniels' boats fish the east coast from North Carolina to the Gulf Of Maine, the Daniels' fish company processes scallops and fish fillets to be shipped across the nation and around the globe. Fortunately for diners, some of the catch stays at home for the restaurants up and down the Outer Banks—none fresher than the straight-from-the-docks seafood at the Daniels' own restaurant. As you sip some iced tea and wait for your made-to-order meal, you can watch one of the Daniels or his neighbors heading out to sea anticipating the next catch.

The seafood is fresh, just like the homemade coleslaw and the faces of the young servers who make you feel at home. No matter what you have, if it originally lived in the sea, it hasn't been away from home long. Start out with a cup of thick Fisherman's Wharf She-Crab Soup or go straight to the Miss Maude's Crab Imperial topped with white sauce. Most everything on the menu can be either fried, broiled, or sautéed, and although it seems a shame, there are plenty of non-fish entrees available, including the "Never Did Like Fish" fried chicken breast strips on the children's menu. Everything is served with homemade hush puppies and coleslaw, and from noon to 3 P.M. there are daily seafood luncheon specials and luncheon platters. If you have room (which is highly unlikely), finish off your meal with a slice of one of the Daniels' special homemade coconut or chocolate pies—it's a secret family recipe.

Secret information:

Location: In Wanchese on Roanoke Island, North Carolina.
Address: Highway 345 South, Wanchese, NC 27981.
Phone: 252-473-5205.
Fax: 252-473-5004.
Hours: Noon to 9 P.M. Monday through Saturday.
Price: Lunches range from $6 to $11; Dinners range from $10 to $17.
Reservations: Not accepted.
Credit cards: Diners Club, Discover, MasterCard, Visa.

TOP SECRET

If you're on the Outer Banks the last weekend in June, head on over to the Wanchese Seafood Industrial Park just up the road from the Fisherman's Wharf Restaurant for the annual Wanchese Seafood Festival. There's the traditional Blessing of the Fleet, live music, commercial fishing-oriented displays, kids' activities, arts and crafts, and best of all, there's no admission fee. Talk to the commercial fishermen and learn about life in a real fishing village, then chow down on fresh seafood platters and steamed crabs. Call Angie Brady-Daniels at 252-441-8144, 9 A.M. to 5 P.M. weekdays for more details.

15

Nags Head Woods Preserve

Where the Wild Things Are

Think Nags Head and you're likely to picture sand, sun, waves, wind, and kites—not acres of untamed forest filled with towering trees, wild creatures, and miles of trails to explore. The reason is that The Nature Conservancy, which operates the Nags Head Woods Preserve in Nags Head, North Carolina, hasn't been anxious to publicize the existence of their pristine slice of the otherwise populated central Outer Banks. They've mostly been concentrating on the slow and steady work of arranging for such prime real estate to be preserved in its natural state, not on advertising that it's open for visitors to explore. Therefore, those who do know about the site are generally left to wander the woods undisturbed by civilization, only miles away from the bustle of the beach.

The preserve lies partly in Nags Head and partly in the neighboring town of Kill Devil Hills. It features the thickest concentration of wooded wilderness in the area. There are beeches, hickories, and towering oaks, including a five-hundred-year-old beauty that's reported to be the oldest known tree in the woods and probably shaded the area's first inhabitants—the Algonkian Indians. The wilderness's entrance, marked by a visitor's center featuring an introductory film and kids' activities as well as a gift shop selling all manner of nature-related stuff, is hidden at the end of a Kill Devil Hills residential neighborhood. The preserve covers fourteen hundred acres of maritime swamp forest (known to exist in fewer than five locations in the world) and boasts a diverse collection of plant and animal life that's downright unbelievable on such a wild and windy barrier island. More than three hundred plant species have been identified here, including woolly beach heather (*Hudsonia tomentosa*) and mosquito fern (*Azolla caroliniana*), both of which are considered rare in North Carolina. There are cottonmouth snakes and marbled salamanders in the swamps; woodpeckers and prothonotary warblers and 150 or so other bird species in the trees; river otters and wood ducks in the water; and white-tailed deer and gray fox roaming the woods with opossums and raccoons.

Since this is a preserve, not a zoo, you probably won't see all of the creatures who call this natural treasure home. But if you walk softly, carry a big pair of binoculars (and some bug spray), and try a different trail each time you visit, you're sure to see your fair share of wildlife in the woods and thirty-four freshwater ponds. There are more than five miles of public walking trails through the preserve, ranging from the quick quarter-mile Center Trail loop to the 1.6-mile, out-and-back Nags Head Town Trail that climbs several ridges on its way to the shore of Roanoke Sound and takes about an hour or so to complete. The most popular, yet rugged, trail is the Sweetgum Swamp Trail. It's two miles long and leads up several steep ridges. This trail branches off from the easy Center Trail and makes a partial loop, so you can send the teenagers ahead and sit in the shade and silence while they hike their little hearts out.

Although the preserve today is home only to the webbed and woolly types, not so long ago families made their homes in this forest. In the early twentieth century, there were houses on the edge of the sound and at the forest's southern boundary. The residents were farmers, hunters, and fishermen. Some even made a living hauling in goods that washed ashore from shipwrecks in the wild waters a couple of miles to the east. Children attended a neighborhood school, and families worshipped in two churches located here. The last resident, Maggie Tillett, left in 1948, but several cemeteries and some remnants of the homesteads can still be seen in the preserve.

Any day is perfect for wandering through the woods. Be sure to call first since the hours differ with the seasons. Whatever time you choose, there'll be plenty to see and appreciate. In March and April the wildflowers are in bloom, in spring and fall the birding is at its peak, and on a hot-enough-to-fry-a-flapjack Outer Banks summer day, the shaded preserve is definitely the coolest place to be for miles around. And when under a live oak that's older than our nation itself you stop to think about it, this slice of natural wonder is one of the coolest places on earth.

Secret Information

Location: About one mile west of the intersection of West Acres Drive and U.S.Highway 158 at milepost 9.5 in Kill Devil Hills, North Carolina.
Address: 701 West Ocean Acres Drive, Kill Devil Hills, NC 27948.
Phone: 252-441-2525 or 252-441-4381 for recorded message about weekly programs.
Fax: 252-441-1271.
E-mail: jmcninch@tnc.org.
Web site: www.tnc.org (Nature Conservancy site).
Hours: 10 A.M. to 3 P.M. Monday through Saturday.
Season: Year-round but hours and days open may vary by season; call ahead for schedule.
Price: $3 suggested donation per person; fees charged for special programs and guided tours.
Reservations: Not needed except for special programs.
Credit cards: MasterCard, Visa.

TOP SECRET

The best way to experience the Nags Head Woods Preserve is through one of the special programs offered throughout the year. For summer tourists, there are guided field trips and kayak tours, children's eco-camps, and a popular Friday Family Fun program that gives parents and kids the chance to participate in hands-on nature activities. Enrollment is limited for every program, so call the Nags Head Woods Preserve office a few months before your vacation to see what's scheduled when you'll be on the Outer Banks.

16

Run Over to the Rundown

When Will Thorp closes down his Rundown Cafe in Kitty Hawk, North Carolina, for December and January, he likes to escape to a warm, sunny island far from his Outer Banks home. The Cayman Islands are his favorite, and his ideal resort is one that doesn't allow kids.

"After you deal with the public and children a lot, you want to find a resort that doesn't allow children and where someone will cook for *you* for a change," says Thorp. "I've found a place in the Caymans where you can hole up for a week and get the local flavor."

The name of that resort is a secret Thorp is keeping, but he is willing to spread the word about his own Caribbean-style restaurant. And despite his desire to spend his free time in a kid-free environment, Thorp isn't at all anti-rugrats. In fact, he runs one of the most family-friendly restaurants on the northern end of the Outer Banks. That's precisely why (as any parent knows) he needs an annual well-deserved break from the small frys.

"We get a lot of families from Duck and Corolla who can't afford to go out to eat with their kids up there," says Thorp, whose kids' menu includes the standard corn dog, PB and J, chicken fingers, grilled cheese, and cheese pizza. "With retail space going for twenty to thirty dollars a foot up there, they have to charge thirty to forty dollars per person. When customers ask about the stroller and the kids, they tell them to go down to the Rundown."

Whether or not you have kids in tow, you also need to go down, or up, to the Rundown. It's Thorp's second restaurant on the Outer Banks. The youthful Rocky Mount native opened his first restaurant, Tortuga's Lie Shellfish Bar and Grille, down in Nags Head in 1989, at age twenty-seven. Besides the same creative Caribbean-style fare dished up at the Rundown Cafe, Tortuga's signature feature is the ceiling filled with more than a hundred license plates from all over the world. Thorp started with only four tacked up to a beam, and customers supplied the rest, often taking off their plates in the parking lot during a visit. Look

Tortuga's Lie Shellfish Bar and Grille in Nags Head is an older sister restaurant to The Rundown Cafe in Kitty Hawk.

for one of Thorp's favorite plates ("one of only a couple I've ever coveted," he says) that reads "4N6DOC." That stands for forensic psychologist and belonged to one of Thorp's regulars.

Rundown is the Jamaican name for a dish served throughout the Caribbean made with fish boiled in coconut milk. Thorp's Rundown Cafe actually serves the dish ($3.25 a cup and $3.75 a bowl), plus a wide variety of creative Caribbean dishes ranging from Vandaloo—shrimp or roasted pork with onions and potatoes in a spicy Indian curry sauce—to a local favorite, St. Martin Shrimp—fettucine with sautéed shrimp, onions, bacon, garlic, tomatoes, and white wine.

"The dinner specials that we change nightly are our most creative items," Thorp says. "We put the seafood on special because it changes fast depending on what's fresh. Most of the people come to the beach for the seasonal crab and shrimp, and the tuna is a standard you've got to have on the menu. Our vegetarian dishes are also very popular, and we'll be adding more because of the demand."

Thorp developed the Caribbean style out of a desire to be different. When he opened Tortuga's Lie, only two restaurants served food all winter—Kelley's and Awful Arthur's, which are both big, popular eateries specializing in seafood and standard landlubber fare. After consulting with friends who had worked in Caribbean-style restaurants and assembling menus from places he and his friends had traveled, Thorp came up with a menu heavy on blackened, jerked, and anything spicy. With the addition of the Rundown in 1993 (located in the former Journey's End Hotel restaurant), Thorp was able to expand upon his original menu, since a bigger kitchen and dining room provided more opportunities for culinary creativity.

Don't let the bright Caribbean hues and the unusual menu items scare you away if you're more a meat-and-potatoes or fried-shrimp-and-slaw kind of diner. The Rundown Cafe has a little bit of something for everyone. One of the tastiest little bits is an order of the Tuna Bites off the appetizer menu. The chunks of tuna are lightly fried and served with a honey and jerk spice dipping sauce. If you'd rather not make your meal an adventure, munch the bites plain. But if you're ready to take a taste trip to the Caribbean, dip the bites in the delicious sauce, and wash the whole thing down with a frothy Black and Tan—a pint-sized combo of Guinness Stout and Bass Ale.

"We like to think of the Outer Banks as the family man's Caribbean," says Thorp, who also notes that the cafe's gooey, fresh baked desserts are worth a visit to the Rundown by themselves. "Most of these guys would much prefer to be like their single co-workers and go to Jamaica or somewhere, but they can't. At least here they can say that they got the cracked conch and black beans and rice and all the stuff you'd get at the islands right here at the beach."

Secret Information

Location:	Kitty Hawk, North Carolina.
Address:	5300 North Virginia Dare Trail, Kitty Hawk, NC ZIP 27949.
Phone:	252-255-0026.
Hours:	11:30 A.M. until "whenever," daily.
Season:	Usually closed on Sundays in October and November and in early spring. Closed December and January.
Price:	Lunches range from $5 to $7; Dinners range from $6 to $15.
Reservations:	Not accepted.
Credit cards:	American Express, Discover, MasterCard, Visa.

TOP SECRET

One of the best things that the Rundown Cafe offers isn't even on the menu. It's on the roof. The rooftop deck (designed as a holding area for patrons waiting for a table) is the perfect place to sip Jamaican Red Stripe beer and watch the sunset. In season, there's live music up there from 7 P.M. to 11 P.M. When you're swaying to the reggae beat and inhaling those jerk spices floating up from the kitchen below, it's not too difficult to look out over the moonlit ocean and imagine that you're in the Caribbean. (Okay, so maybe it will take more than one beer, but you get the idea.)

17

Tranquil House Inn

On The Waterfront

The first thing you notice when you cross the bridge from Whalebone Junction to Roanoke Island on North Carolina's Outer Banks is the wind. Somewhere along the way the wind disappears. You don't have to hold your baseball cap on anymore. You can roll down the windows without losing every map and anything else that isn't bolted down. All is calm. All is right with the world. It's the perfect setting for a place called the Tranquil House Inn.

Although the inn is located in the postcard-perfect village of Manteo, North Carolina, its chocolate brown shingles and nineteenth-century architecture evoke memories of grand New England waterfront manor homes on the rocky coast of Maine or Massachusetts. There are three sprawling levels, a rooftop widow's walk, and a broad back sundeck where innkeepers Donnie and Lauri Just serve a continental breakfast in the mornings and wine (or lemonade) and cheese at sunset. Despite the look and feel of a grand home (reinforced by lots of custom cypress wood and stained glass), the inn is thoroughly modern. It was rebuilt in 1987 after fire destroyed the previous structure and was modeled after the hotel that occupied the site from the late 1880s until the 1950s. This new oldness gives visitors all the charming nooks and crannies of a historic inn without the less appealing features older homes are famous for, like no air-conditioning or cable television, and limited hot water.

Most people visit Manteo to tour the Lost Colony and climb aboard the replica of the *Elizabeth II*, a full-scale reconstruction of a sixteenth-century sailing ship named for one of Sir Walter Raleigh's vessels that brought the first colonists to the New World in 1585. That ship (when it's not out on an occasional commemorative voyage), sits in Shallowbag Bay, the watery front yard of the Tranquil House and can be reached via Ice Plant Island (see Top Secret), a short trek across the footbridge beside the inn. Or better still, check out one of the free rental bikes at the front desk and explore the island's walking trail in early evening.

Local legend has it that the Lost Colonists probably traveled inland with the local Native American tribe when they ran out of food and supplies, but there's no reason for you to leave the Tranquil House Inn for sustenance. The inn's sophisticated 1587 Restaurant is noted for its world-class chefs who use herbs grown in the inn's own gardens to prepare fresh Atlantic seafood, free-range and certified angus meat and fowl, and vegetables fresh from Outer Banks farms. Since Donnie Just, general manager of both the 1587 and the Tranquil House, strives to use the freshest seasonal ingredients, the menu changes regularly. Favorite selections available at various times throughout the year include: Pepper-Seared Salmon atop Shrimp-Studded Wild Rice, surrounded by a Dijon Mustard Cream and finished with Fried Spinach; and Cajun Grilled Filet Mignon fanned over a White Cheddar, Prosciutto Ham, Potato and Corn Hash, finished with a Mixed Baby Greens-Roasted Red Pepper Salad. The restaurant also features a children's menu (well-mannered graduates from high chairdom would feel most comfortable here), and Executive Chef Donny King and his staff welcome vegetarian requests. One of King's most colorful (and delicious) vegetarian creations is the Southwestern Sauté of Bell Peppers, Sweet Corn, Spring Onions, and Roma Tomatoes surrounding Smoked Gouda Cheese Polenta. Although on the upscale range (vegetarian dishes are about $14.95, while other offerings range from $16.95 to $22.95), the quaint harbor view setting, romantic candlelit ambience, and the respite from the tourists are worth it. If you (or your wallet) are not up to a full-blown dinner, at least pull up a chair at the copper-topped bar and toast a summer moonrise.

The twenty-five guest rooms at the Tranquil House vary in size and price. There are canopy, four-poster, queen, and king beds. The mini-suites even have separate bedrooms and comfy sitting areas. The decor in each is as distinctive as the beds. No two rooms are exactly alike, except in quality and charm. Berber carpets, Oriental rugs, designer wallpaper, hardwood floors, and custom-sewn comforters are the norm. If you have your choice and can swing it, ask for one of the third floor harbourside end rooms. You'll have to hike up a couple flights of stairs, but the end rooms are spacious with high ceilings and dormers providing the illusion of even more space. There's a writing desk, a view of the *Elizabeth II* (which is illuminated in the evenings),

The Tranquil House Inn lies in the heart of Manteo's calm waterfront area.

two comfortable queen size beds, a sitting area, a television, a huge walk-in closet, a private tiled bath, and three windows perfect for watching the boats docking in the harbor and people strolling along the sidewalk in front of the inn.

All the comfy nooks and crannies at the Tranquil Inn are perfect for curling up with a good book. You could bring your own, of course, but it's much more fun to stroll up the street to the equally charming Manteo Booksellers (252-473-1221). The homey bookstore boasts an impressive collection of titles relating to pirates, the Outer Banks, and coastal history, culture, and lore. There's an extensive children's section, cards and gifts, and plenty of chairs and carpet where you can stretch out as you browse. After you pick up the perfect beach book, there's plenty more to do within walking distance of the inn—ice cream and coffee shops, kayak rentals, a small park with swings, boutiques featuring clothing, toys, and antiques—so once you park your car in the Tranquil House's wildflower-lined lot, you'll probably never need it again until check-out. Unless, of course, you miss the wind, the blowing sand, the crowds, and the mini-golf. Then you'll have to head back over the bridge where life will never be so tranquil.

Secret Information

Location: Manteo, North Carolina.
Address: 405 Queen Elizabeth Street, Roanoke Island, NC 27954.
Phone: 800-458-7069 or 252-473-1404
Fax: 252-473-1526.
E-mail: djust1587@aol.com.
Web site: www.1587.com.
Rates: Off season $79 to $129 per night. In season $124 to $144 per night.
Reservations: Recommended.
Credit cards: American Express, Discover, MasterCard, Visa.
Details: Rates include evening wine reception and continental breakfast.

TOP SECRET

The island you see from the deck of the Tranquil House Inn is home to Manteo's newest educational and cultural attraction—Roanoke Island Festival Park. Completed in 1998, the park features an eighty-five hundred-square-foot exhibit hall filled with interactive displays designed to transport visitors back to the days when the first English settlers arrived on Roanoke Island through the early 1900s. Tour guides dressed as Elizabethans escort visitors aboard the *Elizabeth II* sailing ship and classical and popular musicians provide the sounds for frequent summer concerts at the outdoor performance pavilion. A forty-five minute film, *The Legend of Two Path*, provides tourists with a Native American perspective on the English landing at Roanoke, and a small theater hosts other historical plays and films throughout the year, except when the park is closed in January and February. Kids will especially enjoy the Museum Store, which is filled with Lost Colony toys and trinkets that will add a dose of historical accuracy to any playroom. Rates are $8 for adults, $4 for students, and no charge for children under five. The hours vary depending on the month, so call the Roanoke Festival Island Park twenty-four-hour events line at 252-475-1500 for the most up-to-date information.

18

Risky Business Seafood Market

Fish To Go

Steve Bailey admits that some people are put off by the name of his pair of shops on Hatteras Island, North Carolina—Risky Business Seafood Market. He chose the name years ago when he was younger and more foolish but still thinks it makes sense. "Anytime you gotta buy fresh and sell it before it gets old…I don't know of a riskier business than that."

It's not only risky, but exhausting. In season, Bailey starts work at 4 A.M. seven days a week and doesn't stop until as late as eight at night. "I've got to make a living while the tourists are here," he explains. "If I don't have what they want, they go elsewhere. I've got to have fish, shrimp, scallops, and crabmeat from week to week. A lot of business is repeat here on Hatteras. People come back year after year, and I need to have what they want or I lose business. I've been selling seafood long enough that I'm getting the kids of old customers." Bailey opened his first store on the water in Hatteras Village in 1984, "then I got a wife and built one for her" up the island in Buxton. He runs the southern branch of the business; his spouse, Beth, the northern. ("Mention her name or she'll kill me," he asked when we talked with him. There you go, Steve.)

Although you cannot sit down and have a meal at Risky Business, we've put it in the category of Places to Eat because they are the best folks in the lower Outer Banks from whom to buy fresh seafood. The Baileys' three hundred-square-foot, cooler-filled shops tucked in buildings with other Maritime businesses may not prepare it for you, but they do offer the best seafood for you to cook in your rented beach house or condo. Bailey is a stickler about selling the finest quality ocean fare. "There is nothing in my store I wouldn't bring home. We have Norwegian salmon flown in, tuna, mahimahi, black tip shark, mako shark, swordfish, Spanish mackerel, flounder fillet and whole flounder, red snapper, large shrimp, jumbo shrimp, sea scallops, bluefish, crabmeat, Alaskan crab legs—everyone likes that—and on Tuesday and Wednesday, fresh soft-shell crab, steamed male and female crabs, and a live-crab tank. We have all the herbs, spices, and marinades for fried and broiled fish—anything I can sell to a bunch of Yankees."

Risky Business's services extend to helping inexperienced customers prepare seafood just right. One key is to choose what you buy carefully. "Fresh fish looks clear, not translucent, but shiny," Bailey reveals. "And it has no odor at all, except for shrimp which start to smell as soon as they're caught, but not with an offensive odor. Any strong odor means the fish is not fresh." Fresh fish should also be firm to the touch; Risky Business is one of the few seafood markets that lets customers pick up and inspect the catch. "That doesn't mean they can feel the fillet," Bailey adds. "We have health requirements, but customers can put the fish up to their nose to check the smell."

As for cooking seafood, the key is not to overdo it. "The thing most people don't know," says Bailey, "is that fish continues to cook after being removed from the heat. Most people cook fish too long. A fish fillet should flake or open like the pages of a book when pierced with a fork." Both of the Risky Business stores have herb gardens, and you can ask the staff for recipes and advice on how best to whip up the perfect homemade seafood feast.

Secret Information

Location: In Buxton and Hatteras Village on Hatteras Island, North Carolina.
Address: P.O. Box 106, Hatteras, NC 27943.
Phone: 800-691-5569.
Fax: 252-986-1432.
E-mail: riskyb@interpath.com.
Web site: www.riskybseafood.com.
Hours: 9 A.M. to 7 P.M.
Season: Easter to the end of October.
Price: Shrimp $8 to $12 per pound. Scallops $8 to $11 per pound. See Web site for more prices.
Credit cards: MasterCard, Visa.
Details: Both stores are located inside much larger buildings that house other businesses. Look for the signs.

TOP SECRET

To make his business less risky, Risky Business Seafood Market owner Steve Bailey has diversified and set up shop on the World Wide Web. With just a few clicks you can order shrimp, scallops, red snapper, tuna steaks, swordfish, flounder fillets, sea trout, or soft-shell crabs straight from the waters of the Outer Banks. The seafood is packed fresh and shipped overnight to your doorstep. Though it's more expensive than in your local supermarket, it's likelier to be fresh and free-range, as opposed to farm raised. You can order over the Internet at www.riskybseafood.com or, if you're not cyber-savvy, you can call 800-691-5569.

Frisco Woods Campground

Camping Lite

19

In our minds, there are two kinds of camping: hard-core and soft-core. Hard-core is the kind of camping that you do in spots such as Portsmouth Island (Secret 36). These are truly wild places where it's just you and nature, and the appeal is to completely escape from everyone and everything in modern life—traffic, telephones, television. Soft-core camping, or camping lite, has a whole other appeal. Staying at a developed campground offers the chance to sit under the stars without giving up all the conveniences of life—a swimming pool, cable television, and shooting the breeze with someone in the next site.

Fortunately, the Outer Banks has the best of both camping worlds. The camping lite variety is represented by Frisco Woods Campground in Frisco, North Carolina, on Hatteras Island. Unlike many commercial campsites that are no more than parking lots for RVs, the twenty-five-acre site on the sound side of the Outer Banks has retained a true natural feeling. "One of the things people like most about our campground is all the tall pines and oak trees native to the island," says Kathy White, who manages Frisco Woods with her husband, Gordon Thompson. "They create a low canopy that's neat to camp underneath. We refer to ourselves as a naturalized campground. We don't have concrete pads, and we think it's important to keep the original landscape. It has the true feeling of being out in nature."

This is all thanks to the good graces of owners Ward and Betty Barnett, who live on the property. They started the campground in 1975 and have expanded it to include 100 sites with no hookups, 150 sites with water and electricity, and about 40 sites with full hook-ups, including cable television. Frisco Woods is the only commercial campground on the Outer Banks to offer true waterfront living, with sites just a few feet from the sound's edge. There are also eight comfy one- and two-room cabins (bring your own bedding and linens). Amenities include a pool, bathhouses, hot showers, laundry facilities, and a large campground store.

Along with relaxing under the canopy, there are such activities as fishing, kayaking, and windsurfing (see Top Secret), all popular diversions.

It's something more subtle than the fun and facilities, though, that draws regular campers back to Frisco Woods—it's common to encounter folks who've been coming back annually for twenty years. "It's the feeling that this place has," says White, grasping to explain what makes the campground special. "It has the sense that everyone is one big family, and yet you can also have your privacy. My husband and I came to Hatteras on vacation, camped here the first time, and never went anywhere else after that. Something about this place grabs you."

Secret Information

Location: Frisco, North Carolina.
Address: P.O. Box 159, Frisco, North Carolina 27936.
Phone: 800-948-3942 or 252-995-5208.
Fax: 252-995-6257.
E-mail: friscowd@pinn.net.
Hours: Check-in office open 8:30 AM to 6 PM. On holiday weekends, hours are extended
Season: March to December.
Price: $22 and up.
Reservations: Recommended.
Credit cards: American Express, Discover, MasterCard, Visa.
Details: Pets allowed.

TOP SECRET

Besides being a prime place to pitch your tent and watch the sunset over the sound, Frisco Woods Campground is also one of the best places on the East Coast to windsurf. Fans of jumping the waves while striding a surf board and hanging onto a sail flock here for the ideal combination of wind and water off the campground's private launching area. It's the site of the annual Windfest celebration, which brings windsurfers, equipment manufacturers, sponsors, and others together for three days of fun and events in the spring. You don't need to stay at Frisco Woods to windsurf from the campground—they'll sell you a day pass for five dollars per person, which not only gives you access to their launching site, but lets you use their pool, bathhouses, and other facilities. Call the campground for details (see Secret Information).

Flying Fete

20

The folks living on the Outer Banks year-round feel like they owe you an apology. You see, during the summer they get about seven million visitors, and it's rush, rush, rush all the time. It isn't that they don't care, but with all that company they don't often get the chance to spend a lot of quality time showing off the area, of which they are so proud. To make up for that, they started the annual Wings Over Water Festival in 1997. The November event, which now draws thousands of people, is held in part to expose visitors to the true Outer Banks experience, particularly the multitude of feathered fauna that live in or migrate through the North Carolina barrier islands.

"In the fall, we have extra time to spend with visitors," explains Angie Brady-Daniels of the Outer Banks Chamber of Commerce (252-441-8144), one of several area groups that co-organizes the festival. "It's also a good time of year to sneak up on nature, to get up close and personal, which is more difficult with all the people here in the summer. The festival's focus is to draw attention to the area's wildlife and wetlands, and it consists of more than thirty expert-guided field trips all along the Outer Banks and on the mainland."

The excursions are rated A, B, or C—with A being for serious birders (if you can recognize the call of the orange-crowned warbler, this is the level for you), B for more casual bird watchers , and C for those with more general interest in wildlife, landscape, and history. Past festivals have featured the A-rated trek to Bodie Island to hunt for King Rails and American Bitterns, for example, while a typical C-rated outing is a canoe trip to the Pea Island area. The dedicated birders log their sightings—more than two hundred species were spotted during the 1998 festival.

There are also dozens of other workshops and seminars on subjects such as identifying shore birds, photographing wildlife, and doing Japanese fish printing (creating fish print designs on rice paper or T-shirts).

Bird lovers flock to see both familiar fauna like pelicans and gulls and rarer feathered wildlife during the Outer Banks' Wings Over Water festival. (COURTESY OF DARE COUNTY TOURIST BUREAU)

Special events include a keynote speech by a noted naturalist, a photo contest, and a family festival at a local school. The entire program gives those of us interested in the environment the chance to learn about the wild world straight from world-class scientists, naturalists, and nature lovers, whom they would probably never meet under normal circumstances.

"During the festival, visitors can come to the Outer Banks and spend quality time with experts," says Brady-Daniels. "We're thought of as a summer beach community, but there's much more to us than that. Wings Over Water gives people the chance to see that firsthand and get a whole new perspective on the Outer Banks."

Secret Information

Location: Throughout the Outer Banks and on the mainland.
Address: Dare County Tourist Bureau, P.O. Box 399, Manteo, NC 27954.
Phone: 800-446-6262 or 252-473-2138.
Fax: 252-473-5106.
E-mail: dctb-info@outer-banks.com.
Web site: www.northeast-nc.com/wings.
Season: Takes place annually for three days in early November.
Price: The trips range from $10 to $75 per person.
Reservations: Recommended.
Credit cards: MasterCard, Visa.

TOP SECRET

One of the most popular field excursions during Wings Over Water is the Red Wolf Howling Safari. As darkness falls, participants leave from the Creef Cut Wildlife Trail, which is on U.S. Highway 64 west of Roanoke Island, and travel to the Red Wolf Camp in the Alligator River Wildlife Refuge (Secret 1). They try to "howl out" the endangered wolves that the U.S. Fish and Wildlife Service is trying to reintroduce into the wild throughout the country. The population is slowly coming back from a low of just one hundred red wolves in the world in 1970. The refuge, in fact, hosts howlings not only during the festival but on most Wednesdays during the summer and on other days during the spring and fall, including a "Christmas Howling." For more information, contact the organizers of Wings Over Water (see Secret Information) or call Alligator River at 252-473-1131, extension 12.

21

Outer Banks International Hostel

Hostel Environment

The Outer Banks International Hostel is anything but—hostile that is. "People tend to stay with us for the friendly atmosphere," says Jim Hornbrook, who owns the spot in Kitty Hawk with his wife, Barb. "The biggest thing here is talking about where you've been, where you're going, what you have to see, and what other hostels you've stayed in. A lot of people check in for one day until they meet other people and start doing things together, then they decide to extend their stay. You can be as sociable or as unsociable as you want, but there are always people to talk to."

It is important to understand that hostels aren't just for scraggly-looking youths bumming their way from shelter to shelter. Hostels draw individuals, couples, and families of all ages who like the simplicity and authenticity of a style of travel that was born in Europe in the 1930s. It was inspired by a German school teacher named Richard Schirrmann, who started taking his students for weekend field trips to the country, during which they bunked down at local schools. That sparked not only the basic concept of a cheap place to sleep, but the idea that traveling is an educational and growth experience—a spirit that still pervades the hostel movement today. There are now 4.5 million members of hosteling associations and a network of five thousand hostels in seventy countries around the world—including the Outer Banks.

If you're on a tight travel budget, hostels are the way to go. The men's and women's dormitory at the Outer Banks facility, which was formerly the Kitty Hawk Elementary School, built in 1920, have basic bunks, or if you want more privacy with your significant other or family, the hostel has private rooms for a bargain compared to the pricey beach areas. Although you need to bring (or rent) your own sheets, the hostel has a full kitchen; a common room with cable television, books, and games; and a ten-acre site a mile and a half from

A former elementary school, the Outer Banks International Hostel is a sociable, affordable alternative to area hotels and motels. (COURTESY OF OUTER BANKS INTERNATIONAL HOSTEL)

the beach for campfires, picnics, and volleyball games. The hostel is air-conditioned, and unlike some others around the world, guests aren't required to do any chores, except for cleaning up after themselves. There's no curfew, so the doors aren't locked for the night. The clientele tends to be the outdoorsy type, and the hostel offers a whole range of activities, including guided kayak and canoe tours, bike rentals, even free use of crab nets and lines. Because of its affiliation with the Hosteling International, you're also likely to encounter travelers from Europe and other parts of the globe.

It's true that the Outer Banks International Hostel is the biggest bargain on the beach, but that's not really what makes it special. "We're not the Sheraton, and we don't try to be," says Hornbrook summing up the appeal of a hostel lifestyle. "We offer the chance to make friends from around the world and stay in a place that has a sense of adventure."

Secret Information

Location: Kitty Hawk, North Carolina.
Address: 1004 W. Kitty Hawk Road, Kitty Hawk NC 27949-4307.
Phone: 252-261-2294.
Fax: 252-261-2294.
E-mail: outerbankshostel@msn.com.
Web site: www.hiayh.org (Hosteling International/American Youth Hostels home page).
Hours: Office hours 8 A.M. to 10 A.M. and 4 P.M. to 9 P.M.
Rates: Basic bunks, $15 per night for members; $18 per night for non-members. Private rooms, $50 per night.
Reservations: Accepted.
Credit cards: MasterCard, Visa.
Details: Bring your own towels and sheets.

TOP SECRET

To get a discount at the Outer Banks International Hostel, and thousands of other hostels around the world, join Hosteling International–American Youth Hostels (HI-AYH). In the United States it's an association of thirty-five local or regional councils that oversee the network of hostels stretching from Bar Harbor, Maine, to Nilichik, Alaska, to Honolulu, Hawaii. Besides offering bargain accommodations, the councils organize a variety of programs, events, and trips designed to expand its members' understanding of the people of the world. No, you don't have to be young to join—hosteling is for people of all ages. Those under age eighteen get free HI-AYH memberships, adults eighteen to fifty-four pay $25 a year, and seniors fifty-five and older are $15 a year. You can also get a lifetime membership for $250. For details about memberships and hostel locations, visit the HI-AYH Web site (see Secret Information), send e-mail to hiayhserv@hiayh.org, call 202-783-6161, or write HI-AYH National Office, 733 15th Street, N.W., Suite 840, Washington, D.C. 20005.

Down Under Restaurant and Lounge

Good Eats, Mate

22

The bad news for those who've already discovered the Down Under Restaurant and Lounge in Rodanthe, North Carolina, is that Australian Brent "Skip" Skiperdene and his wife, Sheila—who made it the best spot on Hatteras Island to bring the family for breakfast, lunch, or dinner; to try kangaroo meat or vegemite for the first time; or to spend happy hour sipping a Foster's Lager, downing ten-cent shrimp, and soaking up the spectacular water views—have sold the place. The good news is that the new owners, Ron and Debbie Lemasters, who took over in 1999, know a good thing when they see it and have kept everything at the Down Under pretty much the same, which is sure to please all those who already know about it, as well as newcomers.

The Down Under is the only island eatery on the ocean. It's located on Rodanthe Pier and is part of the Hatteras Island Resort (see Top Secret), though it's separately owned. Its Australian theme is unique among Outer Banks eateries and is reflected in decor dotted with koalas, kangaroos, boomerangs, and other icons of the continent's culture. The menu features specialties such as 'Roo Stew and 'Roo Burgers. Yes, they are made with real kangaroo meat, which tastes like beef but is lower in fat and cholesterol. For those who like more traditional fare, there're also plenty of seafood, chicken, and pasta choices. Popular items include Down Under Shrimp—shrimp stuffed with cream cheese and jalapeños, wrapped in bacon, and browned. A burger topped with cheese and crabmeat is the perfect choice for lunch, and besides the standard array of bacon, biscuits, eggs, and pancakes, you can get items like a crabmeat omelet for breakfast. If you're really adventurous, try vegemite, a grease-like bread spread that must be an acquired taste.

The Down Under is family friendly with a good kids' menu and a corner with toys and a picnic table where tykes can play while waiting for their food. Get to the restaurant early or make reservations to avoid a sometimes lengthy wait for a table. Happy hour is a popular time for people both young and old to regroup after a day at the beach; have a beer or ice tea, munch on cheap shrimp or onion rings served on a foot-long skewer, and watch the sun slowly set over the sound.

Secret Information

Location: Hatteras Island, North Carolina.
Address: 24221 Marine Lane, Rodanthe, Hatteras Island, NC 27968.
Phone: 252-987-2277.
Hours: 7:30 A.M. to 9 P.M.; lounge open to 11 P.M.
Season: Easter to end of October.
Price: Breakfasts average $7; Lunches range from $6 to $7; Dinners range from $13 to $15.
Reservations: Recommended.
Credit cards: American Express, Discover, MasterCard, Visa.

TOP SECRET

Though a separate operation, the Down Under Restaurant and Lounge is part of the Hatteras Island Resort, a throwback to the days of families staying in simple cottages along the beach. Built in 1960, it includes thirty-five cottages, a thirty-two-unit motel, a swimming pool, and the fishing pier upon which the Down Under is perched. Guests generally rent by the week and spend their time sunning at the beach, fishing or crabbing from the pier, seeing sights such as the Cape Hatteras lighthouse (Secret 7), or playing basketball, volleyball, badminton, shuffleboard, or horseshoes. Rates run from fifty dollars a night for a room or efficiency in low season to nine hundred dollars a week for a four-bedroom oceanfront cottage in season. The resort is open from about Easter to Thanksgiving, depending on the weather. For more information or reservations, call 800-331-6541 or 252-987-2345 or visit www.insiders.com/outerbanks/wwwads/hatresrt/hatres.htm.

Hatteras Village Aqua Farm

Clam Up

23

Kevin Midgett and his family are as deeply dug into the Outer Banks as the untold millions of clams he's scattered in the eighteen acres of undersea muck at the Hatteras Village Aqua Farm. He's lived on the sea his entire life. He got his first boat at age nine and recalls huge storms battering the barrier islands while he was growing up. "We just opened up the front door and the back door, let the water flow through the house, and bailed it out the kitchen window."

The Aqua Farm, located in Hatteras, is a commercial operation raising two to five million clams a year, supplying restaurants throughout the United States. Inside a large, white, wooden building, Midgett tends huge flat sinks of water in which the clams are raised. At their earliest stages of fertilization, they are so small as to be invisible in the constantly recycling water. As they move from holding vat to holding vat, they grow bigger and are eventually transferred to the salty waters of Pamlico Sound, where they are harvested at about two years of age. Midgett's operation has gained a reputation for being one of the highest quality producers of clams in the country and is one of only two operations that soaks the clams in clean water after harvesting them to purge the mud (and grosser substances) from inside the shells before they wind up on your plate.

The farm drew in so many curious people wondering what it was that, a few years ago, Midgett also opened a small area for rake-your-own clamming. For four dollars per person (children under five are free), vacationers get a special rake, a net bag, and the chance to wade out a few hundred yards in the knee-deep water to dig up as many mollusks as they want. Midgett cautions clammers to wear sneakers or water shoes so the scads of sharp shells on the bottom don't cut your feet.

Capturing clams requires a little work. You have to stick the rake into the sandy bottom, then push it and pull it until you hit a hard shell. Then you scoop the shellfish out of the water and plop it in the bag.

Grab a rake and wade into the water for some classic clamming at the Hatteras Village Aqua Farm. (COURTESY OF NORTH CAROLINA COASTAL FEDERATION)

"It's basically set up for kids," says Midgett, who sees a lot of moms and dads bringing their offspring to recreate cherished memories of clamming as children. Some folks harvest hundreds of little necks, middle necks, top necks, cherry stones, top cherries, and other clam categories, which don't refer to different varieties but simply to the size. After they've had enough wading in the water, the clam hunters take their haul back to the farm office where their catch is graded. Anything over 7/8 inches is automatically thrown back, but you can decide which ones and how many to keep of the remainder. Most folks cull from their captives about a couple of dozen to eat later, though occasionally Midgett will steam them on the spot. If you don't care to catch your own clams, you can also buy them by the dozen or order them from one of the several local restaurants that the farm supplies, including Dirty Dick's, the Breakwater, Slammin' Sammies, and the Roadside Cafe.

Secret Information

Location: Hatteras, North Carolina.
Address: 56406 NC Highway 12, P.O. Box 238, Hatteras, NC 27943.
Phone: 252-986-2249.
Fax: 252-986-1323.
E-mail: KMidg99828@aol.com.
Hours: 9:00 A.M. to 7:00 P.M.
Season: Easter to Thanksgiving (barring a hurricane that churns up the water so that clamming is barred until the waters settle). Open all year for retail sales.
Price: $4 per person to rake your own clams plus 24¢ per clam you keep, or $3.95 per dozen.
Credit cards: Discover, MasterCard, Visa.
Details: Wear clothes and shoes you don't mind getting soaked.

TOP SECRET

Never cooked a clam in your whole life? No problem. The Hatteras Village Aqua Farm folks have created *Cooking with Clams*. The slim, self-produced booklet sells for $3.95 a copy at the farm. It features basic information on *Mercenaria mercenaria*—the Latin name for the quahog or hardshell clam, which is native to North Carolina—and more than thirty recipes, from a Backyard Clam Bake to Uncle Doug's White Beans with Clams. Aqua Farm owner Kevin Midgett's favorite is Big A's Clam Stuffed Manicotti, which blends minced clams with mushrooms, bread crumbs, parmesan, mozzarella, and ricotta cheese all stuffed in a large tube of pasta and baked in marinara sauce.

24 Eco Exploration

Seining anyone? One of the greatest things while traveling is happening upon something you've never heard of before—especially in this information age. That is exactly what happened when we encountered seining for the first—and so far only—time in our lives. The non-profit North Carolina Coastal Federation (NCCF) is located in Ocean, North Carolina—between Morehead City and Swansboro—and offers a variety of quality eco-excursions as part of its Coastal Adventures program, including seining outings. Seining involves two people wading out into shallow tidal waters holding wooden poles eight feet apart with a five-foot-tall net strung between them. Keeping the net on the bottom, you walk around and scoop up sea creatures, such as crabs, squid, shrimp, and fish, to examine and release. Kids, especially budding naturalists like our middle daughter, love to see up close what lives under the sea. As part of an NCCF trip, this bit of marine education is done in an environmentally responsible way.

The NCCF was started by executive director Todd Miller after he graduated from the University of North Carolina at Chapel Hill in the early '80s and got involved with an environmental fight over peat mining along the coast. Its mission is to help restore and protect the water quality and wildlife habitats of the coastal wetlands. It has about five thousand members—mostly from North Carolina—and is affiliated with about a hundred other environmental organizations around the world. Among its activities are scientific demonstration projects that show landowners and managers how to repair or avoid damage to an ecosystem threatened by pollution and development. Go Todd!

Public outreach and education are another part of its purpose, and its Coastal Adventures programs are among the best ways to see firsthand the fantastic flora and fauna living along the shore, marshland, inlets, and estuaries in and around Bogue Sound. Besides the Trawl and Seine Expedition, there are such treks as the Croatan National Forest Safari,

The North Carolina Coastal Federation's Coastal Adventures program offers affordable educational excursions for families. (COURTESY OF NORTH CAROLINA COASTAL FEDERATION)

which takes you on a nature trail deep into the old-growth pine forest, and the Open Beach and Inlet Investigation, which takes you by a small boat to explore the marine environment on and around Bear Island in Hammocks Beach State Park (Secret 37). These eco-adventures are a bargain and are led by expert naturalists.

The big difference between the Coastal Adventures program and more commercial programs is that the people at Coastal Adventures don't try to pack in as many people as possible. Water excursions take place in a twenty-two-foot Bateau flat-bottom boat that holds a maximum of six passengers, making it perfect for a family outing. Unlike more massive vessels, the boat can easily navigate the shallows of the area and land pretty much anywhere along the shore. Guests get a lot of individual attention and trips can be customized based on what a group wants to see or do, like learning to crab.

"Kids love the trips," says NCCF development director Sally Steele. "They aren't just for those with a strong interest in the environment but for the general public who's looking for something unique and different."

Secret Information

Location: Coastal Adventures trips leave from the North Carolina Coastal Federation office on NC Highway 24 in Ocean, North Carolina.
Address: 3609 Highway 24 (Ocean), Newport, NC 28570.
Phone: 800-232-6210 or 252-393-8185.
Fax: 252-393-7508.
E-mail: nccf@nccoast.org.
Web site: www.nccoast.org.
Hours: Office hours 8:30 A.M. to 5 P.M. Monday thru Friday.
Season: May through October.
Price: Ranges from FREE to $25 per person.
Reservations: Recommended.
Credit cards: American Express, Discover, MasterCard, Visa.
Details: Wear shoes and clothing that you can get wet. Bring water and snacks.

TOP SECRET

The North Carolina Coastal Federation is one of the environmental groups across the country taking part in CLEAN—Children Linking Across the Nation. In North Carolina, the program creates environmentally oriented curricula, educates teachers about the natural world during one-day to week-long workshops, guides field trips for classes of students fifth grade and up, and publishes an environmental newsletter for children age five to twelve. The program, though, can be adapted for any church, civic, community, or professional group that wants to learn about and get involved with protecting the coastline. To find out about participating in their program or about CLEAN activities in other parts of the country, contact the NCCF (see Secret Information).

El's Drive In

25

We Deliver

In 1959, Alaska and Hawaii became states; Buddy Holly, Ritchie Valens and the Big Bopper were killed in a plane crash; the Barbie doll debuted; the microchip was invented; and El Franks opened El's Drive In in Morehead City, North Carolina. Don't expect one of those drive-ins where you pull up under a concrete canopy and give your order through a speaker, then have it delivered by a carhop on roller skates. El's isn't into faking the '50s. Instead it's a real road-side hangout where generations of local folks have gathered to visit while munching on the original Super Burger (El's boasts that its burgers are all made with fresh ground beef from a local market, not the frozen patties of fast food places), shrimp burgers, oyster burgers, Poor Boy's hot dogs, BLTs, barbecue, and other American classics. You can walk in and order takeout at the counter, but there's no space to sit inside. Forty years has changed the world a lot, but at El's you still park in front of a small brick building and flash your lights to get the attention of a server who comes to your car for your order and to deliver your food. Having survived so long basically unchanged, El's has become an institution and a must-stop spot along the Crystal Coast.

Until recently, when it finally got a computer, El's had no printed menu, only the one on the sign out front. Still you can ask for any kind of drive-in-style food, and they'll make it for you. Getting a side of onion rings or french fries is a must; in fact, it's customary to get two orders of fries, one for you and one to share with the seagulls that constantly hang about (sometimes landing on car hoods) looking for handouts. And, of course, you can get vanilla, chocolate, strawberry, and even cherry milkshakes. Best of all, the prices seem like they are straight from the '50s. The most expensive thing on the menu is the large oyster or shrimp plate for $9.75.

El's isn't fancy, but it is consistent. It is a true survivor without compromise in this ever-changing world. Here's hoping that it's still around serving the Original Super Burger in the 2050s.

Flash your lights for service at El's Drive In. (COURTESY OF GAIL

Secret Information

Location: Morehead City, North Carolina.
Address: 3706 Arendell St., Morehead City, NC 28557.
Phone: 252-726-3002.
Hours: 10:30 A.M. to midnight Sunday through Thursday; open until 1 P.M. on Friday and Saturday.
Price: Ranges from $1.25 for the grilled cheese and $2.70 for the Original Super Burger to $9.75 for the oyster or shrimp plate.
Credit cards: None.

TOP SECRET

The folks who told us about El's Drive In say it's the last place on earth that delivers beer to your car. We don't know if that's strictly true (maybe there's another place in Tibet that will), but at El's you can indeed get an assortment of domestic brews delivered right to your car window—a convenience that may be more appealing to some of us (Dad) than others (Mom). Don't overdo it, and certainly don't drink and drive, but if you want a frosty beverage with your El's burger and fries, you won't even have to leave the comfort of your car.

Carteret County Home Bed-and-Breakfast

26

Going to the Poor House

If you come across a brochure for Carteret County Home Bed-and-Breakfast, one of two things will happen. You'll either be scared away by the owners' promise of "grumpy hosts, a nasty cat, and lumpy beds" or you'll be curious enough about what a poor house turned bed-and-breakfast looks like that you'll drive the few miles out of downtown Beaufort, North Carolina, to have a look. The first choice may seem the wiser one, but opt for the second. You'll be pleasantly surprised, and you'll decide either the owners—Terry and Nan O'Pray—have a great sense of humor or simply a misguided marketing campaign.

Carteret County Home was indeed a poor house from 1914 when it was built until 1942 when Social Security was enacted and Carteret County decided it didn't need to lodge its poor, aged, and infirm. The next year it re-opened as a place to house farm laborers helping with the war effort, and then it was converted into apartments. By the mid-sixties the place was abandoned and was one step away from the wrecking ball in 1996 when Terry purchased it, unbeknownst to Nan.

"I was living on our boat back in Naples, Florida and came home one day to find Terry rocking in a deck chair with a cigar and mint julep in hand announcing that *we* are the proud owners of a 'plantation' in North Carolina," recalls Nan. "Then he showed me pictures of this place that was literally falling down, and though pictures are worth a thousand words, I only had two, 'oh, no!'"

After the shock wore off, or maybe before it fully set in, the O'Prays set sail for Beaufort and began the backbreaking work of turning an eyesore into a unique and comfortable home away from home for travelers. With lots of sweat, probably more than a few tears, and perhaps some Irish luck, Terry and Nan have resurrected a pearl from what could have easily become a parking lot. And their pride and joy is far from poor or grumpy or lumpy.

The Carteret County Home is the only place in the Carolinas where you pay to stay in a poor house.

The Carteret County Home doesn't bear the least resemblance to the stereotypical Victorian home most people imagine when they picture a bed-and-breakfast. It's a long Federal-style building of ten rooms, each with private entrances strung along long porches that run along the front and back of the building. Each room is actually a tastefully decorated studio apartment complete with sink and dining area, a small refrigerator stocked with juices and yogurt, and some rooms even have stove tops for heating up mugs of late-night cocoa or preparing a light supper. There are private baths with showers, cable television, and phones in every room, plus the O'Prays' careful attention to quality and detail. Terry, a building contractor, and Nan personally renovated each unit. And since there was no running water, electricity, or insulation back in 1914, the O'Prays basically kept the shell of the original building and created everything else from scratch. The gleaming hardwood floors, freshly painted walls, crisp linens, and warm, antique accents make each unit a welcoming place to call home for a night, a week, or even a month.

Morning brings the O'Prays, wicker basket in hand, to the door delivering cereal, milk, fresh muffins and bagels, and juices of every variety. And if there's a nasty cat she keeps herself scarce; instead Nan is often accompanied by the lovable Charlotte, a golden retriever mix who found the O'Prays one day and decided to call the Carteret County Home her home.

Sitting out on the long front porch where the less fortunate county residents once swapped tales of woe, you can watch your kids play soccer on the front lawn or wave to the neighbors walking by. You get the idea from their quizzical looks that some of them couldn't imagine paying good money to stay in the poor house, but obviously they've never been on a tour of the updated, O'Pray version, which is now listed on the National Register of Historic Places.

"Some long-time residents of the county remember being afraid of the home when they were children," says Nan. "Since we moved in we've been embraced by the community for taking on this project, though. Their words of encouragement really kept us going when we got overwhelmed."

Secret Information

Location: Beaufort, North Carolina.
Address: 299 Highway 101, Beaufort, North Carolina.
Phone: 252-728-4611.
Fax: Same as phone.
E-mail: Opent@bmd.clis.com.
Web site: www.carteretcountyhomeb-b.com.
Rates: $75 to $95 depending on season.
Reservations: Recommended.
Credit cards: MasterCard, Visa.
Details: Pets welcome.

TOP SECRET

When Terry and Nan O'Pray need a respite from renovating, yard work, laundry, muffin baking, and all the other endless chores that come with renovating and operating the Carteret County Home Bed and Breakfast, they go back to what brought them to Beaufort in the first place—the ocean. The O'Prays own the thirty-four-foot Catalina sloop *September Morn*, which they lived on in Florida before moving to North Carolina. They offer paid charters aboard their boat to their bed-and-breakfast guests—just ask and they'll be happy to take a break from being innkeepers and sail away with you.

27

Core Sound Waterfowl Museum

Down East

The folks who live on Harkers Island are a fiercely independent bunch. Over the years, they've made their living building boats, fishing, and pretty much depending only on themselves and their neighbors for everything they need to live. Although the tiny, six-square-mile barrier island is the gateway to the Cape Lookout National Seashore (Secret 36), it's largely resisted changing to accommodate outsiders. That's not to say they are unfriendly or unwelcoming; it's just that they take pride in their roots Down East, an ill-defined area just north of Beaufort. Many of the families on the island have lived and worked there for generations, and because of the rising real estate prices for the island's simple homes, newcomers are rare.

"Down East is a state of mind," explains Karen Amspacher, the director of the Core Sound Waterfowl Museum on the island. "There's a sense of community, of living off the land. You have to be talented and resourceful to live on the coast. You can't see Harkers Island from the road. You've got to get to the back porches and boat houses. All the old houses face the water because that's the way people would come and go, by boat."

The museum is a good place to start getting into the Down East state of mind. It began back in the early '90s with the idea of preserving the culture of the area smack in the middle of the flyway through which countless waterfowl migrate annually. In particular, it's dedicated to honoring decoy making—the traditional craft of carving and painting wood into replicas of ducks and other birds. Decoys were originally designed for hunters to float on ponds and marshes to draw live fowl close enough to kill, but they've developed into art forms unto themselves—three dimensional *homages* to the elegant and colorful birds that live along the coast. Plans are to build a large museum next to the Cape Lookout Visitor's Center on sixteen acres of maritime

Decoy carvers hang out on the porch of the Core Sound Waterfowl Museum to demonstrate how to create Down East art.

forest at Shell Point and establish a waterfowl sanctuary, but organizers are still in the middle of raising funds toward that lofty goal. They've cleared the land and started construction, but still need about one million dollars to finish. Contributions are gratefully accepted.

For now, the museum is housed in a homey building a few miles up the road from the permanent site. On display are hundreds of examples of the decoy-maker's art, including antiques from as far back as the 1920s. There are replicas of pintail ducks, woodtail ducks, Canada geese, and loons—many of which are for sale and are coveted by an active community of decoy collectors across the country. The museum also features wildlife paintings, pillows, chimes, books, and jewelry—it's a great place for shoppers to pick up the perfect gift for nature lovers, no matter whether he or she is an avid hunter or a rabid environmentalist. Proceeds from the gift shop go to support the museum and its programs to educate the public about the area's wildlife heritage. The highlight of the museum's year is the annual Core Sound

Classes of schoolchildren often come to the Core Sound Waterfowl Museum to learn about local wildlife and paint their own duck decoys.

Decoy Festival in December, a sort of Woodstock of waterfowl that draws thousands of people to take part in decoy carving and painting contests and to buy and sell collectibles—some decoys go for twenty thousand dollars or more.

If you want to get some real insight into the decoy-carver's craft, take some time to hang out on the front porch with the members of the Core Sound Decoy Carvers Guild, who take turns spending the day working wood. They'll be pleased to leisurely explain such things as why Tupelo wood from stumps left by loggers upstate is so good for making decoys (it's got no grain, is light and soft, and holds detail well). The museum also often hosts classes of school children, who get to go outdoors and get messy painting their own decoys. If you're traveling with kids, call ahead and ask the staff about setting aside some blank decoys and paint so they can make their own souvenirs of their visit Down East.

Secret Information

Location: On Harkers Island east of Beaufort, North Carolina.
Address: P.O. Box 556, Harkers Island, NC 28531.
Phone: 252-728-1500.
Fax: 252-728-1742.
E-mail: amspacher@mail.clis.com.
Web site: www.coresound.com.
Hours: 9 A.M. to 5 P.M. Monday through Saturday; 2 P.M. to 5 P.M. Sunday.
Season: All year.
Price: Admission is FREE; $5 to paint a decoy.
Credit cards: American Express, MasterCard, Visa.

TOP SECRET

"Come aboard!" is how J. A. Rose enthusiastically greets visitors to his home and workshop on Harkers Island, just down the road from the Core Sound Waterfowl Museum. The talkative former fisherman is a master model-boat builder, creating intricate miniature versions of everything from multi-masted schooners to simple skiffs—an art form practiced throughout the Down East region. Harkers Island is a center of boat building, and Rose has personally constructed seventy-five full-sized boats in his forty-year career. He starting making model boats at age ten and is somewhat surprised that his hobby has turned into a business that earns him up to eight hundred dollars per boat and has drawn him recognition from the North Carolina Folklore Society and the North Carolina Museum of History, where one of his works is on permanent display. Rose is also known as a musician. He was part of the original North Carolina Coastal Playboys that started in 1947. Look for the sign on the island's main road that marks his home and feel free to pull around back and see examples of his work on display in his small showroom, including replicas of craft owned by his family. Some of the petite ships are for sale, but not many. Most of his work is pre-sold to buyers, who pick a particular design out of a photo album of his previous creations or who want him to carve a small copy of their own treasured boat. If you drop by, be prepared to chat and listen to stories, like how the pirate Blackbeard's ship, the *Queen Anne's Revenge* (Secret 31), wrecked in the waters nearby. For more information or to make sure that Rose will be around when you visit, call him or his wife, Barbara, at 252-728-7504.

28

Crab Shack

Simple Seafood

You've got to wonder who was the first person to eat a crab. What could that first man—yes, we'll assume only a man would be so foolish—to sample such shellfish have possibly been thinking? *Let's see, what I can find here dwelling in the mud and muck beneath the ocean? Hmmm...OUCH! What's this? A dirty, hard, kinda round thing with kicking legs, snapping claws, and beady black eyes. I bet if I cook it, crack it open, and clean out the guts, it'll be some* goooood *eatin'.*

Whoever that pioneering gourmand was, those of us who love the sweet taste of fresh blue crab caught off the Carolina coast owe him a debt of gratitude. There are dozens of ways to prepare the crazy-looking creatures, but we're partial to Maryland style—whole crabs steamed with Old Bay seasoning. The recipe is popular in the Chesapeake Bay area, but the Crab Shack in Salter Path is the only place along the North Carolina coast that prepares crabs Maryland style, according to owner Vernon Guthrie. We'll take him at his word.

Part of the fun of eating a plate full of Maryland-style crabs (caught locally and sold by the half-dozen or dozen) is figuring out how to take them apart to get to the meat. After a lesson from our server, we were able to grasp the process of snapping off the top of the crab, cleaning out the inedibles, and cracking out the good stuff; with practice, we got it down to a science. The kids were grossed out but liked seeing Dad and Mom make a big mess.

For those who aren't into working for their food, the Crab Shack offers plenty of other choices, including soft-shell crab, which are caught while molting so you can cook them whole and eat them shells and all. Other popular items include shrimp, oysters, crab legs, and crab cakes, plus non-seafood entrees like steaks and chicken. "We just cook local seafood, no fancy stuff," says Guthrie. "We just fry up oysters and shrimp, just like local people used to cook." Don't worry, the health conscious can get seafood other ways than fried, including broiled, pan cooked, and grilled.

Guthrie started a seafood business more than twenty-five years ago and eventually began cooking what he caught. The Crab Shack started with just five tables and slowly expanded, but not too much. Guthrie has resisted packing in as many people as possible, believing that folks would rather wait to get a table that overlooks the waters of Bogue Sound, over which the edge of the restaurant juts, rather than a view of nothing but a crowd of other diners. Tucked behind the United Methodist Church on the road running between the Atlantic Beach and Emerald Island bridges, the Crab Shack was around long before the high-rise hotels along the beach and is a classic seafood place that draws beach vacationers back year after year.

Secret Information

Location:	Salter Path, North Carolina.
Address:	100 Shore Drive, Salter Path, NC 28575.
Phone:	252-247-3444.
Fax:	252-247-0015.
Hours:	11 A.M. to 10 P.M. in season; 5 P.M. to 9 P.M. on weekends during the off season.
Season:	Easter to December.
Price:	Lunch special $5.95; Dinners range from $13.50 to $15.50, children $6, and senior citizens $8.
Reservations:	Not accepted.
Credit cards:	MasterCard, Visa.

TOP SECRET

The Crab Shack is on the edge of Bogue Sound, which runs east-west along the mid-North Carolina coast—actually the building juts out over the water. You can sit inside or outside on the deck and enjoy the scenery and boats passing by on the Intracostal Waterway. If you really want to see the sound, though, rent a kayak, canoe, or paddle boat at the restaurant. Price range from $10 an hour to $80 a day and are available from 10 A.M. to 5 P.M.

29

Bald Headed Men of America Convention

Bald Bonding

When you think about it, Morehead City, North Carolina, is the perfect spot to be home to the Bald Headed Men of America Convention. After all: “more head” means less hair. We wish we could take credit for that line, but it comes from John T. Capps III, who founded the No Hair Club for Men in 1974 and has been promoting bald pride ever since.

Capps started losing his hair at age fifteen and was completely bare by age thirty, causing him to experience society’s anti-bald bias. “The Bald Headed Men of America is meeting the prejudice against baldies head on—with humor,” he says. “Unlike other self-help groups, we have no serious goals, hopes, or plans other than to make those who lack hair feel good about being bald. All we want is to have some fun and build pride in having a chrome dome. It’s hard for some men to accept being bald. But if God meant for you to be bald, you’re going to be bald.”

The group does have its serious side and gives people young and old the chance to share experiences and get support as they lose their hair, sometimes from serious medical conditions. “Besides the support and laughter, you’ll find some compassion, too. For instance, some of our members are regulars at several children’s hospitals, where children are treated for cancer. During chemotherapy the children lose their hair. We visit and promote Bald is Beautiful month or week and give them Proud to be Bald buttons and bumper stickers. And we put a smile on their faces. That really makes it worthwhile. There’s no need to exist if you just exist for yourself.”

Mostly, though, this group of guys—and gals—is dedicated to having a good time. Their three-day convention, held the second weekend in September annually, is a relatively loose affair with few formal events and a lot of time for rubbing elbows—or perhaps scalps—with their fellow baldies. The event usually draws a couple hundred people and gets media attention from all over the world. Surprisingly, most of the attendees are women. "They want to be in line to be a judge for the contests to find a bald headed man," Capps says. "They think there'll be a few bachelors there, and they realize bald men don't use their hormones on growing hair." Apparently several romances have been born as a result of unused-hormone-driven encounters at the convention.

Regular events include the Friday night topless (as in no hair) cruise on a paddle wheeler that serves "bald" (no topping) ice cream. Saturday culminates at an evening picnic. At the event, judges recognize the best baldies in such categories as Shiniest Bald Head, Softest Bald Head, Sexiest Bald Head, Most Kissable Bald Head, and Best All Around Bald Head. Just about everyone in attendance wins something. The rest of the weekend is spent swapping stories, eating out, playing golf, and generally doing bald bonding. The convention doesn't cost anything, and as for accommodations, "special rates are available because bald people don't use shampoo or shower caps, and we don't clog the drains," Capps jokes.

At other times of the year, the Bald Headed Men of America is run out of Capps' printing business on Bald Drive (naturally), and although there's nothing to see there, he's always open to meeting those interested in his cause. The organization also sells merchandise such as Bald is Beautiful shirts and a Bald Hair Brush—a cloth on a brush handle that one can use to achieve that perfectly shined scalp. As for the future, Capps sees a continuing boom in bald pride. "Ours is the only organization," he says, "that grows because of lack of growth."

Secret Information

Location: Morehead City, North Carolina.
Address: 102 Bald Dr., Morehead City, NC 28557.
Phone: 252-726-1855.
Fax: 252-726-6061.
E-mail: jcapps4102@aol.com.
Web site: members.aol.com/BaldUSA.
Dates: The BHMA Convention is held annually on the second weekend in September.
Price: Admission is FREE; Special events are $30.
Reservations: Reservations for the convention are optional; hotel/motel accommodations are handled individually.

TOP SECRET

The Bald Headed Men of America's self-proclaimed vice-president is Dave Beswick, who has made a part-time career out of his "cranial nudity." Beswick, who started to shed hair at age fourteen, has penned two tongue-in-cheek books about bald life—*Bald Men Always Come Out on Top* and *Bald Men Never Have a Bad Hair Day*. He offers such observations as these advantages to being follicularly challenged:

- You can shampoo in seconds with a washcloth.
- Now you can get a total body tan from head to toe.
- You'll feel a natural skinship with other bald men.
- It opens up more space for face painting.

For more hairless humor, you can buy autographed copies of the books from Beswick for $9.95 each. Just call 888-BALD101.

Clawson's 1905 Restaurant

30

Historic Hangout

You can't walk a block in Beaufort, North Carolina, without tripping over a piece of history. Every home and headstone has a story. Even the horses grazing across Taylor Creek on Carrot Island can trace their roots back farther than most Americans. But no other slice of Beaufort history tastes as good as our favorite hangout located smack dab in the middle of the historic downtown waterfront—Clawson's 1905 Restaurant.

Whatever you're hungry for, Clawson's has it. There are sandwiches, burgers, salads, and other light fare at lunch; and there's local seafood, ribs, steak, and pasta dishes for dinner. Co-owner Joey McClure says the seafood bisque is a "big time favorite," and he encourages everyone to sample the huge homemade onion rings and the distinctive shrimp and grits. "It's a southern thing," says McClure, who runs Clawson's 1905 with his wife, Elana, and partners, Fred and Joyce McCune. "We take stone ground grits and mix in cheddar cheese. Then we sauté shrimp with garlic, fresh mushrooms, sweet red peppers, and the main ingredient—bacon juice. We sauté everything in that juice and serve it over the grits with a little Tabasco sauce. There's nothing else quite like it."

If all that sounds too filling, don't pass Clawson's by. Inside the antique doors is not only a full-service restaurant but also Fishtowne Java and Ice Cream, which serves gourmet coffees and creamy ice treats. Or, if you'd rather, you can pull a stool up to the antique mahogany bar in Clawson's Pub and sample the many microbrews on tap. The food is fresh, filling, and quite good, but actually, it's the taste of Beaufort history that sets Clawson's apart from other eateries on the waterfront.

Clawson's 1905 got its name from a grocery store opened in 1905 by immigrants Charles and Mary Clawson. He was from Sweden; she was from Ireland; and somehow they ended up together in Beaufort. Their store was actually located across the street, on the water side. They also ran a bakery in what is now the Backstreet Pub. In 1910 a hurricane destroyed the original Clawson's building, and a newer (and obviously sturdier) structure, which today houses Clawson's 1905 Restaurant, was built over the next couple of years.

Clawson's Grocery and Bakery flourished on the Beaufort waterfront and according to local historical records, the breads, cakes, and cookies baked in its fireplace were legendary throughout Carteret County. The Clawsons closed up shop in 1934 (turns out the Depression was bad for business), but the building the couple built lived on. Over the years it housed a hat shop, a dress shop, a children's shop, a piece goods shop, and finally in 1977, a restaurant named Clawson's 1905. The owners have changed a couple of times since then, and the eatery expanded to include the old P. H. Rose Five and Dime Store next door, but the spirit of the family business the Clawsons built remained. The current owners, the McCunes and the McClures, pay tribute to Charles, Mary, and their sturdy brick building by prominently displaying memorabilia and photographs from the grocery store in the restaurant. There are old copies of the *Beaufort News* posted along the stairwell, and period antiques and treasures are tucked in every nook and cranny.

With all the brick, wood flooring, and old Beaufort memorabilia, you could almost close your eyes and pretend you're back in Charles' and Mary's store waiting for the fresh loaves of bread to come out of the fireplace. But don't start daydreaming until you get seated. Clawson's one nod to present day technology is a funky seating system that involves a soft plastic child's toy and a computer screen. If there's a wait for a table (which is a good thing because it gives you time to explore), the host or hostess will hand you a colorful plastic dog or some other toy out of a basket. When a photo of that toy appears on the computer screens in the entrance area, your table is ready. While you're clutching your toy (don't walk off with it) while waiting for your table, take a quick trip upstairs to the third floor dining room, if there isn't a private party in the house. From the window there, on a clear day, you can see all the way to the Cape Lookout Lighthouse on Core Banks.

"My partner Fred owned a television station locally, so he came up with the idea for the seating system. We have some television equipment that superimposes things that we have on our computer system," says McClure, who adds that the system uses a hundred-foot-long mouse cord that runs from the computer upstairs down to the lobby where the photos of the toys flash up on various television screens. "We looked at

The buildings that house Clawson's 1905 Restaurant have been fixtures on the Beaufort waterfront since the early 1900s. (COURTESY OF CLAWSON'S 1905 RESTAURANT)

using the traditional beepers to page our customers, but they cost eighty dollars and if someone walks out of the building with one, it's kind of tough. Since the toys are only $1.50, we only have to take pictures of them every time some body walks off with one. It's amazing. The plastic toys go away all the time. We can't keep them."

Secret Information

Location: Beaufort, North Carolina.
Address: 429 Front Street, Beaufort, NC 28516.
Phone: 252-728-2133.
Fax: 252-728-2692.
E-mail: joey@claswsonwsrestuarnt.com.
Web site: historicbeaufort.com/clawson1.htm.
Hours: 11:30 A.M. until 9 P.M. Monday to Thursday; 11:30 A.M. until 9:30 P.M. Friday and Saturday.
Price: Lunches range from $2.50 to $11; Dinners range from $2.50 to $18.
Reservations: Accepted.
Credit cards: Discover, MasterCard, Visa.

TOP SECRET

Down the street from Clawson's 1905 Restaurant and around the corner up Turner Street is the best place to discover the in-depth history of its quaint hometown—the Safrit Historical Center, which houses the Information Center for the Beaufort Historical Association (BHA). That's where the double-decker bus tour sponsored by the BHA starts. The red 1946 English bus, which was imported by a South Carolina film company, was donated to the BHA by a group of local fishermen and put into service as a tour vehicle in the 1970s. For a few bucks you get to climb aboard (sit outside on top, but watch for low tree limbs) and enjoy an hour-long narrated tour of the historic district. If you're lucky, you'll also have unobstructed views of the wild horses grazing on Carrott Island across the harbor. On the tour, you'll see such sights as the Old Burying Ground on Anne Street, which guides will tell you is the final resting place of a young girl whose body was stored in a whiskey keg when she died on the voyage back from England and of a British sailor who was interred standing upright facing his homeland so he could salute his king for eternity. Buy tour tickets at the center, which includes a gift shop featuring handmade and historic Beaufort gifts and collectibles; it's open Monday to Saturday from 9:30 A.M. until 5 P.M. in season; 10 A.M. to 4 P.M. in the off-season. For more information, call 252-728-5225 or 800-575-SITE (7483).

North Carolina
Maritime Museum

31

Oceans of History

Although the North Carolina Maritime Museum sits near the end of Front Street in the historic waterfront district of Beaufort, North Carolina, the museum's Public Information and Volunteer Coordinator Jane Wolff considers the place a secret to most coastal visitors.

"Many people stumble upon us when they're walking around the historic district," says Wolff. "Since we're a state run museum we're not as well known as some of the other places in the area, but anyone who wants to learn more about maritime history, coastal plant and animal life, and participate in some hands-on environmental programs needs to spend a day with us on their vacation."

The eighteen thousand-square-foot museum, whose all-wood interior and exterior design reflects the style of the early U.S. Lifesaving Service buildings, is literally filled to the rafters with full-sized watercraft, shell collections, life-like dioramas, tools, decoys , and other maritime artifacts and natural exhibits (the kids' eye-level saltwater aquariums are a highlight). One of the more unusual items is an 1890s Life Car, a mini-sub-looking vessel once used to rescue people from shipwrecks. The galvanized sheet-iron pod, built to carry five to six adults or nine "half grown" children, was shot by a small cannon to the wreck then hauled back by ropes. What the display doesn't mention is how many of the "saved" didn't survive their own rescue in the cramped silver pod.

Since the boat-shaped building (the thirty-foot wood beamed ceiling looks like a ship's hull) is about to capsize under the weight of its impressive collection, Wolff says plans are underway to expand the facilities on a thirty-six-acre Gallant's Channel site located just beyond the Town Creek Marina in Beaufort. Currently, an old scallop house on the site is being used as a conservation lab where artifacts—like the infamous pirate Blackbeard's booty (see Top Secret)—are painstakingly cleaned and preserved before being put on display. The museum's popular summer Junior Sailing Program (two-week courses for kids eight years old and up) is also held at the Gallant's Channel location.

The eventual move could, for the first time, result in an admission fee, but for now, the best kept secret in Beaufort is also the cheapest. Admission is free, but there is a $1 suggested donation for the Discovery Time sessions. These sessions, designed for children, are offered every Thursday from the middle of June to the beginning of August. The two-hour program offers craft activities relating to sea topics like pirates, sea creatures, and boats. It's particularly helpful to parents when the rain falls on a Thursday afternoon and outdoor activities are out of the question. These special events help draw tourists to the museum, especially in poor weather, but the transient boaters who travel the Intracoastal Waterway in the spring and fall also look to the Maritime Museum as a resource and a comfortable place to spend an afternoon on shore.

"We have families who stay in Beaufort for three weeks or more outfitting and getting supplies before moving on. A lot of these boaters' kids are homeschooled, and they utilize our reference library—bring the kids in here to do research and for classes," says Wolff.

The seafarer's classroom and retreat is the Charles R. McNeill Maritime Library located in the back of the museum. With its warm wood-paneled walls, leather couch, lighted globe, and welcoming fireplace, the reference library looks like it belongs in the captain's quarters of a grand sailing ship. Anyone interested in shipwrecks, boat building, meteorology, sea shells, or sea creatures can pick out a book from the floor-to-ceiling shelves, plop into a comfy chair at the conference table, and read. There's even a Sailor's Paperback Exchange where boaters and landlubbers alike can drop off a book and take one in return. Even if you're not ready for research or even to read, the library is a quiet haven and the perfect place to rest your feet after a day of sightseeing.

If you're up for more active adventures, the Maritime Museum also has popular field programs. The museum offers what Wolff terms "painless learning" experiences for adults, children, groups, and families. There are afternoon kayak trips and overnight kayak camping trips; stargazing and birding programs; and marine-life collecting cruises aboard a research vessel. One of the most unusual offerings is the Cape Lookout Studies Program, where participants travel out to the Cape Lookout lighthouse (which can only be reached by boat), participate in

Visitors to historic downtown Beaufort often bypass this jewel—the North Carolina Maritime Museum. Those who do step inside are treated to a treasure chest of nautical and maritime artifacts. (COURTESY OF NORTH CAROLINA MARITIME MUSEUM; PHOTO BY DIANE HARDY)

barrier island-related field workshops, then stay overnight in the field station. "Many of the summer programs fill up fast, so plan ahead by getting your name on the museum's free mailing list," advises Wolff. For more information and to receive museum calendars, contact the museum (see Secret Information below).

After you visit the museum's main building, be sure to walk across the street to the annex, the Harvey W. Smith Watercraft Center. Although only shipbuilders and their students are allowed on the floor of the cavernous building, the side ramp provides access to an overlook where visitors can watch wooden ships being built from scratch or craftsmen lovingly refurbishing the hull of an antique vessel. A studio on the observation floor is reserved for model boat builders who volunteer their time to talk about their craft and show their works in progress. Skilled artisans like Fred Wildt share their priceless knowledge of this vanishing art with anyone lucky enough to hear.

"Model kits you buy in the store are cheap and aren't accurate," warns Wildt, a retiree who's been building model boats for close to forty years. "Real model boat builders draw the plans, select the wood, cut the pieces, and finish the models to be *exact* replicas of the full size boats. It's not an easy thing to do, and not many people do it any more. I guess people these days don't like to do things that are hard. It's the things that take time that are the best. They last the longest."

Wildt and the other volunteer model boat builders are on hand Tuesday through Saturday and Sunday afternoons. They'll show you pictures of boats they've built, tell a few stories, and let the little ones step up to the boat they're working on. The smell of sawdust and sea air is infectious, and you just might find yourself wanting to shape some soft wood into your own model ship. If so, walk back across the street and ask about upcoming Boatbuilding Carpentry classes and Lift Half Model Making for adults and Boat Modeling classes for kids. Class size is limited, so you may have to return to the Maritime Museum in the fall or next summer to take your course. That's not so bad, though, because once you discover Beaufort's best kept secret, coming back again is exactly what you'll want to do.

Secret Information:

Location: Beaufort, North Carolina.
Address: 315 Front Street, Beaufort, NC 28516-2124.
Phone: 252-728-7317.
Fax: 252-728-2108.
E-mail: maritime@ncsl.dcr.state.nc.us.
Web site: www.ah.dcr.state.nc.us/sections/maritime/default.htm.
Hours: 9 A.M. to 5 P.M. weekdays; 10 A.M. to 5 P.M. Saturday: 1 P.M. to 5 P.M. Sunday.
Price: FREE.
Details: Field programs and workshops require reservations and fee.

TOP SECRET

Although the North Carolina Maritime Museum houses thousands of treasures, the most popular with tourists are the artifacts recovered from the *Queen Anne's Revenge*, Blackbeard's flagship, which ran aground at Beaufort Inlet in June 1718 and was lost for more than 250 years. On November 22, 1996, Intersal Inc., a private research and survey group, discovered the fluke of an anchor from an eighteenth-century ship in shallow water off the Beaufort coast, which could have been that of the English pirate who terrorized sailors in the Caribbean and the Colonies. That first discovery has been followed by thousands of others, all of which point to the conclusion that the ship buried just off the coast did indeed belong to Edward Teach (or Thatch, no one's sure), a.k.a. Blackbeard. The North Carolina Maritime Museum is part of the North Carolina Maritime Heritage Trail consortium, which was formed to share artifacts recovered from the wreck site and to encourage the enhancement and preservation of the state's maritime history and culture. Currently, the shipwreck site is protected by an electronic surveillance system linked by computer to local law enforcement (so don't grab your scuba gear and go searching for buried treasure out there). You can, however, see many of the artifacts (including cannonballs) from the *Queen Anne's Revenge* at the North Carolina Maritime Museum and in a traveling exhibit. In addition, brief programs to update the public on ongoing preservation efforts are regularly offered at the museum's conservation lab (any program with the word "pirate" in the title always attracts lots of visitors, so if you're interested in a Blackbeard-related event, sign up or show up well in advance). A model of the *Queen Anne's Revenge* is also being built for the museum, which also plans to construct a model of the site of the shipwreck. For more information about learning about booty from Blackbeard's ship, contact the museum or visit the *Queen Anne's Revenge* Web site at www.ah.dcr.state.nc.us/qar/default.htm.

32

Driftwood Motel, Campground, Restaurant, and Gift Shop

Drift Away

The ferry to and from the south end of Ocracoke Island is located on Cedar Island, North Carolina. The area is a couple of hours north of Beaufort and is largely deserted—home to 350 permanent residents, many from fishing families that have been there since the 1700s. It feels completely cut off from the modern world of subdivisions, malls, and movie megaplexes. If you're taking the ferry, that means that the only spot for miles around to get a meal, stay overnight, or pick up some supplies is the Driftwood Motel, Campground, Restaurant, and Gift Shop located right next to the Cedar Island landing. While we've included it in Places to Eat because it's the best place (and pretty much the only place) to get a bite before or after the two-and-a-half-hour ferry ride, its various parts can't really be separated out. It's more like an anything-you-need outpost perched on the edge of America.

The place is owned by the same people who opened it forty years ago—Clay and Iris Fulcher. It's got the feel of an old-time motel—nothing fancy, just simple rooms, basic amenities, and functional buildings designed to survive the wind and weather of the coast. The restaurant—technically called The Pirate's Chest but known as The Driftwood—is one of those great places where the most popular fare is Carolina seafood cooked Calabash style—breaded and fried. There you can get a heapin' helpin' of shrimp, oysters, fish fillets, crab cakes, clam strips, and deviled crabs. In a nod to lighter eaters, frying isn't the only option; they'll also serve seafood broiled, steamed, boiled, or sautéed. Prime rib, chicken, pastas, soups (try the Cream of Crab), salads, and other fare round out the menu. The decor is straight from *Treasure Island*, with a view of the water through porthole windows.

The motel or campground is a good place to stay the night before if you don't want to drive a long way and rush to catch the first—and generally less crowded—ferry to Ocracoke in the morning. Don't expect the Ritz but count on feeling isolated from the rest of the world.

Secret Information

Location: Cedar Island, North Carolina.
Address: NC Highway 12, Cedar Island, NC 28520.
Phone: 252-225-4861.
Fax: 252-225-1113.
E-mail: deg@clis.com.
Web site: www.clis.com/deg.
Hours: 5 P.M. to 9 P.M. daily for dinner and Sundays from 11 A.M. to 2:30 P.M. for lunch.
Season: Easter to the last week of January.
Price: $11 to $17 per entree.
Rates: $55 per night for two people.
Credit cards: American Express, Discover, Visa, MasterCard.

TOP SECRET

If you share our fantasy of riding horseback along the beach, waves lapping at your mounts' hooves, your hair flapping in the sea breeze, your butt aching from bumping in the saddle, then stop by the Outer Banks Riding Stables. It is just a stone's throw away from the Driftwood Motel, Campground, Restaurant, and Gift Shop and the arrival point for the ferry from Ocracoke Island on Cedar Island. Beach tours are guided and horses are matched with riders according to temperament, ability, and the weight of the rider. No riding experience is necessary, and there is no age limit; little kids to seniors are welcome. "The ride is on the beach the whole time, sometimes through inlets, and occasionally galloping is allowed. People come back and ask for the same horse again and again, even though there are eleven other gorgeous horses to choose from. So we give them the horse they want," says owner Cheryl McMahon. The cost is $25 an hour, with $35 an hour for those weighing two hundred pounds or more (three hundred pounds is the limit for the horses). The reason for the difference is that "the bigger horses eat more, therefore we charge more when they are used." Call McMahon's home at 252-225-1885 or the barn at 252-225-1185 to arrange a ride—you do need an appointment, as rides go out only whenever people book them. McMahon, who works year-round, and one other guide, hired for the summer, will take from one to eleven people per trip.

33

Olympus Dive Center

Grave Diving

Although you can't see it, a violent collision is constantly taking place off the coast of North Carolina. From the North comes icy arctic water; from the South comes the comparatively balmy Gulf Stream. The two meet in the thousands of square miles of the Atlantic Ocean east of the kink in the Carolina coast that marks the southern end of the Outer Banks. The result is a constant churning of currents, causing choppy seas and severe storms. When you add the constantly changing maze of capes, islands, channels, and sandbars, you get the Graveyard of the Atlantic—the final resting place of an estimated four thousand sunken ships and the sailors who went down with them.

For divers, the area is a treasure trove of ruins and relics ranging from the earliest days of North American seafaring until today. It is so rich in underwater wonders, both wrecks and wildlife, in fact, that readers of *Rodale's Scuba Diving Magazine* recognized Morehead City, North Carolina, as having North America's Best Wreck Diving, Best Big Animal Encounters, Best Advanced Diving, and as Best Overall Destination in 1999. And, in the same issue, readers picked Morehead City's Olympus Dive Center as the second best dive operator on the entire continent.

You can't miss the Olympus Dive Center on the waterfront in Morehead City—just look for the giant statue of King Neptune out front. It had been a landmark for years at nearby Atlantic Beach. Olympus owners George and Linda Purifoy rescued it from destruction when it fell in the path of a new bridge being built. Part of the reason Olympus is so highly rated is because George found a sunken German U-352 submarine in 1975 along with several more vessels that went to their watery graves off the Carolina coast. He and Linda are Morehead City natives who started dating when she was sixteen and got married three years later. The couple had a diesel mechanics shop where they fixed the engines of local boats before they started

The home water of the Olympus Dive Center has been honored as the best spot in North America to swim with large marine life. (COURTESY OF OLYMPUS DIVE CENTER)

guiding diving excursions. Their son Robert, now in his thirties, started as his father's first mate at the age of twelve and now captains trips for the family business.

Using its two boats—the *Olympus* and the *Atlantis*—Olympus takes guests out to the sites of various wrecks, including the submarine for which George looked for ten years before locating it twenty-six miles off the coast in 110 feet of water. Mired in muck with rusted metal and rotted wood, the dozens of wrecks Olympus visits—ranging from the torpedoed Russian freighter *Ashkabad* to the late nineteenth-century iron steamship *City of Houston*—are eerie underwater apparitions. They jut at all angles from the sea floor and are perfect for poking around or photographing. Swimming above, below, in, and out of them are all manner of sea creatures: Atlantic Sand Tiger Sharks, turtles, manta rays, eels, grouper, red snapper, dolphins. The gulf stream water is clear, providing excellent visibility, and warm—Olympus has guided guests on dives in February in seventy-two degree water. Typical trips start early in the morning and give divers the chance to swim around two different sites in 70- to 120-foot deep water before ending in the late afternoon. They also offer some multi-day, live-aboard trips that give undersea explorers a chance to pretend they're Lloyd Bridges in *Sea Hunt*.

This kind of offshore adventure isn't for amateurs, and Olympus takes only experienced scuba divers out to the wrecks. They do give lessons, though, and can help you get your feet wet if you've always wanted to learn how to dive. And, with a little planning, you can prepare for wreck diving by taking scuba lessons at a local dive shop or recreation center back home before booking a voyage to the bottom of the sea with Olympus Dive Center.

Secret Information

Location: On the waterfront in Morehead City, North Carolina.
Address: 713 Shepard St., Morehead City, North Carolina 28557.
Phone: 800-992-1258 or 252-726-9432.
Fax: 252-726-0883.
E-mail: olympus@olympusdiving.com.
Web site: www.olympusdiving.com.
Hours: 6 A.M. to 9 P.M. in summer; 10 A.M. to 5 P.M. in winter.
Price: $55 for half-day charter; $85 for full-day charter.
Reservations: Recommended.
Credit cards: MasterCard, Visa.

TOP SECRET

Even if the sum total of your diving experience is doing cannon balls in the motel pool, the Olympus Dive Center is worth a visit, especially for kids. The shop is an informal museum featuring artifacts gathered from the hundreds of shipwrecks off the North Carolina coast. Check out the World War I water-cooled machine gun and Civil War-era medicine bottles (still filled with cocaine), which are among a fascinating array of maritime, military, and personal items. If you ask, a staff member will also be glad to give children a tiny taste of the world of diving by showing them videos of wreck diving and allowing them to try out equipment, including breathing with a scuba tank.

King's Restaurant

Hog Heaven

34

"Eastern Carolina barbecue is a different kind of animal," says Wil King. "East of I-95, barbecue is cooked dry and mixed with a vinegar-based sauce, not basted with tomato-based sauce. Everyone here over age twenty-five knows how to cook a pig and everyone has their own recipe for sauce. There's no bad barbecue, but some is better than others. And ours is superior."

A bit of bragging? Maybe, but King can back up his boast. You see, he has barbecue in his blood. His family has been serving up some of the best barbecue on the Carolina coast for decades, and King's Restaurant on U.S. Highway 70 in Kinston, North Carolina, has been a regular stop for generations of families heading to and from the beach.

The operation started as a general store back in the '30s. The story of how they got started serving food depends on who you ask. Wil King's version is that a couple of people got caught in the store during a snowstorm and wanted something to eat, so his great grandfather heated up a can of food on the pot belly stove. Hot dogs followed until the regular patrons, P. E. Sholers and his wife, got tired of them and asked for something different. The management cooked up a fried bologna sandwich, the first plate meal served there. In the '40s King's started cooking whole hogs at a time, and since then, they've been "set up to put you on path of soul food salvation," says King.

King says the secret of his family's barbecue is the way they prepare it. First, they put the meat into clam-shell ovens about the size of beds equipped with infrared heating rods. Next, they set the ovens to turn on after everyone has gone home for the night, and the machines heat the pork at a medium temperature overnight before turning off at nine the next morning. "Low and slow gets you good, tender pork," King confides. Then, the cooked meat is put on a large board and chopped—not "pulled" mind you, that's different—by hand, with all the bone, gristle, and skin being thrown out. "Everyone else chops the pork with a machine

Put the South in your mouth no matter where you live with meals-by-mail from King's Restaurant.

like they use for coleslaw," King reveals. The final step is to hand mix the pork with King's sauce and two secret ingredients "until the meat and seasonings become one. The trick is to hand blend the white and dark meat so you come up with a not too greasy or not too dry mix that's mouth perfect," King says. Our tastebuds can testify that this is true.

The Restaurant's fare is by no means limited to just East Carolina barbecue, though. They also specialize in fried chicken, and the massive menu includes every kind of southern food from trout and oysters to fried chicken livers—all at really reasonable prices. They cook collard greens sixty gallons at a time and massive amounts of other vegetables—peas, squash, beans, corn, you name it. One specialty is the Pig-In-A-Puppy—pork stuffed in a big hush puppy, a culinary invention King says came to his grandfather in a dream. Our favorite dish—besides barbecue—is Brunswick Stew: a mix of pork, chicken, and vegetables that seems like it's made by just throwing whatever's left over at the end of the day into a pot. And though they tout East Carolina barbecue as the best, King's serves ribs cooked in its own traditional tomato-based barbecue sauce, bottles of which, as well as samples of other King's ingredients, are for sale to take home.

The main restaurant—King's also has five other locations in the area—seats more than eight hundred people, which cuts down on the wait during busy times on Friday and Saturday night and after church on Sunday. It has an eclectic atmosphere that mixes decor of the '50s through the '90s. Kinston and King's were hit hard by floods from 1999's hurricane Floyd, so some recent remodeling has been done. The staff is like family—the dining room manager, Hazel, was the restaurant's first female employee; she started in the '40s. King himself has worked his way up from the trash room—throwing out grease and other refuse—to general manager of the King's distribution center.

If eating at King's seems like inviting a heart attack, Wil points out that they have all kinds of dishes, including grilled chicken that's sure to please the health conscious. "According to the federal government, there are only eight grams of fat in our large portion of pork, while there's fifty-six in a Whopper," he adds. If barbecue is a healthy food, then serve us up another large plate of pork and throw on some extra hush puppies.

Secret Information

Location: On U.S. Highway 70 in Kinston, North Carolina.
Address: 409A East New Bern Rd., Kinston, North Carolina 28504.
Phone: 800-332-OINK (6465).
Fax: 252-527-OINK (6465).
E-mail: Kingsbbq@icomnet.com.
Web site: www.Kingsbbq.com.
Hours: 10:30 A.M. to 9 P.M.; open at 9 A.M. for breakfast Saturday and Sunday.
Price: Ranges from $5 to $10.
Reservations: Accepted.
Credit cards: Discover, MasterCard, Visa.

TOP SECRET

Wil King and his family pride themselves on serving authentic old-fashioned Carolina comfort food at King's Restaurant, but that doesn't mean they're not savvy about using technology to peddle pork and other specialties. They've set up shop in cyberspace with their Pig Pages (www.Kingsbbq.com), which features their Oink Express service. Started about a decade ago when a local mom wanted to ship some true southern food to her son serving in the military in California, King's BBQ-by-mail service has evolved into an operation shipping up to one hundred orders a day overnight (or two-day) via Federal Express. The $49.27 (plus shipping) Carolina Oink Sampler, for example, includes a pound of hand-chopped barbecue; one rack of barbecued pork ribs; a pint of each of Brunswick Stew, collards, black-eyed peas, coleslaw or potato salad; five dozen hush puppies; and a bottle of King's Delight Barbecue Sauce. Mmmmm. Demand for King's care packages is particularly strong during holidays because it's traditional to eat black-eyed peas on New Year's for good luck. To order, call the Oink Line at 800-332-OINK between 7 A.M. and 9 P.M. Eastern time.

35

Oriental's School of Sailing

Sail Away

Let's face it. One afternoon spent fumbling around with the Sunfish you rented from the cabana boy at the Hyatt Regency is not going to turn you into a sailor. If you want to know how to sail a boat, you have to learn from people who can already sail. And if you want to know everything there is to know about sailing, then you have to spend a week at Oriental's School of Sailing in Oriental, North Carolina.

Oriental is the self-proclaimed Sailing Capital of North Carolina, and no one has put up a challenge to the title. The small North Carolina village on the Neuse River was originally saddled with the more pedestrian name of Smith's Creek. One day, though, some local folks found a floating name board from a Yankee cargo ship, the USS *Oriental* that wrecked off the Outer Banks in 1862, and that's the name that stuck when the town was incorporated in 1899. That accidental link to the sea is only fitting, however, since many of Oriental's 850 full-time residents still make their living in the marine supply, equipment, or repair business or as commercial fisherman or sailmakers. Plenty of others have retired to this boater's haven to sail and surround themselves with seafaring soul mates. And then, in the warm weather, there are the sailing-challenged outsiders—tourists with America's Cup-sized dreams and *Gilligan's Island* abilities—who learn about the legend of Oriental and make the pilgrimage here to learn to sail from the best.

Oriental's School of Sailing is one of the premier sailing schools anywhere and the oldest sailing school in North Carolina, producing top-notch sailors for more than twenty years. Owner John Poole and his wife and fellow instructor, Juliana, promise "A week of instruction...A lifetime of adventure" to anyone who signs up for one of their comprehensive five-weekday or three-weekend sailing sessions. Once you complete their course, you're prepared to safely charter your first boat. Poole says some students head off on their first cruise from Oriental right after graduation. Still others plunk down big bucks for their *own* vessel after "learning the ropes" at the school.

You don't have to have yacht-sized sailing ambitions to participate in the program. Poole designed his rigorous sailing course for anyone and everyone who wants to learn to sail properly. "The course covers a lot, but it is not difficult," says Juliana Poole. "You learn small details that are done correctly and in the right order." Young adults to seniors and every age group in between are represented at most sessions.

A blend of half days in the classroom and half days on the water prepares students with the skills and confidence required to take to the waves on their own. The Pooles and their staff of instructors (all U.S. Coast Guard Licensed Captains) stress safety first and offer personalized instruction designed to meet the needs of each student. In the mornings, novice sailors cover sailing terminology and learn how to read and use charts, tie knots, anchor, handle lines, and even how to open drawbridges. Afternoons are spent aboard one of two sloop-rigged cruising boats. One is a safe and stable twenty-seven-foot Erickson, named *Babe*, that sports a mainsail with two reef points and five headsails, two of which are reefable. The larger boat, *Starchaser*, is a thirty-foot Pearson 303 that boasts a roller furling/reefing 140 percent headsail similar to those found on most charter boats. Both have diesel auxiliary power and a full array of electronics. If none of that made any sense to you, don't panic. Most people who come to the Oriental school are inexperienced and don't understand such terms either, so don't be intimidated if you don't know a sloop from a schooner.

Before committing to a week-long class, you may want to test the waters, as it were, with a two-hour evening sail; call the school for reservations. They go out every evening, weather permitting. If you're ready to climb aboard for a full week of intense learning and fun, though, call or write Oriental's School of Sailing for a brochure on exact session dates. Classes are strictly limited to six people—three per boat—so make your reservation early in the season. Also, lodging and meals are not covered in the tuition price. There are two local motels close to the school: Oriental Marina Motel (252-249-1818) and The River Neuse Motel (252-249-1404). For more lodging options, call Oriental's Town Hall at 252-249-0555.

Spend a week studying seafaring skills at Oriental's School of Sailing.

Secret Information

Location: Oriental, North Carolina.
Address: P.O. Box 127, Oriental, NC 28571.
Phone: 252-249-0960.
Fax: 252-249-1247.
E-mail: captjohn@coastalnet.com
Web site: www.sschool@pamlico-nc.com.
Season: April through October.
Price: Sailing school tuition is $595 per person; Two-hour evening sail is $15 per person with a minimum charge of $60 (maximum of six persons per boat).
Reservations: Required.
Credit cards: American Express, MasterCard, Visa.
Details: While sailing school students are primarily adults, teenagers fifteen and older are accepted.

TOP SECRET

"In Oriental, you can work whenever you want, sleep whenever you want, eat whenever you want." That response was to a question of whether we could park in an unmarked spot. It came from a couple of locals sitting on the front porch of the Ol' Store in Oriental and pretty much sums up the town's laid-back attitude toward life. Even if you aren't interested in expanding your seafaring skills at Oriental's School of Sailing, take a day trip to this cool waterside community of 850 year-round residents. From the Morehead City area, hop the free ferry from Havelock to Minnesott Beach, then go up North Carolina Highway 306 and follow the signs. While passing through Janiero, stop for a moment at Dawson Creek, the inspiration for television's *Dawson's Creek*, which was created by Kevin Williamson, who grew up in Oriental. Once you're in town, stop at the Ol' Store. It's stuffed with decades' worth of antiques, collectibles, and just plain junk; kids especially love to poke among the piles of stuff looking for treasures. On the day we were there, the owner, Lucille Truitt, sat in her well-worn recliner and explained that folks in Oriental don't wear watches, don't lock their doors, and let their children roam the quiet streets confident that neighbors will keep an eye on them. Although Oriental today resembles Andy Griffith's Mayberry right down to the freckled-faced boys, the town has grown and changed in recent years. Truitt, who used to fish for a living, paints scenes of Oriental Harbor in the '30s and '50s (and sells prints in her store) to preserve the town's past for her grandkids and to inspire them to work at preserving it for the future. "I only paint in January and February," says Truitt, who keeps a spare chair nearby for visitors to sit and chat a spell. "The rest of the year I pickle vegetables." For a bite to eat, head across the lane from Truitt's place to M&M's Cafe (252-249-2000) or around the corner to The Trawl Door (252-249-1232). And if you're in town in September, don't miss the Oriental Cup Regatta (call the Inland Waterway Treasure Co. at 252-249-1797, and ask for Jay Winston), which is really an excuse for a fine three-day party with a sailboat race in the middle. All types of sailors—weekenders and competitors alike—are encouraged to join in the fun.

36 Extreme Camping

We have friends who, when they want to get away, really like to *get away*—away from running water, electricity, anything resembling modern civilization. That makes their favorite place on the Atlantic coastline remote Portsmouth Island, which is also known as the Northern Core Bank and lies just south of Ocracoke Island and east of Cedar Island.

The twenty-two-mile long stretch of sand is protected as part of the Cape Lookout National Seashore, which has its visitor's center on the mainland at the end of Harkers Island. Portsmouth is what our friends call a "manly" place, where guys go—though you do see a few females and children—to pitch a tent between dunes and cast their line into the surf in search of a monster red drum, flounder, or the other sea life that inhabit the coastal waters. There are miles of treeless windswept wilderness to explore, birds to watch, mounds of shells to collect, even a ghost town (see Top Secret). The appeal of camping out there on the edge of nowhere is more spiritual—the Zen of fishing, the communion with nature, the male bonding over coolers of beer.

To get to Portsmouth Island, the man to see is Captain Don Morris, who runs Morris Marina Kabin Kamps and Ferry Service (252-225-4261) across the sound in the town of Atlantic (not to be confused with Atlantic Beach further south). For $10 to $15 per person and $75 per vehicle (get a permit to use a four-wheel drive on Portsmouth from Cape Lookout National Seashore headquarters in Beaufort), he'll ferry you to the southern part of the island at Drum Inlet. There are a limited number of fisherman's cabins that you can rent—talk to the Captain about them as well, or contact the other company offering basic accommodations on the island, Alger G. Willis Fishing Camps (252-729-2791). If you bring your own tent, pitch it wherever you like. Either way, bring everything you'll need, including water, and don't count on getting off the island on schedule if bad weather disrupts the three-times-a-day ferry service.

Secret Information

Location: Cape Lookout National Seashore, North Carolina.
Address: Cape Lookout National Seashore, 131 Charles Street, Harkers Island NC 28531.
Phone: 252-728-2250.
E-mail: CALO_Information@nps.gov.
Web site: www.nps.gov/calo.
Price: No entry or camping fee. Cabins rent for $22 to $150 per night.
Details: Before camping on Portsmouth Island, get a complete set of rules and recommendations from the National Park Service office or by visiting its Web site.

TOP SECRET

If you're not into extreme camping, Portsmouth Island is still worth a visit to see the ghost town of Portsmouth Village. The remnants of the abandoned community are at the northern end of the island and visitors have to follow a road that's generally covered in water (stakes mark the route) to get there. The settlement was once home to more than six hundred people, and the economy was built on the business of "lightering." When large, heavy ships from afar encountered the treacherous and often shallow shoals of the barrier islands, people living in Portsmouth, on Ocracoke Inlet, one of few stable inlets in the area, would unload their heavy cargo, making the ships *lighter*, and transfer it to shallow-draft boats that could make it to the mainland. Due to shifting transportation routes, the lightering business died out, and the Civil War caused the villagers to flee the island, most never to return. To tour Portsmouth relics such as the lifesaving station, Methodist church, and general store, call Captain Rudy Austin (252-928-4361 or 252-928-5431), who runs a ferry trip from Silver Lake on Ocracoke Island. All Terrain Vehicle tours are also available by calling Portsmouth ATV Excursions, which was founded by the owner of Carolina Outback Adventures (Secret 5) then sold to a friend, at 252-928-4484 or 252-928-2644.

37

Hammocks Beach State Park

Deserted Island

Hammocks Beach State Park isn't for everyone. That's what makes it so cool. Because if it were easier to get to, everyone would be there. No, this is the beach for the few, and if you're lucky enough to get up early and be one of them, you'll get to savor one of the best—and most secluded—stretches of sand on the Carolina coast.

Hammocks, or Bear Island as the actual chunk of island is called, is a little 3.5 mile-long and less than a mile wide slice of sea and sand heaven, an unspoiled barrier island accessible only by boat, canoe, or kayak from Swansboro, North Carolina. (An additional thirty-three acres of the state park is located on the mainland.) Unlike most of the other remaining pristine and undisturbed islands on the Carolina coast, this one belongs to the state. That means you don't have to own or rent your own watercraft to spend a day in the unspoiled splendor.

You see, one of the main reasons Hammocks Beach State Park annually earns accolades as one of the top beaches in the nation is that only a limited number of visitors are allowed on the island at any given time. To get there, you have to take a ride on the twenty- to twenty-five-minute, 2.5 mile state-operated passenger ferry, that is, if there's a seat to be had. There aren't any advance reservations, so arrive early at the mainland park office (it opens at 8 A.M.) and buy a ferry ticket. Even if you have to wait in line awhile, it's worth it if your idea of the beach is peace, quiet, nature, and miles of blue sky and crashing waves.

But before you even think about getting up early and driving up (or down) to Swansboro, take the time to think this trip through. Although there's a snack shop on the island and modern bathrooms, that's it. So you'll want sunscreen, the pails and shovels, maybe a kite, and of course some beach blankets, but most importantly you'll need to bring along the two *F*s—food and sturdy footwear. The food can be picked up at one of the grocery stores in Swansboro then packed in your cooler, but you'll really want the shoes from home. It's a half-mile walk across the dunes from the ferry stop to the beach on the island, and although that may not sound far, summer sand can French-fry tender feet, and carrying a load of beach supplies requires steady steps and comfortable footwear. Pack wisely, but not like you're moving in. The passenger ferries are small (twenty-four passengers maximum), and you don't want to make enemies with people you'll be spending several hours with on a virtually deserted island. Travel light.

On the ride out to Bear Island, you'll travel through the Intracoastal Waterway, then through the shallow Cow Channel, named for the animals that were once herded over to the island to graze on the rich sea grass. Along the way you won't have to look hard to see egrets, herons, and osprey. Once on land, gather up your gear and head for an empty stretch of sand. Even at maximum capacity, there's plenty of private space for everyone. Once settled, tread lightly and go on a nature quest. Between mid-May and late August loggerhead sea turtles come ashore at night to nest, and after a two-month incubation the hatchlings emerge to make a mad dash back into the sea. There are also bottle-nosed dolphins that play just off shore, and both gray fox and white-tailed deer make their homes in the island's interior.

Although they've never said so directly, the wildlife is probably the group most pleased that Bear Island is a wildlife preserve. The island's last private owner, New York neurosurgeon William Sharpe, loved to hunt on the island so much that he bought the entire 892-acre barrier island for his retirement home. His plan was to eventually will the property to his hunting guide, John Hurst, but luckily for the animals, Hurst convinced Sharpe to instead donate Bear Island to an organization of black educators—the North Carolina Teachers Association (NCTA). In 1950, the group got the deed to the island and over the next few years unsuccessfully attempted to develop it. By 1961, the NCTA had given up plans for the remote island and decided to donate the land to the state for use as a park for blacks. The Civil Rights Act of 1964 nixed that plan, however, and from then on Hammocks Beach State Park has been open to everyone. Thankfully for true natural-beach lovers like us, *everyone* doesn't get to come at the same time.

Secret Information

Location: Swansboro, North Carolina.
Address: 1572 Hammocks Beach Road, Swansboro, NC 28584.
Phone: 910-326-4881.
Fax: 910-326-2060.
E-mail: habe@nternet.net.
Web site: www.ncsparks.net.
Hours: The state operated passenger ferry runs every half hour from 9:30 A.M. until 6:00 P.M. (last trip back to the mainland), Memorial Day weekend through Labor Day and on a shortened weekend schedule in April and October.
Price: $2 per adults and $1 per child under twelve.
Credit cards: None.

TOP SECRET

The term "primitive camping" takes on new meaning when you pitch a tent and little else on an uninhabited barrier island like Hammocks Beach State Park. There are fourteen family campsites (up to six people each) and three group sites (up to twelve persons each). All are located near the beach and inlet and provide an ideal base for exploration of the same dunes and maritime forests where Indians, pirates, privateers, Confederate soldiers, and hunters once roamed. Unlike those earlier island inhabitants, today's campers have access to water and other facilities at the bathhouse (except from mid-December through mid-March), however, no fires or alcoholic beverages are allowed and all trash must be removed. You can bring a camp stove, though. Camping is by permit only, which can be obtained at the park office near the ferry landing, and reservations are required for the group sites. Although the sites are open year-round, no camping is allowed during full moon periods in the summer when the loggerhead sea turtles are nesting. For reservation and fee information, contact the park (see Secret Information).

Duplin Winery

Fine Vines

38

The roots of winemaking in North Carolina run deep. In 1584, a pair of ship's captains working for Sir Walter Raleigh wrote to their boss to report on what they'd found as they explored the New World. "The coast was so full of grapes that the very beating and surge of the sea overflowed them," they said, perhaps succumbing to a bit of poetic exaggeration. "They covered every shrub and climbed the tops of high cedars. In all the world, a similar abundance was not to be found. Their smell of sweetness filled the air as if they were in the midst of some delicate garden."

Sorry California and New York, North Carolina can lay claim to being the birthplace of winemaking in America. It was the first state in the nation where grapes were cultivated—the variety settlers first called "Big White Grape," which later became known as the scuppernong, a variation on an Algonquin Indian word meaning sweet bay tree or muscadine. The Tar Heel State was the leading producer of wine in the United States until federal prohibition banned alcohol in the early 1900s. It took until the '60s and '70s for the state's winemaking industry to really start growing again, led by pioneering vintners like Dave and Dan Fussell, who founded Duplin Wine Cellars, in Rose Hill in 1976. Duplin, about an hour north of Wilmington, is the best place along the coast to see how wine is made and to sample wines whose heritage stretches back hundreds of years.

The winery has made a go of it by being creative. The brothers, who knew nothing about the art of turning raw fruit into fine wine, originally started making wine to provide a local market for the grapes they and other local farmers had grown after the bottom dropped out of the market elsewhere. Dave eventually bought Dan out, and David Jr. now runs the operation. The winery produces seventeen different wines, including scuppernong, champagne, port, sherry, and burgundy. Wines made with scuppernong/muscadine grapes tend to be sweeter than the drier wines to which many wine drinkers are accustomed.

The winery offers free one-hour tours and tastings daily (except Sunday) and goes out of its way to make sure that guests get a great experience. "We show the best film about winemaking on the East Coast," says Duplin founder Dave Fussell. "Then we have a wine museum, which features the oldest winemaking artifact in America, a grape crusher from the 1700s. On the tours we gauge the interest of the group and go as little or as much in-depth about the winemaking process as they'd like. Then we get to the tasting bar, where we have samples of eight of our wines each day. We're not fancy; we're farmers, but we're very hospitable."

Duplin's hospitality extends to other special events it hosts. Once or twice a month on Saturday nights it puts on wine-and-dinner shows, which are usually sold out. They feature variety-show-style music and comedy that generally draws the fifty-plus crowd. And on the third Saturday of September each year, the winery throws the Grape Stomp, a day-long tour and tasting celebration. The centerpiece of the event is the stomping competition in which visitors shed their shoes, step into a barrel filled with grapes, and see how much juice they can squeeze out of the fruit in one minute of frenzied tromping. Awards are given for the most juice produced, best stomping style, and biggest feet.

The Fussells are constantly looking for innovative ways to expand their business. In response to all the recent research documenting the health benefits of red wine, Duplin has created a "food supplement" that's concentrated Resveratrol, an antioxidant that some think is the reason red wine is good for preventing heart attacks, strokes, and even cancer. "Sometimes I tell people that we look at ourselves as a winery and health spa," says Fussell. "The supplement is made up of ground up grape seeds and skins. It's very tart so you have to cut it with something to drink. It's basically for folks who won't drink wine, although it does have alcohol in it."

All the publicity about the benefits of wine means that business is booming, adds Fussell. "Since the health news came out, we've sold everything we could grow. We've actually sold out of some wines, which is a winemaker's dream."

Secret Information

Location: On U.S. Highway 117 in Rose Hill, North Carolina, about one mile off I-40 Exit 380, north of Wilmington.
Address: P.O. Box 756, Rose Hill, North Carolina 28458.
Phone: 800-774-9634 or 910-289-3888.
Fax:: 910-289-3094.
E-mail: jonathanfussell@hotmail.com.
Web site: www.duplinwinery.com.
Hours: 9 A.M. to 5 P.M. Monday through Saturday.
Season: Year-round.
Price: Tasting tour FREE; wines $5.95 to $15 per bottle; Saturday dinner show $30.25 per person; Grape Stomp $10 per person.
Reservations: Not necessary for tasting tours; recommended for Saturday dinner show and Grape Stomp, which is held annually on the third Saturday in September.
Credit cards: American Express, Discover, MasterCard, Visa.
Details: Tasting tour lasts about an hour.

TOP SECRET

Here's a secret sight that is sure to get the hearts of ardent fans of viticulture (grape horticulture) racing. Although the products of North Carolina's wineries may not command the respect from wine connoisseurs that their counterparts from California do, the Tar Heel state can lay claim to an honor no other wine-growing state can match. It's the home of the fabled Mother Vine, whose feet-thick strands once covered an entire acre. Now trimmed to about a quarter of that size, the bent and beaten plant is the oldest-known grape vine in America. Its existence was noted as early as the mid-1700s, but because scuppernong vines grow at a snail's pace, it sprouted much earlier than that. The vintage vine is still clinging to life and producing fruit. It's on private property, but you can get a look at it from the road by finding the road marker on U.S. Highway 64 just north of Manteo on Roanoke Island, turning onto nearby Mother Vineyard Road, and keeping an eye out just after the loop road takes a tight turn right.

39

Waco Biplane Tour

Fear of Flying

Before you climb onto the lower wing and into the cockpit of a vintage 1942 Waco (pronounced Walk-o, not Way-co like the Texas town) to tour the southern Cape Fear area from the air, you first have to get outfitted by putting in ear plugs, slipping on goggles, and donning your Snoopy hat. Snoopy hat? "We don't know what else to call it," admits pilot Jay Marten. "It's not really a helmet. It's like the hat Snoopy wears when he fights the Red Baron."

The Red Baron is indeed what comes to mind when you first catch sight of the red biplane owned by Ocean Aire Aviation, which flies out of Brunswick Airport near Southport, North Carolina. The craft is one of the last open cockpit, bi-wing planes ever made. It was built by the Weaver Aircraft Company, not for World War I aces, but as a trainer for World War II pilots. After the war the plane had nineteen different owners before Ocean Aire bought it and hired Marten, a former airline pilot who'd flown a similar plane in Las Vegas.

"The company bought it specifically to give air tours," says Marten. "Flying in an open cockpit plane is different than flying in a modern plane. It really does make you step back in time. It wasn't the big airlines that introduced aviation to the world, but barnstormers, little guys like me traveling around in open cockpit planes giving rides to two passengers at a time."

With the front control stick removed, two people can sit side by side in the Waco in front of the pilot's cockpit and behind the seven-cylinder engine and six-foot propeller. Once airborne and flying about eighty-five miles an hour, Marten takes passengers on a thirty-minute bird's-eye tour of Southport, Bald Head Island (Secret 43), and area beaches, including Fort Caswell, which is privately owned and during the summer can be seen by outsiders only from the air. The ocean view can include shrimp boats and schools of fish or dolphins. There's no narration due to the noise, but the front windscreen makes it possible for passengers to talk with each other.

"Before we take off we always ask passengers what they'd like to see," says Marten. "Usually they say they want to fly over the beach house or condo where they're staying. We keep the flights fairly smooth, but sometimes all their friends are there waving, and I've been known to dip a wing and make a tight turn."

Secret Information

Location: At Brunswick Airport on NC Highway 133 near Southport, North Carolina.
Address: 4019 Long Beach Rd. SE, Southport, NC 28461.
Phone: 910-457-0710.
Fax: 910-457-6410.
Hours: 9 A.M. to 5 P.M. daily.
Season: Memorial Day to the end of October.
Price: $99 per flight for up to two people.
Reservations: Recommended.
Credit cards: MasterCard, Visa.
Details: Tours last 30 minutes.

TOP SECRET

If you've always wanted to learn to become a pilot but aren't sure whether you've got the right stuff, take a couple of hours out of your vacation for an introductory flying lesson. Besides Waco biplane tours, Ocean Aire Aviation offers a two-hour-or-so introduction to what it takes to get a pilot's license, including putting you at the controls of a Cessna 172 for a thirty- to forty-minute flight above Cape Fear. The cost of the aircraft and an instructor is $60 an hour; call Ocean Aire to reserve a time. "A lot of parents come down and have kids take a first lesson, even if the kids are too young to get a license," says Chief Pilot Jay Marten. "Many children have spent thousands of hours on a computer flying simulator, and this gives them a chance to compare it to the real thing. Kids need to be at least twelve years old, preferably thirteen or fourteen due to the physical aspect, so they are big enough to handle the controls and mature enough to learn to fly."

40

Holden Beach

Blast from the Past

Going to the beach used to mean simply that. You packed everyting—the kids, the pails and shovels, a week's worth of clothes and bedding—into the station wagon and drove to a seaside cottage. And except for an occasional night out at the miniature golf course, you spent the days swimming, building sand castles, and snoozing under the beach umbrellas.

At nine miles long, Holden Beach is the largest of the South Brunswick Islands. It is named for Benjamin Holden, who planted the family flag on the island in 1756. Over the years Holden's island developed into quite a commercial fishing center, but the beach side of the land wasn't developed until the 1920s when the Holden family decided to open their land to tourists. In 1926, John Holden, Jr. built the Holden Hotel for adventurous city folks looking for an isolated seaside holiday. When the Intracoastal Waterway was built in the 1930s, Holden Beach was cut off from the mainland and became an island. The hotel remained, and Holden's oldest son, Luther S. Holden, owned and operated the place until a hurricane destroyed it in 1934. Back then a small ferry brought vacationers over to the island. Later a drawbridge was built. When the drawbridge was replaced in 1984 with a sweeping, modern bridge spanning the Intracoastal Waterway, tourists and limited development discovered Holden Beach once again. Fortunately, the locals have managed to keep high-rise buildings, hotels, motels, and everything else that can ruin a perfect beach community off the island.

Today there are plenty of Holdens still in town and Alan Holden Vacations helps vacationers find the perfect beach home to rent. More importantly, however, the concept of Holden as a family place has endured. Holden has grown over the years (in 1999 there were two thousand plus homes) with pastel, Charleston-style homes being the latest additions, but there isn't any of the neon and noise that has swallowed up many other family beaches. No condos, no amusement parks, no bars. The island has cottages, a few ice cream and pizza shops, restaurants on the Causeway, and an honor-system library situated in the top floor of the Atlantic Vacation Resorts, Inc. realty company on Ocean Boulevard West.

Bill Kelley, the president of the Holden Beach Merchants Association calls his hometown "the best kept secret in North Carolina." Well Bill, the secret is out but not far enough to ruin the charm or family-centered pace of this place eight to nine hundred permanent residents call home. The high-rise bridge links Holden with the interstate and the outside world, but once you cross over there's little reason to go back. Homes rent from as little as $350 for a week in the off-season for a comfortable two-bedroom cottage to more than $3,400 a week in season for a new six-bedroom seaside retreat. Whatever you're looking for, book early because the families who have been enjoying Holden for generations have no reason to go anywhere else, and after one week here, you'll probably feel the same way.

Secret Information

Location: On the North Carolina coast, between Wilmington and the South Carolina border.
Address: For more information, contact the South Brunswick Island Chamber of Commerce, 4948 Main St. Shallotte, NC 28459 or a local accommodations rental company.
Phone: 800-426-6644.
Fax: 910-754-6539.
E-mail: sbicc1@nccoast.net.
Web site: www.sbichamber.com or www.hbtownhall.com
Rates: Vary depending on season and location.
Reservations: Recommended.

TOP SECRET

On the last weekend of October each year, Holden Beach throws itself a party—The North Carolina Festival By The Sea—and more than twenty-five thousand locals and visitors from across the South pack the place to enjoy food, crafts, a parade along the Causeway, and "family fun" events like sand sculpting, kite flying, and horseshoe pitching. Even with the crowds, Holden Beach holds its own and retains the small town appeal. On Saturday night, couples and kids boogie, sway under the stars, and form long conga lines at the old-fashioned street dance, and on Sunday morning, gospel groups serenade the flock on street corners. For more information, call the South Brunswick Chamber of Commerce (see Secret Information).

41

The Pharmacy Restaurant

Family Affair

What Dan Menna, owner of the Pharmacy Restaurant in Southport, North Carolina, most wants you to know is: "This is a family type of business. One of us is here at all times and we use that to be more personal with people." The "one of us" he's referring to is him, his wife and co-owner, Kelly, and his sister, Lisa, who's the chef and creates the "American Euro-Cusine" that makes up the diverse—and delicious—fare at the elegant eatery near the waterfront.

The Mennas are new to the Pharmacy, having bought it in 1999, and have brought some special changes to what was already a top spot in town. "We exposed the brick on either side of the dining room, have twelve-foot-high ceilings, and have the original tin roof still intact from the original building," Menna says. The name of the restaurant comes from the building's history as the area's only pharmacy from the late 1800s to the 1950s. "The decor is somewhat Victorian, and we have incorporated some antiques from other buildings into the renovations," Menna continues. "Some pieces are from our hundred-year-old Victorian home near Philadelphia in South Jersey. My wife's grandmother's cut crystal glass from Germany is used to serve certain desserts."

At lunch the Pharmacy serves such items as tuna sandwiches, corn crab chowder, and a portobello burger. Fancier dinner fare includes blackened beef, pork, and fresh seafood, including the place's most popular item: crab cakes. "They are of our own design," confides Menna. "We make them in filo dough instead of the traditional breaded way. They are our best seller and our forte." Other specialties include Lisa's duck in a honey and balsamic vinegar sauce. "Some people don't like duck because it is sometimes gamey or fatty," says Menna, "but she prepares it by roasting the whole duck, then renders the fat off the whole bird, removes the breast, and sears it in a cast iron frying pan." Lisa, who attended culinary school in New England, also makes all the desserts, like crème brûlée and a chocolate truffle torte.

The Mennas chose to locate in Southport "because it's in a beautiful area on the coast that's not developed yet," Dan says. "Southport is a special historic town that's not going to change for awhile." So far the new Pharmacy has been a big hit with locals and visitors alike. "We've hit the ground running and done no advertising yet," says Menna. "We've had a phenomenal run!"

Secret Information

Location: Southport, North Carolina.
Address: 110 East Moore Street, Southport, NC 28461.
Phone: 910-457-5577.
Fax: 910-457-5577.
Hours: 11:30 A.M. to 2:30 P.M. for lunch; 5:30 P.M. to 9:00 P.M. Monday to Saturday.
Price: Lunches are $10 or less; Dinners are $20 or less.
Reservations: Recommended.
Credit cards: MasterCard, Visa.

TOP SECRET

Southport, home to the Pharmacy Restaurant, is itself a secret worth exploring. The waterfront area features historic homes, antique shops, art galleries, and a pretty park where you can relax and watch transoceanic ships travel up the Cape Fear River toward Wilmington. The Southport Maritime Museum (910-457-0003) shows off the town's seafaring past with such exhibits as "Pirates: Gangsters of the Sea." A funky find just across the street from the Pharmacy is Etcetera (910-457-6119), which calls itself the "Second Most Unique Gift Shop" and features folk art, metal sculptures, and jewelry. Southport is also the jumping off point for visiting Bald Head Island (Secret 43) and Fort Fisher (Secret 50). For more information, stop by the Southport 2000 Visitor's Center at 113 W. Moore St (800-388-9635), or call the Southport-Oak Island Chamber of Commerce at 800-457-6964 or 910-457-6964.

Beaches for the Real World

There's a line in the sand that separates the year-round beaches from the summer ones. That line falls just about at the North Carolina–South Carolina border. Everything south of here is pretty much oceanfront property that stays popular and packed with bathers, boaters, golfers, tennis folks, and active retirees throughout the year. And to the north are the traditional "school's-out" beaches that anyone who grew up north of the Mason-Dixon line fondly remembers from childhood. They are summer beaches that are buzzing with activity from Memorial Day to Labor Day and refreshingly empty (a great place to let your dog run or harvest a bucket of shells) and often boarded up the rest of the year.

The southernmost "school's-out" beaches fall roughly along what's known as the Cape Fear coast. This title commonly refers to the area immediately bordering the Cape Fear River near Wilmington, North Carolina, but we're stretching the limits a bit to the north and a tad to the south to include all of the state's southern coast. So our Cape Fear Coast stretches from Calabash, North Carolina—billed as the "Fried Seafood Capital of the World" (there are about thirty seafood places packed into one square mile)—in the south to Topsail Island (pronounced "TOP-sull") in the north. In between lies a pristine ribbon of barrier islands linked to the mainland by bridges spanning the Intracoastal Waterway. The area encompasses four oceanfront counties (Brunswick, New Hanover, Pender, and Onslow) and one big port city on the Cape Fear River—Wilmington.

Wilmington's most famous native is basketball legend Michael Jordan, and it seems appropriate that the final leg of Interstate 40 (completed in 1991), which links Wilmington to California, is named for him. Before this stretch of interstate was finished, Wilmington was somewhat isolated from the rest of the state. Although this separation caused economic problems for the area over the years, it also had a positive preservation effect, which is now paying huge dividends in terms of tourist dollars. Since industry and developers didn't have easy access to Cape Fear, the region, for the most part, retains the look and feel of the best summer beach communities of the 1950s. And Wilmington itself boasts a thriving, fifty-five-block restored waterfront downtown district featuring restaurants, shops, clubs, as well as meticulously renovated historic homes with private gardens. Tourists and locals alike enjoy leisurely strolls along Wilmington's Riverwalk by day and club-hopping along the river at night. If you're a fan of the television show *Dawson's Creek*, you may enjoy sharing the sidewalk with one of the stars (Secret 48). Some of the cast live in Wilmington's walkable downtown district (when the series is filming), and others party here when the work day is done.

Yeah, work. While most of the year-round beach communities in South Carolina and Florida are associated mainly with play, the northern, summer beaches, like the ones on Cape Fear, have a real-world atmosphere. People here work for a living. The ocean and river just happen to be in their backyard. When the summer comes, they'll sneak out to the shore after work, on the weekends, and for a week or two on vacation, but most of the time they live lives of mortgages and kids and school and time-cards. That real-world edge gives Cape Fear a grittier feel than its southern cousins in the South Carolina Grand Strand and Lowcountry. If you're looking to be pampered in luxury, you'll find pockets of possibilities on Cape Fear, but you'd be better off heading farther south. But if you're looking for friendly folks, great fishing, and simple beach cottages where Andy and Opie Taylor could have stayed, then the Cape Fear coast is for you.

The closest beach community to Wilmington also happens to be one of the prettiest and most popular on the Cape Fear coast—Wrightsville Beach (Secret 49). The beach communities to the south, along the Cape Fear River have a more remote feel than Wrightsville. Carolina and Kure Beach feature tidy cottages and a few concrete high-rise motels that snuck in under some slip in a zoning ordinance. The further you travel down Route 421 from the city, the farther back in time you seem to go. If you take the narrow, sand-strewn road as far as you can drive, you'll dead end at the Fort Fisher Recreation area (Secret 50). That's where you can venture onto the beach (if you have a four-wheel drive vehicle with plenty of undercarriage clearance) and drive even further south to get a look at the actual point of land known as Cape Fear.

A quick ferry ride from Fort Fisher or a long (really long in summer traffic) ride back through Wilmington is the charming village of

Hit hard by past hurricanes, Topsail Island, north of Cape Fear, is dotted with trees stripped of foliage.

Southport, which is listed on the National Register of Historic Places. There's free street parking in town, so just find a spot and stroll along the oak-lined sidewalks to visit antique shops, art galleries, and restaurants. If you don't mind the crowds, make plans to attend the North Carolina Fourth of July Festival in downtown Southport. It's one of the state's biggest and best red-white-and-blue celebrations, and it ends with a huge fireworks show on the waterfront.

Just off the coast of Southport is environmentally friendly and residentially upscale Bald Head Island (Secret 43), which is also home to

Old Baldy Lighthouse. This summer haven for golfers, and others wealthy enough to afford the seclusion, sits across the water from the more blue collar Oak Island, which includes the communities of Caswell Beach, Yaupon Beach, and Long Beach. The area is older and focused squarely on fishing. There are only a few restaurants on the island and a handful of quaint one- and two-story motels. Mostly, Oak Island is a narrow strip of land with a wide, white sand beach and modest cottages, all within easy walking distance of the ocean.

To the south of Oak Island are the three South Brunswick Islands—Holden Beach (Secret 40), Ocean Isle Beach, and Sunset Beach. Ocean Isle Beach—the middle island—is the most developed but is still considered quaint by today's standards. These are all family-cottage beaches where kids can safely ride bikes. The one-lane pontoon bridge leading to Sunset Beach (each year there's lobbying to replace it with an ugly, modern bridge) only serves to increase the charm (and the wait during the summer to get on the island). Sunset is also where you can walk out to the neighboring, pristine Bird Island at low tide.

While the beaches to Wilmington's south are easily accessible from the city, the neighbors to the north on Topsail Island seem much farther away. The twenty-seven-mile ride from the city takes about forty-five minutes, much of it a pretty boring ride over flat, barren land. This treeless theme continues at the coast where Hurricane Fran wreaked havoc a few years back. There's a wind-swept, weather-ravaged feel to Topsail Island that's appealing to anyone looking for a basic beach for the main course with a splash of adventure on the side. The waves can be formidable and downright frightening up here, but the beach has its gentle side since it's a haven for loggerhead sea turtles. A forty-year-old swing bridge connects Topsail to the mainland at Surf City on Route 50/210. This is the commercial hub of the area and is home to most of the island's handful of restaurants, shops, and food stores.

After all our travels on the Cape Fear coast, we couldn't find one thing to truly fear (okay, except for a winter wave or two on North Topsail Beach). Instead, we found a lot to love. The traditional summer beaches of Cape Fear might be too slow, too old, too plain for some visitors, but we find the old-fashioned atmosphere and historic setting comforting—kind of like Mom's macaroni and cheese on a cold winter day. In fact, maybe Cape Comfort would be a better name for this stretch of coast.

Secret Information

For more information about the Cape Fear coast, contact the following organizations:

- Cape Fear Coast Visitors Bureau, 24 North Third Street, Wilmington, NC 28401; 800-222-4757; www.cape-fear.nc.us; info@cape-fear.nc.us.
- Carolina Beach Chamber of Commerce, 1140 North Lake Park Boulevard, Carolina Beach, NC 28428; 910-458-8434
- Topsail Area Chamber of Commerce and Tourism, 205 S. Topsail Drive, Topsail Island, NC 28445; 910-328-4722 or 800-626-2780.
- Southport/Oak Island Chamber of Commerce, 4841 Long Beach Rd, S.E., Southport, NC 28461; 910-457-6964 or 800-457-6964.
- North Carolina's Brunswick Islands, P.O. Box 1186, Shallotte, NC 28459; 910-765-5517 or 800-795-SAND (7263); www.ncbrunswick.com.

TOP SECRET

As you come into Wilmington, you can't help but notice that thing sitting in the harbor; it's as big as a battleship. Oh, wait! It is a battleship—the *North Carolina*, which was launched in 1941 and was supposed to be scrapped in the '60s. It was saved by school children and others who raised enough money to make it a memorial to the ten thousand North Carolinians who fought and died in World War II. The memorial offers a fascinating self-guided tour that allows you to explore up and down the decks of the 44,800-ton, 728-foot-long war machine. If you're a serious military buff, though, seek out one of the two men who actually served on the *North Carolina* during its time in the Pacific in WWII. They now spend part of their golden years as volunteers telling tourists inside stories of ship life. One of the former sailors is Leo Bostwick, who served on the North Carolina as a Machinist Mate Second Class. He can show you the bunk he slept in and talk about how hard it was to get fresh air below deck. He can take you to the room below the giant rotating guns where the crew loaded ninety-pound packs of explosives that propelled shells through the ship's sixteen-inch guns. He can tell you what it was like to go through the torpedo attack that killed crewmates. He can pass along stuff you never knew before, like the fact that a water fountain aboard ship is called a "scuttlebutt," around which news and rumors were shared. Bostwick reserves his tours for those who are truly serious about listening and learning about the *North Carolina*'s history; he prefers not to give tours with kids, whose attention spans are too short to enjoy the experience. If you're seriously interested in learning about the sacrifices the crew of the *North Carolina* made, though, he'll gladly show you around.

Barely Inhabited

If you listed all the things you didn't like about your last beach vacation, traffic and too many people would probably be near the top. Everyone loves going to the beach, they just wish everyone else would stay home. That's the theory behind Bald Head Island, which is located on North Carolina's Cape Fear coast. There's no bridge access to the island, no cars are allowed, and the rental rates are comparatively steep. The result is few people, more beach space and wildlife, and greater opportunities to explore the outdoors on foot, bike, and kayak (since basically there isn't any other option.) With more than ten thousand acres of the island's salt marshes and maritime forests permanently protected as nature preserves, there's no chance that this piece of paradise will be devoured by the same development monster that has gobbled up other Carolina coastal communities.

The southern end of the island is where Bald Head's gentle version of development is concentrated. Narrow lanes with names like Creeping Cucumber Court and Evening Primrose Path branch off from the two main roads—Federal and South Bald Head Wynd—all of which are for foot, bike, or golf cart traffic only. Visitors take only what they can carry in baskets and backpacks. They greet each other on the street as they head to the beach, golf course, tennis courts, the harbor, or to Harbor Village—the island's retail and restaurant hub where just before sunset, savvy islanders grab a table on the deck at Eb and Flo's Steambar (910-457-7217) for steamed crabs and conversation. Bikes are a necessity on the island, especially to explore the 173-acre Maritime Forest Preserve at mid-island. Your kids will probably be the first ones on the block to ride their bikes into a rain forest—literally. Bald Head's maritime forest is the northernmost tropical rain forest in the country. Pretty cool, huh? Rent your bikes by the hour, day, or week. More of a luxury, but just as popular, are the golf carts, which can be rented by the hour or day. For current rates and reservation information on both or to rent a canoe to explore the marshes, call Island Passage at 910-457-4944.

Exclusive Bald Head Island offers peaceful places to paddle and pursue other vacation pastimes. (COURTESY OF KELLY C. SELLERS)

Whether they vacation on Bald Head Island or not, most Cape Fear visitors become familiar with Old Baldy Lighthouse. When on the island, be sure to visit this 109-foot tower. It was built in 1796 and put into operation in 1817 in order to guide ships through the dangerous shoals of the lower Cape Fear River. Old Baldy retired in 1935 (it was used primarily as a secondary lighthouse because it was too far inland), but it's still standing—making this the oldest remaining lighthouse in the state. Visitors can tour both the lighthouse and Captain Charlie's Station, where the lighthouse keeper and his assistants used to live for free all year round.

In the evenings during the summer, visitors and locals (there are roughly 160 very fortunate permanent residents) flock to the beach for sea turtle walks sponsored by the Bald Head Island Conservancy. Space is limited for the guided walks along the island's ten miles of nesting beach. Nesting season runs from June through mid-October, and the walks help educate visitors about the fragility of sea turtle hatchlings and about the need to protect nesting areas. For more information about the turtlewalks or to reserve your spot, call the conservancy at 910-457-0089.

While today's guests make reservations months in advance to claim a place to stay on the island, early visitors to Bald Head were less enthusiastic about being there. That's because most were on ships lured to the island by false lights placed on the beaches by the British pirate Major Stede Bonnet—"The Gentleman Pirate of Barbados"—and his men. Thirteen ships ran aground during the summer of 1718 and were captured by the pirates. Throughout the years Bald Head has also been home to Indians, British troops during the Revolutionary War and Confederate soldiers during the Civil War, and river pilots who steered ships through the perilous waters of Cape Fear and Frying Pan Shoals. Legend has it that the name Bald Head came from a dune on the island's south beach that was worn bare by river pilots standing on top searching for ships off the coast. Once a ship was spotted, the pilots would race out in rowboats to be the first one to offer his navigating services to the captain. The first man to reach the ship would be paid to steer the vessel safely over the bar and up the Cape Fear River.

Today, Bald Head Island is a quick ferry ride from the quaint village of Southport. Most people who take the Bald Head Island Ferry at the beginning of the week to stay on the island rarely venture back before they have to turn in their key. If you're short on cash and can't stay on Bald Head Island, take a day trip golfing, exploring, or relaxing on the beach. But, if you can afford it, Bald Head Island is the place to be when being away from it all matters most.

Secret Information

Location: Accessible by ferry from Indigo Plantation and Marina in Southport, North Carolina.

Address: Bald Head Island Information Center, 5079 Southport-Supply Road, Southport, NC 28461.

Phone: Information: 800-234-1666 for the management company; rental reservations: 800-432-7368.

Fax: Reservations center: 910-457-7524.

Web site: www.baldheadisland.com.

Rates: $700 to $3,500 per week.

Reservations: Recommended.

Credit cards: Discover, MasterCard, Visa.

TOP SECRET

If you don't have any little ones in tow, check into Bald Head Island's first bed-and-breakfast, Theodosia's. The gabled Victorian inn is ideally located near the marina and provides spectacular views of the harbor, river, and marshes from its numerous porches and decks. Like most things on the island, the rates are expensive ($165 and up in the summer and $150 and up in the off-season) but worth it. Each of the ten rooms is decorated with a Caribbean feel and all include private baths or showers, telephones, and cable television. Along with the bountiful breakfast, guests also get to use the complimentary golf carts and bikes. Later in the day innkeepers Frank and Lydia Love serve guests complimentary *hors d'oeuvres* and a scrumptious evening dessert. The inn was named for Aaron Burr's daughter, who disappeared off the North Carolina coast in 1812. Local lore says that Theodosia's ghost enjoys spending time on Bald Head Island, and if she's smart, she pulls up a rocker and watches the sea from a deck at the inn bearing her name. For information and reservations call Theodosia's Bed and Breakfast at 800-656-1812 or 910-457-6563.

Graystone Inn

Southern Manor

44

As a top executive for Enterprise Rental Cars, Paul Bolda traveled the world, often with his wife, Rebecca; in twenty years of marriage they lived in eighteen different places in the U.S. and overseas. "When we traveled outside major cities we always tried to stay in country inns and bed-and-breakfasts to get the flavor of the local area and people," says Bolda. "When I retired from Enterprise, we decided to start second careers as innkeepers." Bolda contacted the New York office of the world-famous Sotheby's auction house and asked for help locating the perfect place to establish a bed-and-breakfast somewhere in Georgia, South Carolina, or North Carolina. "We're both from Detroit and had our fill of shoveling snow," Bolda says, laughing.

After looking at several places, the couple chose a landmark in Wilmington, the old Bridgers Mansion, built in 1906. "The building was in pretty bad shape," recalls Bolda. "It was already an inn, but it had shag carpet and plastic shower surrounds." In fact, the mansion was so rundown that it didn't even rate one star—the lowest score—in the American Automobile Association travel guide.

With the same energy and skills he'd used to launch Enterprise's operations in Canada and Europe, Paul plunged in and collaborated with Rebecca, an interior designer, to completely restore the mansion. They got the original blueprints and worked with the local historic preservation community to recreate every detail of the original home, which was built by the widow Elizabeth Haywood Bridgers for her seven children. This included hiring a plasterer from Maine to come to North Carolina to painstakingly recreate the molds for interior details. All the work paid off when the Graystone Inn reopened a couple of years ago. "We've just been awarded four diamonds by the AAA and are one of only fifteen places with that rating in the whole state," says Bolda with pride. "The person from AAA said this is the only place he knew about that went from not even making the book to four diamonds overnight."

The secret of the Graystone's success is that the Boldas have tried to take all the best elements of the hundreds of inns they've stayed in around the world and bring them together in one place. With only seven rooms, the inn immerses guests in luxury living, right down to Egyptian cotton linen sheets with a 320 thread count. Rooms are spacious (in fact, one of the suites is thirteen hundred square feet and has eighteen-foot-high ceilings) and all feature clawfoot bathtubs and antique furnishings such as four-poster beds. The largely Victorian decor extends to the public areas that include a parlor, sitting room, and dining room, where breakfast, made by Rebecca, a gourmet cook, is served at a Sheraton-style mahogany dining table. The most popular public room in the inn, though, is the library, which is paneled in Honduras mahogany and lined with glass-front shelves holding thousands of books. In keeping with the feel of a European *pension*, cordials are served in the library each evening.

All this luxury comes at a price. The Graystone Inn is the most expensive bed-and-breakfast in Wilmington. The clientele is definitely upscale and sometimes famous (see Top Secret), although the atmosphere is comfortable and casual, not stuffy. It's a great place to stay for any reason, although it's particularly nice as a retreat for a couple stressed from the day-to-day pressures of work and family life. "We were voted one of the top three most romantic places to stay in North Carolina by two television stations," reports Bolda, who adds: "We're having a blast."

Secret Information

Location: Wilmington, North Carolina.
Address: 100 S. Third St., Wilmington, NC 28401.
Phone: 888-763-4773 or 910-763-2000.
Fax: 910-763-5555.
E-mail: paulb@graystoneinn.com.
Web site: www.graystoneinn.com.
Rates: $139 to $289 per night.
Reservations: Recommended.
Credit cards: American Express, Diner's Club, Discover, MasterCard, Visa.

TOP SECRET

Wilmington is the third largest center of television and film production in the United States, (Secret 48) and when stars are in town, they generally choose to stay at the Graystone Inn. You never know who you'll run into by the sideboard buffet at breakfast—Goldie Hawn, Charles Bronson, Phyllis Diller, David Brinkley, Billy Zane, Alan Alda, all of whom have stayed there in recent years. The stars are generally friendly and like mixing with other guests—Peter Falk a.k.a. Columbo, in fact, insisted on not coming down to breakfast unless other guests were there so he could schmooze with them. Also at breakfast, Anthony Hopkins was asked to do his "Hannibal Lecter face," and did, which "scared the hell out of everybody," reports innkeeper Paul Bolda. The inn itself has also been used as a location for several television shows and movies, from *Dawson's Creek* to the Nick Nolte-Sandra Bullock movie, *Everybody Wins.*

45

Trails End Steak House

Cattle Drive

Just before you finally get to the Trails End Steakhouse there's a warning sign that reads ROAD ENDS. Your immediate reaction may be, "Oh no. We're totally lost." Just ignore the sign, keep driving toward the Atlantic, and soon you'll come upon a restaurant on the Intracoastal Waterway that serves up the best steaks in Wilmington. It takes some navigating through the southeastern part of the city to get there, but as the locals who love it know, eating at the Trails End is worth all the trouble.

The Trails End is one of those unabashedly rough-edged steakhouses that put chain imitators like Longhorn and Lone Star to shame. There's a wooden Indian guarding the entrance (no political correctness here). The door, whose handles are two horseshoes actually worn by the Budweiser Clydesdales, closes after you come in with a set of ropes and pulleys weighted by a Civil War cannon ball. Originally a cinder-block seafood restaurant, the building's decor was changed to cowboy rustic when B. C. Hedgepeth opened the Trails End in 1965. Current owners John and Carole Coble took over in 1983.

The place isn't for vegans. The place prides itself on selling steaks that are hand-cut every day and grilled over open hardwood charcoal. Beef options include New York strip, Delmonico (cut as large as you like and priced at $1.80 per ounce), Sirloin, Prime Rib, Beef-K-Bob, and a ground beef burger. Seafood selections consist of lobster tail, Panned Masonboro Shrimp, and daily catches. The sole chicken dish is the Booze Run Bird, a boneless breast. The menu is kept intentionally simple, without any of the trendy changes in cuisine that sometimes distract other restaurants from what they do well. It's the quality of the beef, seafood, and chicken along with the savory taste that comes from the smoky hardwood fire that makes the Trails End Steakhouse a worthy secret to seek out.

Secret Information

Location: Wilmington, North Carolina.
Address: 613 Trails End Road, Wilmington, NC 28403.
Phone: 910-791-2034.
Fax: 910 799-9617.
Hours: 6 P.M. to "until" every day June to August and in December, and Monday to Saturday the rest of the year.
Price: Range from $12 to $32.
Reservations: Recommended.
Credit cards: American Express, Discover, MasterCard, Visa.
Details: The owners are purposely vague about closing time. The nice thing about a small family restaurant is that they can stay open until everyone is satisfied and ready to leave.

TOP SECRET

You won't go away hungry from the Trails End Steakhouse. Besides big slabs of beef and scads of seafood, the restaurant features a "hospitality table," which amounts to a smorgasbord of sides. It's included in the price of every meal and offers not only the usual salad fixin's, but items like smoked sausages, clam fries, and meatballs. Our advice: don't wear tight pants to the Trails End—you'll need room for your belly to bulge.

46

Carolina Web Sites

FYI

Carolinas in Cyberspace

The Carolinas are well represented in cyberspace. Most of the secrets in this book have Internet sites you can visit, ask questions, request materials, make reservations, or purchase products. There are also some great sources of travel information for both North and South Carolina on the Web that you may want to consult to plan your coastal vacation. The following are some sites worth looking into:

CoastalGuide.com (*www.coastalguide.com*). Enterprising Internet designer Bob Jordan of Elizabeth City, North Carolina, has created a "co-op" site of local chambers of commerce, tourist bureaus, and hospitality and travel businesses that covers every city, town, or wide spot in the road along the coast of North and South Carolina. Links for each spot include information about its history, ecology, weather, legends and tall tales, services, events, lodging, activities, and more.

Connections: A Southern Golf and Vacation Guide (*www.aesir.com*). This site offers travel information in general and about golf in particular for areas from the Outer Banks to Fort Lauderdale, Florida. It includes sections on lodging, events, and recommended reading, but the feature that makes it different than other sites is the "travelogue" area for each location. Web users post comments about things to do, places to eat, and other subjects for each destination. This is the place to turn for recommendations for where to go—and where not to—from average travelers.

South Carolina Tourism (*www.travelsc.com*). This is the official state tourism site for the state of South Carolina. Attractively designed, it features information about Palmetto State things to do and where to stay as well as golf and state park guides. You can also order a free printed travel guide or golf guide on-line.

North Carolina: A Better Place to Be (*www.visitnc.com*). This is the Tar Heel State's official travel site. Check it out for information about attractions and accommodations as well as up-to-date information on such subjects as what's biting for fishermen along the coast.

Great Outdoor Recreation Pages (*www.gorp.com*). The GORP Web site features comprehensive information on outdoor adventure opportunities around the world. It's the place to find spots in the Carolinas to do everything from cycling to scuba diving.

EarthCam (*www.earthcam.com*). Finally, if you can't actually make it to the beach at least you can see live pictures of what's going on there right now on your computer. This site features links to cameras trained on all kinds of sights around the world, including Carolina coast areas such as Wrightsville Beach, North Carolina, and Myrtle Beach, South Carolina.

TOP SECRET

Point your browser to *100 Secrets of the Carolina Coast* Web site (www.100secrets.com) for updates to information in the book that has changed since publication—or that we got wrong. (Nobody's perfect). You'll also find excerpts from our first book, *100 Secrets of the Smokies* (available at a bookstore near you), our biographies, and reader reviews. Feel free to send your comments on this book or secrets we should include in a future edition (see "Send Us Your Secrets" in the back of the book) to Carolinas@100secrets.com.

47

Blue Water Point Marina Resort

Marina Life

Homogenized hotel chains make life easier for road travelers. You see a brand name, and you know what to expect. There's a standard of quality at each facility, and you're rarely disappointed. Unfortunately, all that uniformity eliminates any chance of a pleasant surprise or local flavor. That's what makes treasures like the Blue Water Point Marina Resort on Oak Island worth savoring and saving.

Blue Water Point Marina Resort is one of the few motels on what is mainly a cottage and condo island frequented by native North Carolinians. But Oak Island's location—exactly halfway between Wilmington to the north and Myrtle Beach to the south—makes it the ideal spot from which to launch any Carolina coastal vacation. To get to the complex, make a right off the Oak Island Bridge and drive until you almost hit the water. That's where you'll find the tidy blue and white Blue Water Point Marina Resort. The rooms are large and all have a water view, plus there's room-side fishing available. There's a pool, three sundecks, and beach chair and umbrella rentals, but most of the folks who drop anchor here are more interested in being out on the water. That's where the marina part of the story starts. General Manager Buzz Greene can set you up with pontoon or sailboat rentals; parasailing; deep-sea fishing; a picnic on the beach at sunset; or a nature cruise on the sixty-foot *Blue Water Princess*.

"We're at the end of the road, so we're glad to have anybody," jokes the affable Greene, who manages the Blue Water Point for owner Carl Micky, a Hickory, North Carolina, businessman who bought the marina complex a few years back and spent a million dollars completely renovating the entire operation. "A lot of people don't know we're here the first time they find us. Then they keep coming back, and they know exactly where to go. They don't think of going anywhere else."

No wonder. The place is well-kept, the pool is clear and blue, and the Atlantic Ocean is just across the street 150 yards. Not bad for only $75 per night in season.

The docks of the small and simple Blue Water Point Marina Resort sit at the tip of Oak Island.

"I wanted to create a place where families could come and relax and keep it affordable," says Micky, who enjoys talking with the guests and fishermen who visit his marina. "We have everything right here for them, so they don't spend their vacation driving."

Most people who check into the Blue Water Point are on the island to fish. In addition to the deep-sea fishing, there's great fishing nearby. In fact, back in 1991 Katherine W. Davis caught a world-record 531b 3oz King Mackerel off the Long Beach pier across the street. And if you think that story sounds a bit fishy, then check out the catch and the plaque proclaiming the world record yourself at the marina's restaurant, the Fish House. While you're there, treat yourself to the Blue Water Steam Pot for Two—shrimp, oysters, clams, snow crab legs, mussels, crawfish, sausage, new potatoes, and corn-on-the-cob all steamed to perfection with Old Bay Seasoning and herbs.

The restaurant, which is decorated in, you guessed it, a blue and white nautical decor, has two walls of windows providing views of the harbor, boats, and fishermen returning with their catches. Around sunset, says Greene, everyone gathers on the deck outside the restaurant to toast the day and greet the returning anglers. The assembled crowd cheers and the little kids' eyes grow wide as the fishermen hang their catches and pose for photos in front of the Blue Water Point Marina sign on the dock.

If you don't fish already, you probably will give it a try before you leave the Blue Water Point. Rod and reel rentals are only $10 a day, and Greene and his crew will set you up with bait and give you plenty of free advice. But if fishing is the last thing you want to do on your beach vacation, don't let that stop you from checking out the small resort. Besides the ideal location, reasonable rates, friendly management, access to watersports, and an on-site restaurant, there's volleyball, basketball, the pool, and yes, that little attraction called the Atlantic Ocean.

Secret Information

Location: At the eastern end of Oak Island, in Long Beach, North Carolina.
Address: 57th Place, W. Beach Drive, Long Beach, NC 28465.
Phone: 910-278-1230.
Fax: 910-278-1212.
Hours: Restaurant: lunch served from11:30 A.M. to 2:30 P.M. in summer, dinner served spring, summer, and fall from 5P.M. to 10 P.M., restaurant closed in winter.
Season: Motel open year-round, but restaurant closed in winter.
Prices: Lunches range from $6 to $7; Dinners range from $15 to $18.
Rates: Motel is $75 per night.
Reservations: Recommended.
Credit cards: Discover, MasterCard, Visa.

TOP SECRET

On the opposite end of Oak Island from the Blue Water Point is Caswell Beach. Few tourists find their way up this narrow strip of sand and salt marsh. It's quiet and residential. In fact, the only thing commercial here is the private Caswell Dunes Country Club. There is, however, an interesting historic site located at the end of narrow Caswell Beach Drive. It's the remnant earthworks of Fort Caswell, which was built in 1826 to protect the entrance to the Cape Fear River. During its active tenure, the fort was under both Confederate and Union control and was considered a prime protector against coastal invasion during the Spanish-American War, and World Wars I and II. Today, the fort is owned by the North Carolina Baptist Assembly and used as a summer youth camp. But during the off-season, for $2 you can drive through the assembly grounds and visit the fort. For more information, contact the North Carolina Baptist Assembly, Oak Island, NC 28465, or call 910-278-9501.

Filmington

Quick! Name the top three centers of television and movie production in the United States. The first two are a cinch—Los Angeles and New York. The third, though, probably comes as a surprise. It's Wilmington, North Carolina, which, like any unknown who suddenly hits the big time, should probably change its name to something more glamorous, like Filmington.

The Cape Fear area's most prominent ongoing production is the teens-in-trauma television series *Dawson's Creek*. In typical Hollywood fashion, the waterways, historic buildings, restaurants, and hangouts around Wilmington substitute for the show's coastal Massachusetts setting. Hundreds of other productions, though, have called the area home since 1983 when filmmaker Dino DeLaurentis made the movie *Firestarter* there. (Remember Drew Barrymore as the Stephen King creation who could incinerate bad guys with her mind?) Other Cape Fear movie credits include *Muppets from Space*, *Elmo in Grouchland*, and *I Know What You Did Last Summer*. Television series shot locally include *Matlock*, which starred North Carolina resident Andy Griffith. When you're in town, keep your eyes open for cameras filming scenes on the Wilmington waterfront or stars grabbing supper at a local restaurant. And if you're really ambitious, try to get your face on film by being an extra for a day (see Top Secret).

The same natural beauty, quaint scenery, and welcoming attitude of the locals that brings tourists to the Cape Fear area is what has also attracted so many filmmakers. Plus the mild weather (hurricane season excluded) is an added advantage for location shots. There's also plenty of studio space in Wilmington, thanks to DeLaurentis, the master of disaster films like *The Towering Inferno*. Back when he shot *Firestarter*, he built a state-of-the-art, $1.5 million studio complex in town, which has since changed hands several times. Currently, EUE Screen Gems Studios, Ltd. owns the thirty-two-acre site, and none other than Frank Capra, Jr. (son of the director of *It's A Wonderful Life*) is company president.

For a guaranteed glimpse of moviemaking in Wilmington, take a walking tour of the complex. Understand, though, that this is a working studio (not a tourist attraction like Universal in Orlando), so tours are limited to weekends when they won't interfere with production activity. For $10, you get to walk through the largest production studio east of Hollywood, which includes a three-block, four-story urban studio backlot modeled after New York's Chinatown and the world's largest blue screen, which is used to film actors for scenes into which backgrounds or special effects will be added later. The hour-long tours are provided through a private operator, Silver Screen Tours, and are led by industry insider James Crews. Most weekends, tours begin at 10 A.M., noon, and 2 P.M. on both Saturday and Sunday at the studio gate. No cameras and no one under twelve is allowed, and reservations are recommended during the summer.

Secret Information

Location: Wilmington, North Carolina.
Address: EUE Screen Gems Studio, 1223 N. 23rd. St., Wilmington, NC 28405.
Phone: Silver Screen Tours: 910-675-8479.
Web site: www.screengemsstudios.com/tourinfo.html.
Price: Studio complex tour is $10. No children under 12 are allowed.
Reservations: Recommended for tours.
Credit cards: None.

TOP SECRET

How about this for a vacation memory? You head to Wilmington, North Carolina, where *Dawson's Creek* is filmed. You get cast as an extra for a day, but during a scene with lead hunk James Van Der Beek, he spots you in the crowd and tells the director that you'd be perfect for a part on the show. You join the cast and are a big hit, decide you really want to be in movies, quit your job, and go on to be the next Harrison Ford or Julia Roberts. Okay, so most of that's a complete fantasy, but it's entirely possible that you could get cast as an extra in a production in the Cape Fear area. To give it your best shot, contact Fincannon and Associates (1235 North 23rd Street, Wilmington, NC, 28405, 910-251-1500), the biggest casting company in town and the one that hires extras for *Dawson's Creek* and other productions. They'll give you an information packet to fill out, which they'll keep on file. To increase your odds of being called for an extra while you're in the area on vacation, give the casting office a call when you arrive in coastal North Carolina to remind them that you're available. Often a phone call is enough to pull your photo to the top of a pile or at least put your name at the front of the brain of the person doing the casting for the next job. If you are picked for a production, don't expect star treatment. You'll earn about fifty dollars a day and probably spend hours standing around on the set. If you've always wondered what it takes to shoot a movie or television scene or if you simply enjoy once-in-a-lifetime experiences, being an extra for a day can be a blast.

49

King Neptune Restaurant

Caribbean Getaway

How would you like to work at a place that closes down for one week every year and takes the entire staff on a vacation to St. John in the U.S. Virgin Islands of the Caribbean? Start writing your resume and send it to the King Neptune Restaurant in Wrightsville Beach, North Carolina. Be warned, however, there aren't a lot of openings. Most of the key people who work there have been with the restaurant since it was bought by owner Bernard Carroll in 1986, and the average length of service for the general staff is about five years. "We're a very tight group, more friends than employees," Carroll explains. "Owning a restaurant allows me to express my philosophy of life and become very good friends with the staff. There are no managers here, because each person knows what to do. If something needs to get done, it gets done."

The staff's annual January treks south aren't just for bonding, though. The trip has a practical purpose. It allows employees to stay in touch with the latest trends in Caribbean culture and cuisine, which they then bring back to the restaurant. Carroll grew up in St. John, and the King Neptune's food and atmosphere come straight from the islands. "The decor is Caribbean, and most of the art is custom work from Tortola or St. John," Carroll says. "The bar is mainly nautically decorated as though the pirate Blackbeard could walk through any minute. We feature a lot of rums." The restaurant boasts bright Caribbean colors, and the background music consists of reggae and other island tunes that the staff discover on their trips.

Carroll started out serving traditional Carolina seafood dishes, and the menu still has the standard fried seafood platters, crab cakes, and steaks. It's the Caribbean selections that make the place unique, though. There's Rasta Pasta, noodles blanched in soy sauce with grilled shrimp and sun-dried tomatoes, then topped with peanut sauce; grilled mahi-mahi with black beans and rice topped with pineapple salsa; Jamaican

The King Neptune restaurant brings Caribbean flavor to the cool white sands of Wrightsville Beach.

Jerk Tuna (prepared like they do chicken) with grilled bananas and pineapple; and East Indian curried shrimp with coconut-garlic peppers served over rice; and more. There are also plenty of choices for children, and as a nice touch, Pam Carroll has had students at Wrightsville Elementary School do drawings for the kids menu.

As you've probably gathered, the King Neptune cultivates a laid-back island attitude. It extends to taking no reservations for his 125-seat restaurant. "I hate reservations," Carroll reveals. "We take people as they come. It's real casual."

Secret Information

Location:	Wrightsville Beach, North Carolina.
Address:	11 North Lumina Avenue, Wrightsville Beach, NC 28480.
Phone:	910-256-2525.
Fax:	910-256-2522.
Hours:	5 P.M. to 10 P.M. daily for dinner; lounge open until 2 A.M.
Season:	Year-round except the first week of January.
Price:	$9 to $16.
Reservations:	Not accepted.
Credit cards:	American Express, MasterCard, Visa.

TOP SECRET

We've seen a lot of sand researching this book, and for our money, some of the prettiest is at Wrightsville Beach, home to the King Neptune Restaurant. The island, which has been a summer retreat for Wilmingtonians for decades, has a reputation for being squeaky clean and insect free. It boasts both big complexes, like the Blockade Runner's Resort (800-541-1161), as well as classic beach cottages, but both the tacky, t-shirt-shop-every-other-few-feet feel or stuffy, no-poor-people-allowed attitude of some other vacation areas are missing. For day visitors, finding a place to park is a problem but not impossible, and it's worth it to have some sun and fun on the beach; to fish or engage in other watersports; to visit the Wrightsville Beach Museum of History (910-256-2569), which is housed in the fourth oldest surviving cottage on the island; or to check out the Johnny Mercer Pier. (For those of you under age sixty, Johnny Mercer was a famous songwriter and penned "Moon River," "The Days of Wine and Roses," and about a thousand other tunes.) For more information about Wrightsville Beach, call its Chamber of Commerce at 800-232-2469.

Fort Fisher

Playing Fort

50

South of Wilmington, North Carolina, past Carolina Beach and Kure Beach, nearly at the land's end lies Fort Fisher—the spot where one of the major turning points of the Civil War took place way back in 1865. The Confederate outpost had been forged out of sand and earth, which could withstand bombardment from Union forces better than buildings, thanks to the labor of up to one thousand slaves and freemen. Its forty-five guns, mounted on batteries up to sixty feet high, protected the approach to Wilmington from both land and sea. An attack in December 1864 failed, but another assault by an estimated fifty Union warships lobbing explosives at the earthen fortress for two days caused the Confederate soldiers to finally call it quits in January 1865. That Union victory sealed up the last Atlantic avenue for the ships running the Union naval blockade to supply the Rebel army and pretty much shut the door on any Confederate hope of victory.

Today you can head to the Fort Fisher State Historic Site and view what's left of this mighty Confederate fort—the third most visited historic site in the state. There's also a cool underwater archeology exhibit, Hidden Beneath the Waves, and a museum that tells the story of the fort and the men who served there during the Civil War. It features a collection of items belonging to the blockade runners. If you're lucky, you'll arrive in time for one of the uniformed demonstrations or reenactments scheduled that day. Civil War buffs love it, but even if you don't know Robert E. Lee from Bruce Lee, the eclectic collections of attractions and activities at Fort Fisher still make it worth a day trip.

Where else, for example, can you see a World War II bunker that housed a hermit for nearly twenty years? A stone's throw away from the fort is the spot where Robert Harrill lived without electricity, plumbing, or other conveniences from 1955 to 1972. He became something of a tourist attraction himself to the more than seventeen thousand visitors—especially '60s hippies seeking cosmic truth from the recluse—who would stop by and soak up his thoughts on the shortcomings of modern society. Many would leave money in an old frying pan; after his death one thousand dollars in change was found buried near his makeshift home. People still come to see the bunker or to visit his grave at a cemetery in Carolina Beach, where his final resting place is marked with a stone that reads "He Made People Think."

More conventional attractions also in the area include The Cove, a perfect place to picnic on the water, and the Fort Fisher State Recreation Area. The latter is four-wheel-drive heaven, especially for families whose four-wheel-drive vehicle spends most days sitting in the school carpool lane or battling suburban traffic. On a crowded weekend you're bound to get four-wheelin' yahoos doing donuts on the sand, but in the off-season, the four-mile stretch of beach is empty (except for the fishermen) and provides the perfect chance for anyone with a little courage and a lot of faith in his or her vehicle to explore off-road. The white sand is soft and shifting, so you have to hold on tight and follow the ruts left by your fellow four-wheelers. Near the shore the sand is packed, and it's like driving on Daytona Beach without all the bathers and other cars to get in your way. There's just miles of blue sky above, an endless blue ocean to your left, and a beach in front as far as you can see. Stay an hour and play, fish, or just revel in the discovery.

Unfortunately, another of our favorite things to do at Fort Fisher is temporarily out of commission. The North Carolina Aquarium at Fort Fisher, which was always fun and a bargain compared to the excellent but expensive Ripley's Believe It or Not Aquarium further south in Myrtle Beach, is undergoing an expansion. It is being redesigned to focus on the "Waters of the Cape Fear River System" and will feature exhibits on plants and animals indigenous to the area, such as American alligators and loggerhead sea turtles. The highlight of the new facility will be the 180,000-gallon Ocean Habitat, a two-story tank filled with sharks, barracuda, and other sea life. The facility won't be open until the spring of 2001, but the surrounding trails and beach are still accessible. Take a quick hike along the self-guided Marsh Nature Trail, which leads through the surrounding salt marshes and near the front doors of many coastal feathered, finned, and leatherbacked creatures. The trail also passes the hermit Harrill's home.

Finally, it's fun to take the ferry to or from Fort Fisher to the town of Southport (Secret 41). The thirty-minute ride across the churning waters of the Cape Fear River is only $3 per car—there isn't a better boat cruise deal available on the Cape Fear Coast. Once you're safely parked on the ferry and cleared to get out of your vehicle, venture to the top deck where in winter the wind is icy and in summer the sun is the strongest. Okay, so it would probably be more comfortable in the warm (or air-conditioned depending on the season) cabin, but outside is where you can smell the salt air, see the wonders both natural—dolphins and pelicans—and historical—Price's Creek Lighthouse.

Secret Information

Location: South of Wilmington, North Carolina, near the tip of Cape Fear.
Address: P.O. Box 243, Kure Beach, NC 28449.
Phone: 910-458-5798.
Fax: 910-458-3722.
E-mail: fofisra@isaac.net.
Web site: www.ils.unc.edu/parkproject/fofi.html.
Hours: November through February: 8 A.M. to 6 P.M.; March and October: 8 A.M. to 7 P.M.; April, May, and September: 8 A.M. to 8 P.M.; August: 8 A.M. to 9 P.M. Office hours 8 a.m to 5 P.M. Closed Christmas Day.
Price: FREE.
Details: The above information is for the Fort Fisher State Recreation Area, which should be able to provide general information about the area. Call 910-458-8257 for specific information about the North Carolina Aquarium at Fort Fisher, which is scheduled to reopen in spring 2001; or 910-458-5538 for the Fort Fisher Historic Site.

TOP SECRET

If you have a tad more courage than common sense and don't have any pint-sized explorers with you, then a trek out to Zeke's Island at Fort Fisher just might be the highlight of your vacation. Zeke's is at the end of U.S. Highway 421 beyond the Fort Fisher/Southport ferry dock. It includes a four-mile-long barrier spit that extends south from the Federal Point access area. The cool thing is that you can walk out to the island across a breakwater at ebbing tide (the path is covered at high tide). If you stand at the boat ramp beyond the ferry landing at low tide, you'll be able to see the breakwater called "the Rocks." This is your staircase to Zeke's. Before you attempt the journey, put on some old clothes and sneakers and bring water, sunscreen, and bug spray. The rocks are slick, so walk softly and slowly. Once you make it to the island, and let out a heartfelt "Thank God," then swim and explore. There aren't any facilities or lifeguards out here (but you knew that already) so play smart. After you've played *Gilligan's Island* for the day, head back over the rocks again at ebbing tide. For more information on Zeke's Island, contact the North Carolina National Estuarine Research Reserve at 910-256-3721.

South Carolina Secrets

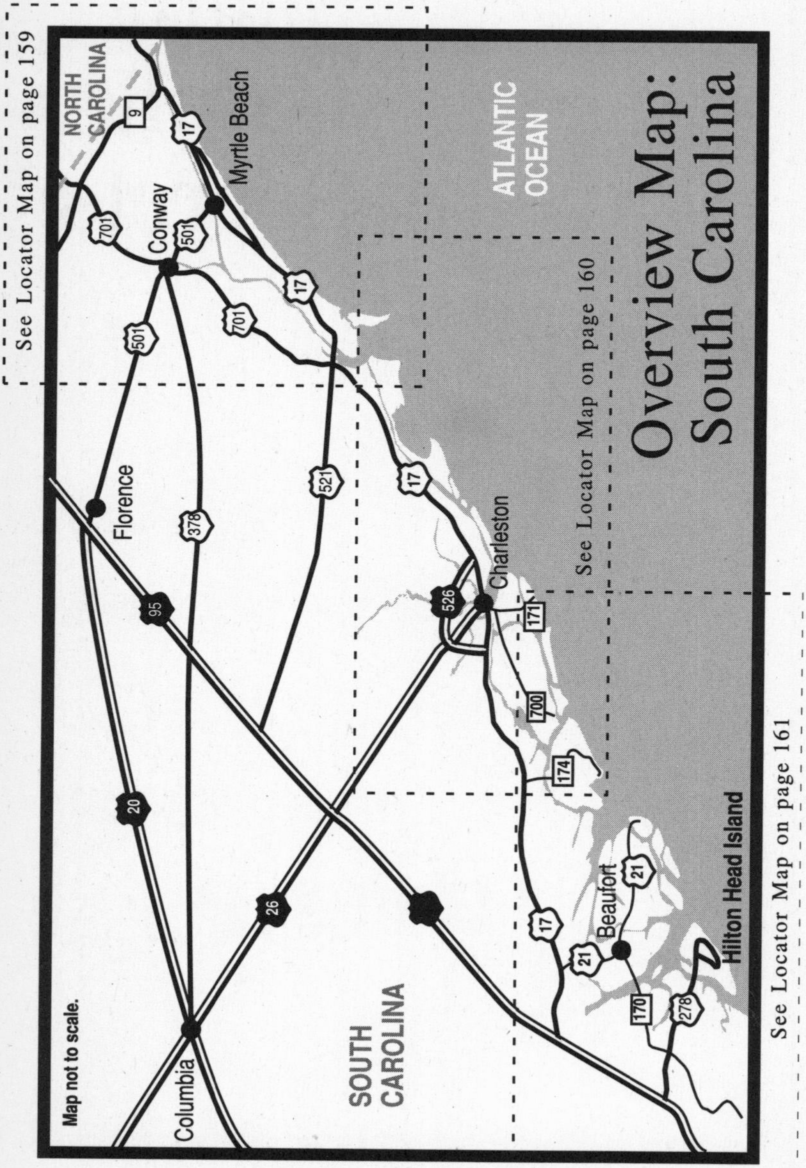
See Locator Map on page 159
NORTH CAROLINA
9
17
Myrtle Beach
ATLANTIC OCEAN
Overview Map: South Carolina
701
Conway
501
17
701
501
See Locator Map on page 160
17
521
Florence
378
Charleston
526
171
95
700
174
20
26
SOUTH CAROLINA
Hilton Head Island
21
17
Beaufort
21
170
278
See Locator Map on page 161
Map not to scale.
Columbia

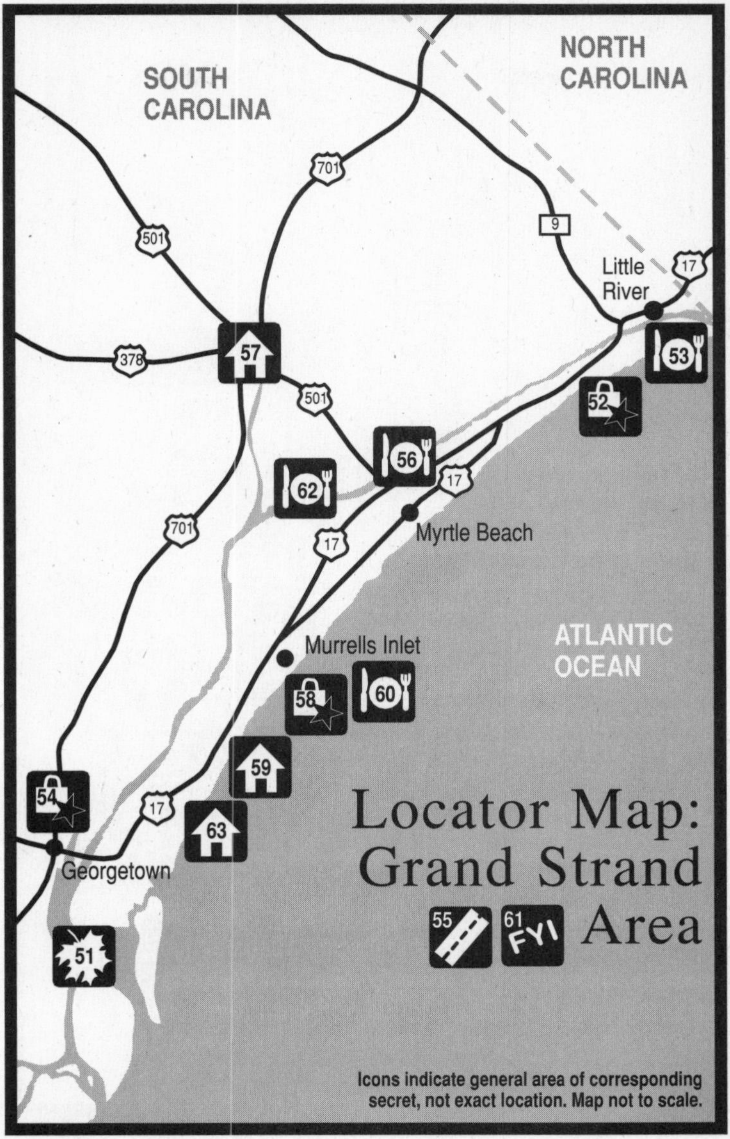
NORTH CAROLINA
SOUTH CAROLINA
701
501
378
57
501
9
Little River
17
53
52
56
62
17
701
17
Myrtle Beach
ATLANTIC OCEAN
Murrells Inlet
58
60
59
54
17
63
Georgetown
51
Locator Map: Grand Strand Area
55
61 FYI
Icons indicate general area of corresponding secret, not exact location. Map not to scale.

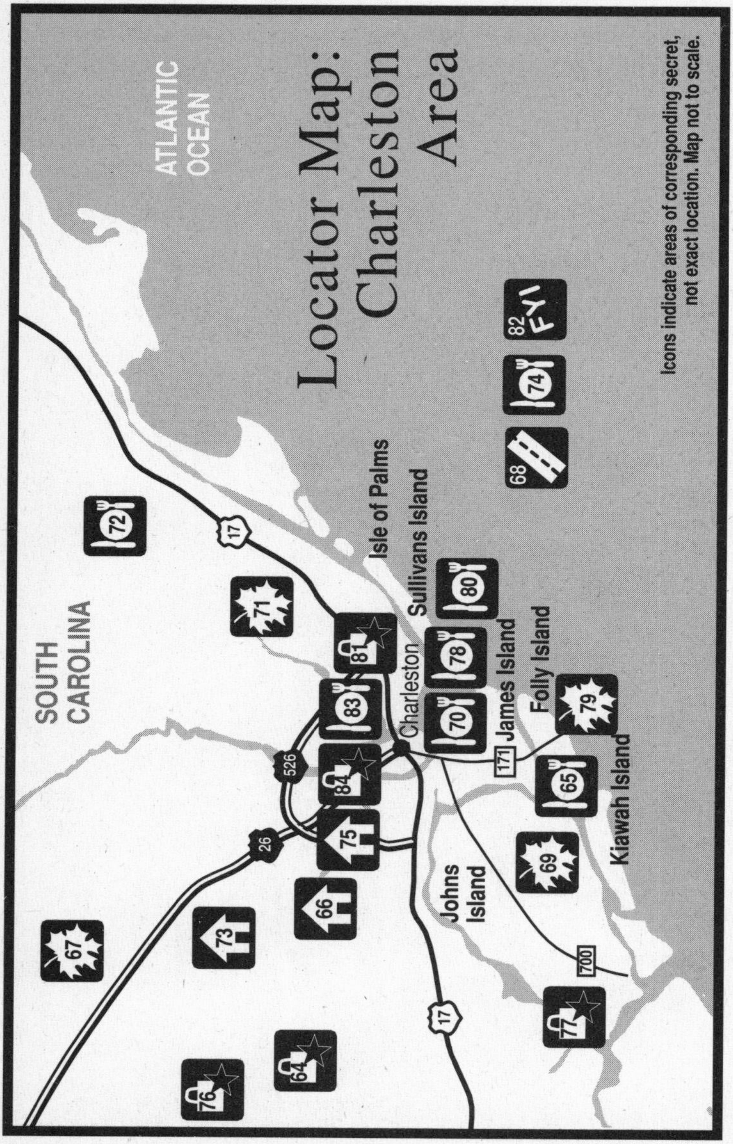
Locator Map:
Charleston
Area
ATLANTIC
OCEAN
SOUTH
CAROLINA
Isle of Palms
Sullivans Island
Charleston
James Island
Folly Island
Kiawah Island
Johns
Island
17
526
26
171
700
17
64
65
66
67
68
69
70
71
72
73
74
75
76
77
78
79
80
81
82
FYI
83
84
Icons indicate areas of corresponding secret,
not exact location. Map not to scale.

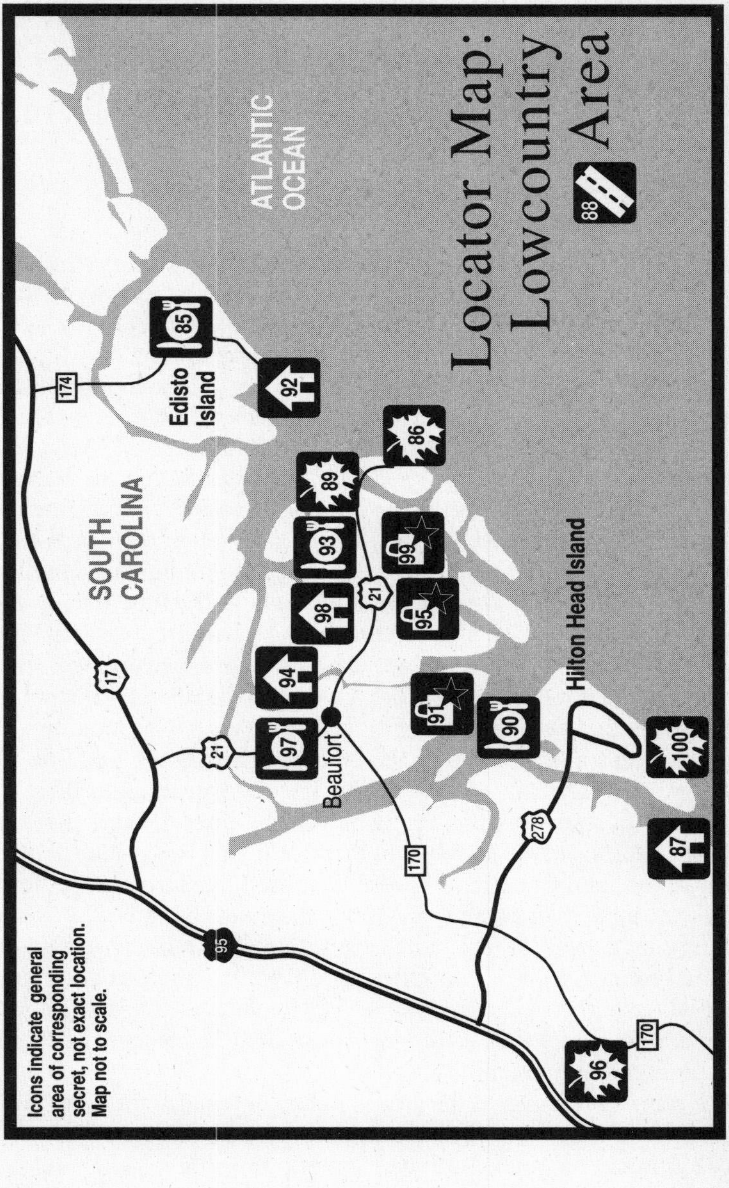
Locator Map: Lowcountry Area
88
ATLANTIC OCEAN
SOUTH CAROLINA
Edisto Island
Beaufort
Hilton Head Island
Icons indicate general area of corresponding secret, not exact location. Map not to scale.
95
17
21
174
170
278
85
86
87
89
90
91
92
93
94
95
96
97
98
99
100

51

Tom Yawkey Wildlife Center

Off Limits

One of the toughest pieces of wilderness to get to in the world is the Tom Yawkey Wildlife Center, which lies about midway between Charleston and Myrtle Beach near Georgetown, South Carolina. It's not blocked by towering mountains or cut off by raging rivers—it's just off limits, except to a handful of humans who are lucky enough to get a glimpse of this refuge for waterfowl and other wild animals.

"This is one of the most pristine areas left on the East Coast," says Robert Joyner, who's been the resident biologist at the site for more than twenty years. "We don't encourage a lot of visitation." To say the least. The center offers guided tours only on Tuesday afternoons year-round. Excursions are limited to fourteen people, the maximum that can fit into the large van in which visitors travel through parts of the twenty-thousand-acre preserve. "This is designed as a wildlife research area," explains Joyner. "We're very guarded about its use, because we've seen what's happened to other areas that have been trampled by the public."

The preserve was left to the state of South Carolina by Tom Yawkey, who's most famous as the owner of the Boston Red Sox from 1933 until his death in 1976. (To our knowledge, though, there's no ban on Yankee fans visiting the refuge.) The three islands that make up the wildlife center at the mouth of Winyah Bay—North Island, South Island, and Cat Island—were first used by European settlers as rice plantations, then in the early 1900s they were acquired by wealthy Northern industrialists like the Yawkey family as summer estates and hunting grounds. Yawkey inherited land from his uncle at age sixteen, added other parcels over the years, and for the rest of his life developed land management techniques designed to preserve the area's plant and animal population.

The primary purpose of the area is to be a safe place for waterfowl to flourish. It is right smack in the middle of the Atlantic Flyway—the route migrating birds take to travel south in the cold weather and north in the warm. During the winter, more than one hundred thousand ducks and geese spend time in the protected ponds and marshes of the preserve. "We have more than 250 species of birds—every species in South Carolina, including eight active bald eagle nests," reports Joyner. The area is also home to alligators, wild turkeys, red-cockaded woodpeckers, loggerhead sea turtles, fox squirrels, otters, hawks, and hundreds of other species. The landscape ranges from maritime forest totally untouched by human intervention to areas—many former rice fields—carefully converted to provide prime nesting and food habitats for a duck population that includes mallards, shovellers, pintails, gadwalls, widgeons, teals, canvasbacks, and coots.

On the Tuesday tours, which start with a short ferry trip, Joyner tells visitors about the habitats and history of the area—it was the site, for example, of Civil War forts. The tour tends to draw those interested in ecology and preservation rather than the casual tourist who may prefer to spend Tuesday afternoon sunning on the beach. Winter is the most popular time to visit. It's when the population of waterfowl is greatest, and guests may see great flocks of ducks or geese soaring through the sky. Reservations—made well in advance—are a must, although the center sometimes gets late cancellations, so call to see if there's any space available. In keeping with the center's educational mission, all of the tours are free.

The beauty of the Tom Yawkey Wildlife Center isn't just its serene scenery, but its purpose as a place to study and protect all creatures wild and wonderful. "The reward I get from working here is that the area we're managing is large enough to be challenging yet small enough to see the results of your work," says Joyner, who, like other employees of the center, lives on its islands. "We're maintaining the area the way Mr. Yawkey intended it to be. I feel like I've been blessed to be here."

Secret Information

Location: Near Georgetown, South Carolina.
Address: One Yawkey Way South, Georgetown, South Carolina 29440.
Phone: 843-546-6814.
Fax: 843-527-1221.
E-mail: yawkey_wildlife@compuserve.com.
Hours: Tours Tuesday afternoon only.
Price: FREE.
Reservations: Required.

TOP SECRET

A slice of nature that's smaller and more domesticated than the Yawkey Wildlife Center is the Roycroft Daylily Nursery. Gardeners will love to stroll the official American Hemerocallis Society National Display Garden and check out the stock of about five hundred unusual and award-winning hybrids. The flowers mix every color of the spectrum and sport such names as Anastasia, Blood Stained, Ruffled Perfection, and Midnight Magic. You can purchase plants to take with you or have them shipped home. Some special blooms run up to $80, but much more affordable ones also are for sale. The nursery is open March through October and is located on White Hall Avenue off U.S. Highway 17 South a few miles south of Georgetown. For more information, call the Daylily Farm at 843-527-1533 or order on-line at www.roycroftdaylilies.com.

Shag 'til You Drag

52

Before Austin Powers and the British turned "shag" into a four-letter word, it was just an innocent dance that had its roots in the coastal dunes of the Carolinas. The perfect way to boogie to classic beach music such as "Be Young, Be Foolish, Be Happy" by The Tams, "Under The Boardwalk" by The Drifters, "My Girl" by The Temptations, and "My Guy" by Mary Wells is to shag—the dance looks simple, but takes years to master. (Actually, you could say the same thing about the International Man of Mystery's version of shagging.)

Some think the shag looks like a slow jitterbug or boogie-woogie, with a man and woman standing facing each other and moving their feet to a six or eight count without much upper-body motion. Shagging steps have exotic labels such as the belly roll, boogie walk, kickback with lean, prissy, and sugarfoot. By its very nature, though, the shag shouldn't be thought of as formal or intimidating—the underlying spirit of shagging is the fun, freedom, and recklessness of a vacation at the beach.

No one knows who first created the dance, but it was born sometime in the '30s or '40s on the South Carolina shoreline, blossomed there during the '50s and '60s, and was spread around the country by those who tried it on holiday and took it home. The center of the shagging universe, though, is still where legend says it got its start: the Ocean Drive Beach area of North Myrtle Beach, South Carolina. It's the place to go to truly get into the groove of beach nightlife.

There are several clubs in the Main Street area at which to strut your stuff and learn to shag. At Fat Harold's Beach Club (843-249-5779), for example, soft red lights shine down on a parquet dance floor as the DJ spins not only the classics but also current pop hits. To prepare for a night out there, call ahead for their schedule of free shag lessons. Ducks (843-249-3858) also offers instruction on Wednesday nights. The huge Ocean Drive Resort (843-249-1436) nearby includes two popular dance spots: the casual OD Beach Club and the flashier

Spanish Galleon (843-249-1047) as well as the Shagger's Hall of Fame, which honors the lords and ladies of the dance.

The Ocean Drive area is a dance-a-thon during the entire vacation season, but it really heats up when members of S.O.S.—Society of Stranders—invade. (Please note that except for "Location," all the Secret Information below is for S.O.S.) The big bashes, the Spring Safari in April and Fall Migration in September, last ten days, but the group also gets together for a shorter time for their Mid-Winter Beach Classic. The ten to fifteen thousand attendees see old friends, swap stories, and swing to the music as clubs like Fat Harold's and the Spanish Galleon link together to host one big party. Members (you can join for $35 annually) get free admission to the clubs, discounts on food, and a subscription to the group's publication, *Carefree Times*. There are also workshops, exhibits, contests, and, in the spring, a parade. Mostly, though, you get to hang out with folks who *really* know how to get footloose and have fun.

Think you can't dance? Don't be a drag. Head to Ocean Drive Beach, grab a partner, and just let go and shag.

Secret Information

Location: North Myrtle Beach, South Carolina.
Address: Society of Stranders, P.O. Box 4688, Columbia, SC 29204. (All of the following information is for S.O.S.)
Phone: 888-SOS-3113 (767-3113).
E-mail: mikesmail@mindspring.com.
Web site: www.shagdance.com.
Season: S.O.S. events are held in the Ocean Drive Beach area in January, April, and September.
Price: Events: $20 to $40. (Contact clubs for specific cover charges and prices.)

TOP SECRET

Here's a warning for all you folks who go straight to the Internet to learn about new subjects, such as shag dancing. Since *shag* also has a sexual meaning ("Curse you, Mr. Powers," as Dr. Evil might say), when you enter the word, or any of its variations, in Web search engine sites like Yahoo, Excite, or Lycos, you'll likely get back some sites heavy on dirty and light on dancing. Fortunately, though, there are some great, squeaky clean shag dancing sites. One of the best is Betty B's Bungalow—A Shagging World that is operated by an avid shagger living in Charlotte, North Carolina. (Betty doesn't make her last name plain on the site, so we won't either.) It's not only a safe place on the Web to start learning about the shag, but it also attractively presents information and links that should tell you all you want to know about the Carolina's coolest dance, including a schedule of S.O.S. events at Ocean Drive Beach through 2003. To check out her site, point your browser to *users.vnet.net/bbhunt.*

53

Little River

Fishing Villagers

In 1791, President George Washington dined in Little River, South Carolina, on his southern tour. He was one of the first in a long line of travelers who've visited the tiny village to savor fresh seafood caught by a fleet of local fishermen. Over the years, plenty of other Northerners have found their way south. In fact, for a while the place was known as Yankee Town because of all the New Englanders who'd moved there during the early days of the United States. The folks in Little River swear that if you listen carefully, you can still detect a hint of a British, Massachusetts, or perhaps Connecticut accent in the chatter of the fishermen down at the docks. Others believe the village's unique personality is linked more closely to the combination of pirates, Indians, Spanish explorers, and shipwrecked sailors who founded the place back in the 1500s.

As you travel down the turnoff toward the Little River waterfront from U.S. Highway 17 just south of the North Carolina border, you'll pass tidy homes, fruit stands, ancient cypress trees covered in Spanish moss, tall pines, and signs for fishing boat charters, marine supply, bait, and ice. There are also ads for jet skis and restaurants, but don't get the idea that Little River is a tourist town. Sure, local fishermen like Tommy Long, who captains *The Capt. Vick*, make a living in the summer hauling vacationers out to the inner shore or Gulf Stream to cast for shark, amberjack, king mackerel, and other sea creatures, but fishing—not tourism—comes first in Little River. When the summer people leave, the old salts—a hard lot with a reputation for being suspicious of strangers—still hit the water to pay the mortgage and feed the family. Most any day of the year you can walk down to the docks at Carolina's Best Fish Store and watch the catch of the day being unloaded, weighed, and cleaned. Then you can stop inside the shop and buy some fresh grouper, snapper, shrimp, or blue crab to bring back to your condo and cook up for dinner.

If you'd rather leave the cooking to someone else, there are plenty of places to eat clustered along the horseshoe-shaped, cypress-shaded road that makes up the Little River waterfront. During Crabby Hour on the back deck of Crab Catchers On the Waterfront (843-280-2025), for example, you can watch the boats cruising up and down the Intracoastal Waterway and sip a few brews, while the servers teach you the proper way to eat a blue crab. (Basically you start by peeling off the back, but once it's uncovered you need to know what *not* to eat.) Or if you've been out on a charter, bring your catch over to them, and they'll fry it up for you for a fee and add some hush puppies and fries on the side. Nearby Capt Juel's Hurricane Restaurant (843-249-2211) and the Fisherman's Hide-A-Way (843-249-1785) are also known for their fresh-from-the-docks fare.

The best time to sample both the local recipes and the local atmosphere in Little River is in May during the village's Blue Crab Festival. Since 1982, each weekend after Mother's Day, Little River has thrown itself a party and welcomed anyone who loves live music, fresh blue crabs, and crafts to come on down for a visit. In recent years, thousands of people have accepted the invite. No wonder—every restaurant in town sets up food booths with fresh seafood (blue crab's the specialty, of course); vendors serve a variety of southern taste treats from smoked turkey legs to boiled peanuts, and the music—country, gospel, rock, and more—is non-stop. Then there are the crowd's favorites: crab races and craft booths. Crabs are everywhere. There are bonsai tree topiaries shaped like crabs, orange rubber crabs hung over the bars, and crab emblems on most every T-shirt and baseball cap for sale. Although the Blue Crab Festival is a weekend to party, there are always plenty of fishing charter boats available because, well, it just wouldn't be Little River if there wasn't some fishing going on.

Secret Information

Location: Just below the South Carolina-North Carolina border.
Address: Little River Chamber of Commerce, P.O. Box 400, Little River, SC 29566. (The following phone numbers and Internet addresses are also for the chamber.)
Phone: 843-249-6604.
Fax: 843-249-9788.
E-mail: lrcoc@get.net.
Web site: www.lrcoc.com.
Price: Varies widely.
Reservations: Call restaurants.
Credit cards: Call restaurants.

TOP SECRET

Every small town has a local bar and in Little River it's Admiral's Flagship Restaurant (843-651-3016). It's the place where local fishermen and their families gather to talk about the day's catch, who's doing what around town, and probably about all the obnoxious outsiders ruining the place. You can't miss Admiral's, even though there's no sign posted outside (there's a worn wooden sign inside). It's a two-story wooden building with peeling white paint across from the waterfront that was built in 1936 and re-opened most recently in 1997. Inside it's dark, smoky, and the walls are painted pink (probably to contrast with the aqua blue doors). There's a huge marlin over the bar and a hand-painted sign advertises beef jerky for seventy-five cents. Little boys drink Cokes on ice, and their fishermen fathers sit on the red leather high-backed stools at the bar, which takes up half the space in the place. There are *Soldier of Fortune* and various hunting and fishing magazines to read and a pool table in the back room. If you visit Little River, you owe it to yourself to stop by Admiral's for at least one drink and, if you're feeling particularly adventurous, maybe a piece of beef jerky.

Getting to Know Georgetown

54

About the only things that have changed in Georgetown, South Carolina, since 1732 are the advent of automobiles, indoor plumbing, and electricity. Located midway between Charleston and Pawleys Island, the colonial city stands proudly just as it did in the 1700s when George Washington roamed its broad, tree-lined streets and the Marquis de Lafayette clinked a few frosty mugs at the corner dockside tavern, whose foundation still remains. It was a prime port of entry for indigo, rice, and slaves, but now its economy is driven by commercial fishing and manufacturing, including the giant International Paper plant, the smell of which hits you as you enter the town from the south but quickly fades away.

Today the best way to see this bit of living history is on a walking tour guided by Miss Nell, a.k.a. Nell Morris Cribb, a spry, soft-spoken woman with a genteel, honey-dipped southern drawl. The Georgetown native and retired high school secretary started a small business showing visitors through the shady streets of her hometown in 1988.

On her thirty-minute to hour-and-a-half tours, Miss Nell, sometimes wearing period costumes, explains that everything in Georgetown is laid out just as it was in 1729, and the entire downtown district is on the National Register of Historic Places. Unlike Virginia's colonial Williamsburg, where you see just the foundations of old homes, in Georgetown, more than fifty homes still stand. In addition, they have been carefully restored to protect their historic status. During the town's recent $4.5 million revitalization, construction crews unearthed a Revolutionary War cannon, which experts determined to be part of George Washington's war chest.

Notable landmarks Miss Nell points out are the Town Clock; the Rice Museum (it focuses on the town's past economies, which were driven by the rice and indigo culture); the restored Harbor House Bed-and-Breakfast; and the dockside seafood market, where you can pur-

To follow Miss Nell's footsteps along the quaint sidewalks of historic Georgetown is to journey back in time.

chase almost anything fresh. Along the way, you'll see the Prince George Winyah Episcopal Church and find out from Miss Nell how the square-shaped pews allowed worshippers to stay warm by lighting a fire in the center. Another highlight is the Masonic Lodge No. 40 (circa 1740) where George Washington made a speech following his inauguration. At times during the walk you might even see young girls in hoop-skirted dresses selling lemonade on the corner to parched passersby under the shady live oaks and leafy palmettos.

Secret Information

Location: Georgetown, South Carolina.
Address: Meet Miss Nell by appointment at Harborwalk Books, 732 Front Street, Georgetown.
Phone: 843-546-3975.
Hours: 10:30 A.M. and 2:30 P.M. Tuesday to Thursday; by appointment Saturday and Sunday.
Price: $5 for the thirty-minute tour and $9 for the hour-and-a-half tour.
Reservations: Recommended.
Credit cards: None.

TOP SECRET

Just outside of Miss Nell's hometown of Georgetown lies the Hobcaw Barony, a 17,500-acre wildlife preserve that was once the estate of early twentieth century financier and presidential advisor Bernard Baruch. The site includes two mansions—Hobcaw House and Bellefield; the latter was the home of his daughter who helped put together land from eleven plantations to create a protected wilderness for scientists from South Carolina colleges and universities to study. The Hobcaw Barony Visitors Center at the Hobcaw Barony entrance on U.S. Highway 17 is open from 10 A.M. to 5 P.M. Monday through Friday and from 10 A.M. to 2 P.M. Saturday June through August. Three tours are offered. The Baruch Family Tour of the Baruch estate and Hobcaw and Bellefield houses is three hours and costs $15 per person. The Hobcaw Rice Plantation History Tour that visits rice fields and the only remaining slave street left on the Waccamaw Neck is two hours and costs $10 for adults and $5 for children under 12. The Hobcaw Barony Nature History and University Research Tour that features research being done by Clemson University (forests) and the University of South Carolina (marine biology) lasts two hours and costs $10 per adult and $5 for children under 12. Reservations are required for all tours. For more information, tour times and days, or to make tour reservations call 843-546-4623, fax 843-545-7231, e-mail hobcawbarony@juno.com, or visit www.hobcawbarony.com.

55 Myrtle Beach and Beyond

Myrtle Beach, South Carolina, is the third most visited tourist area in the country behind Disney World and Atlantic City, all three of which are grand spectacles. During the height of the summer, Myrtle Beach—the hub of the Grand Strand—operates on a grand scale with mile after mile of hotels and motels overrun with people; restaurant after restaurant serving untold tons of fried seafood; more holes of putt-putt golf than you could possibly play in a lifetime; and much, much more. To some, the glitz and glamor of Myrtle Beach is tacky. However, to those who crave to be in the center of things and rub elbows, and often bumpers, with his or her fellow humans, the action of Myrtle Beach is a vacation mecca. It offers endless entertainments along with miles of sand and sun. Broadway at the Beach, the area's grandest attraction, for example, is an entertainment/shopping megaplex centered on a huge manmade lake. It features amusements such as the Ripley's Believe It or Not Aquarium, the John Q. Hammonds IMAX Theater, Dragon's Lair Fantasy Golf (which boasts a giant animatron dragon periodically popping up and breathing fire), and restaurants like the NASCAR Cafe and Planet Hollywood.

For the other kind of vacationer, those of you who are looking to get away from the madding crowd rather than be immersed in it, the frenzied Myrtle Beach proper is only one part of the Grand Strand, a stretch of coastline that runs about sixty miles from the North Carolina border south to about Georgetown. Along the way, you can find almost any kind of vacation experience possible, from lavish gated golf resorts to weathered and worn beachhouse communities. Our favorite place to stay and still be close to the action of Myrtle Beach—which the kids in particular cry for—is North Myrtle Beach, a calmer cousin of its sister city and birthplace of the Carolina shag (Secret 52). If you want to stay in a big resort, try the Ocean Creek Plantation (843-272-7724), a huge everything-in-one family complex. There are also good family spots south of Myrtle Beach that people, once they discover them, tend to return to year after year. Surfside Beach and Garden Beach are lesser known family beaches and good places to stay if you want to be within a few miles of all the attractions further north. Further south is Murells Inlet, which features a string of restaurants that are favorites of Grand Strand veterans. Litchfield Beach is a newer and more upscale development along the lines of the plantations on Hilton Head, while Pawleys Island is the classic weathered retreat for those who are wealthy but don't want to show it (Secret 63).

If you want to get an idea of the real contrast between Myrtle Beach and its neighbors, take a drive down to Georgetown (Secret 54). The quiet main street is straight out of *Our Town* and is lined with small shops, restaurants, and bookstores. Filled with historic homes on shady streets, it has an authentic South Carolina coastal town feel that Myrtle Beach proper can never match.

Secret Information

For more information about the Grand Strand, contact the Myrtle Beach Area Chamber of Commerce, P.O. Box 2115-M Myrtle Beach, SC 29578; 843-626-7444; www.myrtlebeachlive.com.

TOP SECRET

If you need a place to stay in the Grand Strand or anywhere else in South Carolina, stop into any of the visitor's centers operated by the state. They're usually located just inside the South Carolina border off major thoroughfares such as U.S. Highway 17, which links Myrtle Beach to its cousin coastal communities in North Carolina. Unlike many visitor's centers, these places aren't just spots to use the restroom and pick up brochures. They also serve as free reservations centers. The people manning the welcome desk will be happy to book a room for you at a local hotel, motel, bed-and-breakfast, or campground—and they know where to find local vacancies even when the beach crowds are at their height.

56

The Parson's Table

Divine Dining

Your mom would be mortified if you told her you wanted to eat in church, but we'll tell you to do just that. Technically, of course, the building that the Parson's Table occupies hasn't been a "house of God" since the 1950s, when the congregation of the Little River Methodist Church built a new sanctuary to replace the building that had been its home for the previous sixty-seven years. The restaurant in Little River, though, is still a good destination for a pilgrimage if you love wonderful food.

Inside, the Parson's Table is an amalgam of antique architecture and decor. The building, built in 1865, was a community center for a time. Then, in 1978 it was purchased and moved about two blocks to its current spot. The doors are more than a century-and-a-half old and are made from solid cypress. The flooring in the entryway is from an 1850s farm house. The stained glass windows in the main room and the chandeliers throughout were salvaged from the Baptist Church of Mullins, South Carolina. Despite additions and enhancements throughout the years, the logs sawed for the original building are still intact. Such an old structure is hard to heat and is the main reason the Parson's Table closes from Thanksgiving through mid-January.

History lovers will find the atmosphere, as well as the food, heavenly. The Parson's Table has garnered a long list of awards for its cuisine, including a ranking as one of the top fifty restaurants in the country. The menu emphasizes beef, fowl, lamb, and seafood and includes such chef's specialties as Roast Stuffed Quail, Char-Grilled Lamb Chops, Wiener Schnitzel, and Veal and Shrimp Bombay. For appetizers, try the Oysters Rockefeller, Mushrooms Copenhagen, or, if you're brave enough to try snails, the Baked Escargot with Portobello Mushroom Cap and Mozzarella. Though more the kind of place adults would go to for an upscale meal, there is a children's menu offering chicken, flounder, or beef.

Secret Information

Location:	Little River, South Carolina.
Address:	U.S. Highway 17 N., Little River, SC 29566.
Phone:	843-249-3702.
Fax:	843-280-0199.
Hours:	4:30 P.M. to 9 P.M., Monday through Saturday.
Season:	Mid-January through Thanksgiving.
Price:	$11 to $24.
Reservations:	Required.
Credit cards:	American Express, MasterCard, Visa.

TOP SECRET

The Parson's Table Restaurant is owned by Nancy Murray and her son Eddie Murray, Jr. Eddie is the executive chef and was named one of the best chefs in America by the Gourmet Diners Society of North America, which first bestowed its Golden Fork Award on him in 1994, an honor also won by such culinary celebrities as Wolfgang Puck. In '97 and '98, Murray received the Award of Excellence as an Executive Chef from the International Resturant and Hospitality Bureau and another Golden Fork Award in 1999. Eddie Murray, Sr., is a food engineer graduate of Michigan State. He worked in the restaurant industry for forty years before retiring. A talented tenor, though, he still comes around the Parson's Table occasionally and performs Irish songs for private parties.

57

Cypress Inn

Peace and Pampering

In the mid-1990s, Jim and Carol Ruddick were looking for an established bed-and-breakfast to buy. At the same time, the city of Conway, South Carolina, happened to be searching for someone to build a bed-and-breakfast in its historic Riverfront District. Along the way, the two searches crossed paths, and the Ruddicks (who had canvassed most of the Eastern seaboard trying to find the "perfect" property and town) ended up building a new, historic-looking inn overlooking the picturesque Conway marina. The city was happy. The Ruddicks were happy. And now road weary travelers (including many business people as well as those looking for a romantic escape) are happy that there's a place of "peace and pampering," as the Ruddicks call their inn, just fifteen minutes from Myrtle Beach.

After a two-year design phase and eight months of construction, the Ruddicks' dream inn opened in 1997 and has already earned a four-diamond rating from AAA. The couple, originally from Atlanta, left careers in retirement planning and personnel to embark on what they call "their greatest adventure yet." Although their distinctive three-story inn, with its long porch and its gleaming wood floors, is a jewel, it's the on-site owners who make the Cypress truly unique. "We offer the privacy and amenities of a small hotel and the personal service of a bed-and-breakfast," says Carol. "Our excellence is in the details because the importance of our guests' total comfort is no small thing."

Those details include being attentive to the needs of every guest. If you want privacy, the Ruddicks will surface only to keep you well stocked with fresh linens, iced tea, cookies, and a bountiful breakfast. If you're in the area on business, the couple can provide wake-up calls, fresh coffee, corporate billing, and a room with a desk. There's also a small meeting facility available, and the phones are equipped

Guests at the riverside Cypress Inn can doze in a rocking chair and watch the boats or walk down to the marina and play captain for the day. (COURTESY OF THE CYPRESS INN)

with data ports. If a romantic getaway is what you're after, for an additional fee the Ruddicks can arrange for everything from champagne, strawberries, and chocolate truffles to a hot-air balloon ride. And if you want to retreat to the Cypress Inn in the evenings, but spend your days exploring the Grand Strand, the Ruddicks can help you plan a fun-filled itinerary including boating, golf, tennis, shopping, and sightseeing (plus arrange for a massage or facial to help you relax when you get back from your adventures).

Each of the twelve guest rooms has a television, phone, Jacuzzi or garden tub, ceiling fan, and a unique theme and special touches. For example, the English country-styled Miss Marple Room, named for Agatha Christie's famous detective, features sixty Christie novels on its shelves. The second-floor Carolina Room was designed specifically with couples in mind. It is one of three rooms in the inn decorated in a distinctly southern style. The guest quarters, named for the Ruddicks favorite state, includes mahogany furnishings, a luxurious four-poster king bed, a romantic fireplace, and a two-person Jacuzzi.

Whichever room you choose, the lodging at The Cypress Inn will be head and shoulders above the cookie-cutter accommodations typically available in the Myrtle Beach area. First, there's the friendly, attentive service provided by the Ruddicks, then there's the other half of this perfect bed-and-breakfast match—the city of Conway. The historic Horry County seat, named for Charleston entrepreneur Robert Conway, prides itself on being close to the action of the Grand Strand, but a world away. You can safely bike or stroll the tree-lined streets here. You can rock on the inn's front verandah and drift peacefully off to sleep. And in the afternoon, you can walk just outside the inn's front door and board the *Kingston Lady* riverboat for a lazy ride down the Waccamaw River or rent your own boat from the marina and play captain for the day.

Secret Information

Location: Conway, South Carolina.
Address: 16 Elm Street, Conway, SC 29526.
Phone: 800-575-5307 or 843-248-8199.
E-mail: acypress@sccoast.net.
Web site: www.acypressinn.com.
Rates: $95 to $155 per night.
Reservations: Required.
Credit cards: American Express, Discover, MasterCard, Visa.
Details: The romantic package of champagne, strawberries, and chocolate truffles is $30, and the hot air balloon ride is $150 per person and includes refreshments.

TOP SECRET

Since many historic inns along the coast have resident ghosts, the owners of the Cypress Inn, Jim and Carol Ruddick, decided to hire a friendly spirit for their bed-and-breakfast. "Quinlan was the only applicant to answer the ad," says Carol, "so he got the job." Unfortunately, Quinlan had apparently been deceased so long, he couldn't remember who he was or what he looked like. To give their ghost an identity, the Ruddicks launched a contest in October 1998 to create a past and image for poor Quinlan. Stop by his room—Quinlan's Quarters—to see his picture and read an account of his last days, which according to the contest winning entry were spent off the Carolina coast.

Atalaya

Sand Castle

58

While my family was exploring Huntington Beach State Park, near Murrells Inlet, South Carolina, we came across an intriguing sight. What we had discovered, was Atalaya, an impressive, foreboding, Moorish-styled structure unlike anything else we've encountered in the coastal Carolinas. With ancient-looking brickwork and ornate, rusted, wrought-iron grillwork covering all the windows, it's an eerie sight, to say the least.

It looks as though it's been there for centuries but actually was built as a summer home and artist's studio during the Great Depression by Collis P. Huntington, son of a transportation baron, and his wife, Anna Hyatt Huntington, a sculptress. Laid out in a perfect square with two-hundred-foot long sides surrounding an inner courtyard, it has thirty rooms and twenty-five fireplaces. In the courtyard's middle stands a forty-foot-tall functional artesian well. This well, which was designed by Mr. Huntington before running water was even an option in the area, drew the water upward, and gravity sent water throughout the house. This well inspired the name of the house, Atalaya, which is Spanish for "a tower overlooking the sea."

Deserted after Collis Huntington's death in the '50s, the home is exposed to the elements and feels like an abandoned medieval mansion. It's open for visitors to wander the maze of long, thin corridors and skinny rooms, except for the large studios in which Mrs. Huntington worked. She used the areas to accommodate the large animals—such as horses, bears, and dogs—who served as models for her sculptures. Outside the studio were stables, kennels, and a bear pen to house them all. These statues became part of the impressive sculpture gardens at nearby Brookgreen Gardens (see Top Secret).

Huntington Beach State Park offers several special programs, including daily tours of Atalaya and the evening Ghosts of the Coast visit to the site, during which rangers recount stories of spooks that supposedly haunt the South Carolina shoreline. The structure is also the site of an arts and crafts

The eerie Atalaya mansion is the setting for Huntington Beach State Park's Ghosts of the Coast program.

show each September. Nature programs centering on alligators, snakes, sea turtles, and other local creatures are also well worth signing up for, and the park has a great beach, camping sites, and a boardwalk into the marsh.

Secret Information

Location: In Huntington Beach State Park near Murells Inlet, South Carolina.
Address: 6148 Ocean Highway, Murrells Inlet, SC 29576.
Phone: 843-237-4440.
Fax: 843-237-3387.
E-mail: scparks@prt.state.sc.us.
Web site: www.travelsc.com.
Hours: 6 A.M. to 10 P.M. April to October; 6 A.M. to 6 P.M. November to March.
Price: FREE; Admission to park is $4 per adult and $2 per child (6 to 12).
Details: Access to Atalaya and programs are free with admission to the park.

TOP SECRET

Collis and Anna Huntington, who built Atalaya, also bought the land that became beautiful Brookgreen Gardens, just across U.S. Highway 17 from Huntington Beach State Park, in the early '30s. The ninety-one hundred acres of lush foliage and flowers is filled with mesmerizing fountains and Mrs. Huntington's striking animal sculptures. Brookgreen also boasts works by more than two hundred other artists; a twenty-three-acre wildlife park, where you can nearly reach out and pet an alligator; horseback ride; enjoy carriage tours; and even take sleepy pontoon cruise. It's open daily from 9:30 A.M. to 5 P.M., with extended hours Tuesday through Saturday in the summer. A seven-day admission pass is $8.50 for adults and $4 for children. For more information about Brookgreen Gardens, call 800-849-1931 or 843-237-4218, extension 250.

Litchfield Plantation

Tara By the Sea

59

Frankly, my dear, if you don't give a damn about price, then Litchfield Plantation in Pawleys Island, South Carolina, is the place to spend a most authentic, genteel southern vacation.

The bed-and-breakfast inn is an actual federal-style, white-columned plantation manor house that looks like Tara from *Gone with the Wind*. It was built around 1750 by rice planter Peter Simons. His property—nineteen hundred acres of original King's grant land—stretched from the Waccamaw River to what was then called Magnolia Beach on the shore. Today, the exquisitely restored manor house is owned by Louise Parsons and is surrounded by six hundred acres of lush Lowcountry land (there's also an 8,250-square-foot guest house with six guest rooms, and several spacious villas on the property). Litchfield is expensive but not outrageous by upscale inn standards. Meals are extra, but the tab is easier to swallow after experiencing Litchfield's unsurpassed elegance, charm, and history.

Litchfield is the only original plantation mansion on the Waccamaw River that faces a live oak avenue, and the only way to see it is to stay there. Unlike other plantations in the area that have been turned into museums, it is not open to the general public. Front Desk Manager Terry Belanger, whose front desk is actually three miles away to preserve the historical integrity of the place, says that guests of the plantation are as likely to be from Germany, Belgium, Switzerland, or France as they are to be from New York or North Carolina. The international clientele and exclusive wrought-iron gate sets Litchfield a world apart from the rest of weather-beaten, wealthy Pawleys Island (Secret 63) area.

There are only four rooms (two over-sized rooms and two magnificent suites) in the Plantation Manor House. All of the architectural features are the originals—fireplaces, floors, windows, and so on. Even the long-grain rice fields out back are real, and rice still.grows but isn't harvested. Each distinctive room and all of the common areas—living room, dining room, and kitchen (where guests can sneak down in the middle of the night to heat up snacks in the microwave) are appointed with period antiques. According to Belanger, one appraiser commented that "the antiques are worth more than the house itself." (No wonder they don't let just anyone walk in here.) The best view in the house belongs to the biggest room, the expansive Ball Room Suite, which could accommodate quite a few dancers if the four-poster king-size bed and living room furniture were cleared away. In addition to the double Jacuzzi and fireplace, the suite affords guests a vista of the plantation grounds, including the Avenue of Live Oaks and the Intracoastal Waterway. The property also includes a private beach club, heated pool, tennis courts, marina, and an exclusive gourmet restaurant, The Carriage House Club.

As with any historic home, the walls of the Litchfield Plantation House could tell quite a tale if given a tongue. There's a slave cemetery on the property (it's inaccessible due to woods and overgrowth) and according to Belanger and more than a few guests, there's a resident spook who makes house calls. As Belanger tells it, the ghost is none other than Dr. Tucker, the son of the plantation's second owners. When he was still breathing, Dr. Tucker would go out at night to call on patients. Upon returning home, he'd ring a bell that hung at the entrance gate to call a servant to meet him and his horse when he reached the mansion. After Dr. Tucker's death, the people who lived in the manor house would still hear the bell ringing at night. For awhile they lived with the noise. Then it started driving them nuts, so they buried the bell. It no longer rings, but apparently that doesn't stop the ghost of Dr. Tucker from making his nightly calls. As recently as August 1999, a guest has confided that on previous trips to the Plantation House he was awakened in the night and saw the ghost of Dr. Tucker sitting by the fireplace. Belanger adds that the guest's wife told her husband "he was insane," but the guest stands by the story. The only way to know for sure, of course, is to visit the Litchfield Plantation yourself. And don't forget to turn the lights off. Apparently, Dr. Tucker disappears when anyone flips the light switch.

A canopy of oaks lines the approach to the eighteenth-century Litchfield Plantation, now a luxurious bed-and-breakfast. (COURTESY OF LITCHFIELD PLANTATION)

Secret Information

Location: Pawleys Island, South Carolina.
Address: 290 River Rd., Pawleys Island, SC 29585.
Phone: 800-869-1410 or 843-237-9121.
Fax: 843-237-1041.
E-mail: vacation@litchfieldplantation.com.
Web site: www.litchfieldplantation.com.
Rates: From $66 to $225 per night.
Reservations: Required.
Credit cards: American Express, Carte Blanche, Diners Club, Discover, Eurocard, MasterCard, Visa.

TOP SECRET

If you can't bear to leave Fido or Fluffy at home when you visit the Lowcountry, then head for the Mansfield Plantation, just down the road from Litchfield Plantation, in Georgetown. The Mansfield Plantation, which is listed on the National Register of Historic Places, is an authentic antebellum rice plantation turned bed-and-breakfast with a four-legged twist—innkeeper Sally Cahalan welcomes pets. The plantation, which also offers public tours, received the top Five-Paw rating from *Pets Welcome* travel guide. In addition to the furry family members often seen on the grounds, there are also plenty of beaver, deer, fox, and alligators who roam this nine-hundred-acre natural wonderland. Spend the night in one of the historic guest houses, enjoy a full breakfast in the manor house, then explore the surrounding rice fields, forest, and dikes on complimentary bikes. Rates range from $100 to $125. For details, call 800-355-3223 or 843-546-6961.

60

River City Cafe

Burgers and Brew

We were hot. We were thirsty. We had just been riding around on wave runners in the ocean when we found it just a stretch up the road from Captain Dick's Marina (see Top Secret) in Murrells Inlet, South Carolina. The area just below Myrtle Beach is known as the place to come for great bars and restaurants such as Flo's Place, Anchovies (one of our favorites), and Bovine's. That makes this tiny little pub easy to miss, particularly when you're craving a frosty brew. Fortunately, though, after a sweaty day on the sea, we stumbled upon the quaint, rustic River City Cafe, where with every step across the worn wooden floors, you crunch discarded peanut shells.

Real license plates with messages like "Try Bud," "Radical," and "Eat Beef" cover the walls. Scrawled graffiti leads your eye to wander over the odd assortment of wall decorations, including boxing gloves in a frame, a jackelope (we swear!), an antique peanut roaster, a plane propeller, and a deer's rear (mounted taxidermy-style). Outside, visitors can sit in chairs or on bench swings while they chow down with the locals.

But we don't go there just for the laid-back atmosphere. The food's pretty darn good, too. The place is famous for its award-winning, bigger-than-your-mouth burgers slathered with cheese, bacon, onions, jalapeños, and other toppings. The made-from-scratch menu choices also include hand-dipped onion rings (the "blooming onion"), fried bologna sandwiches, homemade french fries, a variety of salads, and a couple of seafood sandwiches. With a unique atmosphere, tasty food, and good, consistent service, this hidden treasure that's been cherished by locals for years may not be a secret much longer—*USA Today* recently named it and its sister location up the road in Myrtle Beach one of the top ten places for families at the beach.

Secret Information

Location: Murrells Inlet, South Carolina.
Address: Highway Business 17, Murrells Inlet, SC 29575.
Phone: 843-651-1004.
Hours: 11 A.M. to 10 P.M. daily.
Price: $3 to $8.
Credit cards: MasterCard, Visa.
Details: There is another River City Cafe location in Myrtle Beach.

TOP SECRET

Before you dine at River City Cafe, be sure to work up a hunger at Captain Dick's Marina, also located in Murrells Inlet. From its decks, you can watch fishing boats come and go, or you can book a trip to deep-sea fish, explore the marsh, cruise the ocean, or even parasail. The day we went to Captain Dick's, we were treated to an unforgettable adventure—we were allowed to take its rental wave runners out into the ocean. Though it's probably not the company's usual policy, our guide let us break from the usual ride around a horseshoe-shaped channel and explore the choppier (and far more exciting) waves of the Atlantic. For more information, call Captain Dick's at 843-651-3676.

61

Top Ten Beach Books

FYI

Novel Vacation Ideas

Along with the sunscreen and over-sized towel, every well-stocked beach bag needs at least one thick paperback beach book. No work-related or helpful how-to titles allowed on the sand, however. Beach books are for complete escape only. They are big fat juicy reads with lots of vivid descriptions and probably one or two illicit love affairs. The experience is even more fun when the story you're reading is set where you're vacationing—immersing both your mind and body in a world away, far from the humdrum of home.

To truly get into a vacation on the Carolina coast, take along a work by one of the wealth of writers who've painted vivid pictures of life from the Outer Banks to the Lowcountry. Our favorites are Pat Conroy and Anne Rivers Siddons. Both are locals—Conroy is a 1967 graduate of The Citadel in Charleston and Siddons is a Charleston resident —and they weave such artistic tales and create such compelling characters that, when you're done with one of their totally engrossing books, you'll feel as if you're a local too. To help you pick the perfect vacation read, here is the list of our ten favorite Carolina coast beach books by Conroy, Siddons, and other authors.

1. The Water Is Wide by Pat Conroy. This treasure, which is non-fiction yet reads like all of Conroy's other lyrical tales, chronicles his adventures as a young man teaching fifth through eighth grade Gullah children in the one-room Mary Fields School on Daufuskie Island (Secret 87). Once you finish the book, rent the movie version called *Conrack,* starring Jon Voight in the title role.

2. Lowcountry by Anne Rivers Siddons. Siddons blends Gullah culture and its melodic rhythms with wild island ponies and other natural wonders of the ACE Basin (all of which do exist) to tell the story of Caroline Veneable who, when her mind-dulling cocktail party and country club lifestyle becomes unbearable, escapes to the pristine Lowcountry island her granddaddy left to her.

3. The Prince of Tides by Pat Conroy. Nick Nolte played the lead, Tom Wingo, when this Conroy masterpiece (book reviewers have compared it to Steinbeck's *East of Eden*) was turned into a successful film by Barbra Streisand, who rented a home in Beaufort, South Carolina, while shooting the movie.

4. The Lords of Discipline by Pat Conroy. This famous volume (also a movie) is loosely based on Conroy's years as a cadet at The Citadel in Charleston and the struggles of students to survive in the closed and rigid military institution.

5. Outer Banks by Anne Rivers Siddons. Only about one-third of the book, which links the lives of four college friends in the past and present, is set in the Outer Banks, but those chapters are worth the read for the detailed description and background information on Nags Head and surrounds.

6. The Great Santini by Pat Conroy. Plan a visit to Parris Island (Secret 91), the marine base, after finishing off this story of the struggle between eldest son Ben Meecham and his Marine Corps fighter pilot father, Lt. Col. Bull Meecham, which is crafted after the real-life relationship between Conroy and his late dad, Colonel Donald Conroy, a former USMC pilot.

7. The Outer Banks by Anthony Bailey. The memoirs of a British travel writer is considered by local bookstore owners a "must read" for Outer Banks visitors.

8. An Outer Banks Reader by David Stick. Stick, who has lived on or near the Outer Banks all his life, is often called "Mr. Outer Banks." If you enjoy this volume of essays, check out his earlier work including *Graveyard of the Atlantic* and *Roanoke Island: The Beginnings of English America*.

9. Teach's Light—A Tale of Blackbeard the Pirate by Neil Wise Wechter. This beloved classic for younger readers—a time-travel adventure starring Blackbeard—is now available in paperback and is a great addition to any family beach bag.

10. Hatteras Journal by Jan DeBlieu. Consisting of ten essays first published in hardcover in 1987, this collection captures the distinctive character and spirit of the Outer Banks and its people. It includes chapters on loggerhead turtles, commercial fishing, and the legendary nor'easter that hit Hatteras Island in 1986.

Secret Information

To pick up one of our ten best beach books or to get other recommendations for perfect vacation reads, stop by or call one of these independent bookstores in the Carolinas.

- Manteo Booksellers, 105 Sir Walter Raleigh Street, Manteo, North Carolina, 27954, 252-473-1221; www.manteobooksellers.com.
- Buxton Village Books, Highway 12, Buxton, North Carolina, 27920, 252-995-4240.
- McAllister and Solomon Books, Wrightsville Square, 4402-1 Wrightsville Avenue, Wilmington, North Carolina, 28403, 910-350-0189.
- Port Royal Bookstore, Port Royal Plaza, 95 Matthews – 5A, Hilton Head, South Carolina, 29926, 843-689-9996.
- The Preservation Society of Charleston Bookstore, 147 King Street, Charleston, South Carolina, 29401, 843-722-4630.
- Historic Charleston Foundation Museum Shop, 108 Meeting Street, Charleston, South Carolina, 29401, 843-724-8484.

TOP SECRET

The ride to the beach is the ideal time to prepare the kids for the coastal adventures that lie ahead. Younger readers will relish the two entertaining yet educational paperback series written by local Outer Banks author Mary Maden, which she self-publishes through her Dog and Pony Enterprises (P.O. Box 3540, Kill Devil Hills, NC 27945; 252-261-6905). The first, "Outer Banks Animal Adventure Series," features an adorable dog named Tazz and a lovable pony named Petey (all of Maden's animals are based on real animals she's known), who take readers through historically acurate learning adventures. Titles include: *Flying High With the Wright Brothers*, *The Secret of Blackbeard's Treasure*, and *In Search of the Lost Colony*. The second, newer series, "The Earth Ocean Adventures," includes *The Dolphin Adventure: Touched by a Dolphin*, *The Great Manatee Rescue*, and *The Great Shark Adventure*. All of Maden's delightful books are $5.95 (an Outer Banks Coloring Book is also available for $2.95) and are featured at book stores throughout the Outer Banks or by mail through Dog and Pony Enterprises. Buy a few selections before your trip for the kids to read on the ride to the coast, then pick up some additional titles for the long trek home.

Collectors Cafe

Appetizing Art

62

Before you save room for dessert at the Collectors Cafe in Myrtle Beach, South Carolina, it would probably be a good idea to call and check the spending limit on your credit card. Most nights at least one diner at this upscale bistro opts for a piece of local art work over a slice of the homemade Key Lime pie. And while the restaurant's tempting desserts (such as the award winning tiramisu) could set you back a few dollars, the paintings displayed on the walls can easily cost you a few thousand or more.

The Collectors Cafe is many things to many different people. To the year-round locals of Myrtle Beach, it's "their place," a combination Mediterranean-inspired restaurant and European-style coffeehouse far from the all-you-can-eat grazing grounds on the beach's touristy restaurant row. To artists from throughout North and South Carolina, it's a supportive gallery that invites them to exhibit and sell their finest work. And to owners Thomas Davis and his partners, brother and sister duo Michael and Rhonda Smith, this bright and funky gallery-bistro-coffeehouse-gathering place represents a dream come true.

In their former lives, Thomas Davis and Michael Smith were college roommates and artists—Davis by trade and Smith to "escape the monotony of his everyday job as an engineer," says Sharon, the cafe's manager. In 1994, the pair teamed up to create an unusual place to hang their own art and display works by fellow Carolinians. Smith's sister was brought on board because of her decade-plus experience in the restaurant industry. The final piece of the puzzle was self-taught chef Carlos McGregor, an artist in his own right, whose creative talent can be seen and tasted in every dish he prepares.

The strange equation of artist, engineer, restaurateur, and chef coming together has equaled success for the Collectors Cafe. The off-beat restaurant doesn't advertise, yet the phone rings constantly with requests for dinner reservations. Through the reciprocal support of the arts community, word-of-mouth recommendations, and the repeat business of both locals and vacationers lucky enough to stumble upon the place, Collectors Cafe has quietly become one of the favorite, yet still least known, restaurants on the Grand Strand.

Many of the afternoon visitors to the cafe simply come in to sip cappuccino around handpainted tables. There are five unique rooms in the cafe, and the colorful Coffee Shop is the one you enter first through the front door. The owners traveled out to coffeehouse Mecca—Seattle—to learn the secrets of perfect brewing and cappuccino making from the Java masters. From the mesmerizing aroma of the custom coffees, you can tell they were apt pupils. The servers and assembled coffee lovers in the shop are welcoming to tourists and other strangers. And the Mexican tile floor is a work of art, perfectly complementing the hanging paintings and photographs that vary widely in style, size, and price (roughly $150 for photos to $4,000 or more for an oil painting). A cup of coffee tastes best when accompanied by a homemade fruit cobbler or crisp, but visitors can skip the food and drink completely and simply stroll through the four other "gallery" rooms of the cafe to enjoy the art—including pieces crafted by Thomas Davis and Michael Smith.

One of the rooms is called The Gallery and features a stunning thirty-foot sculpture suspended from the ceiling. Enhancing the dramatic effect are slate stained walls and rich oak floors. The Grill Room, where Chef McGregor creates his masterpieces before your eyes, contains ceramic tile-topped tables and a handpainted ceramic bar. The private Lions Den is decorated with a jungle theme. And stately Greek columns command attention in the main dining room, where starched white tablecloths and sophisticated works of art help create an atmosphere of elegance and romance.

Although the art on the walls, which changes every six months to rejuvenate the look of the restaurant, attracts the bulk of the day visitors, it's McGregor's inventive menu that keeps them coming back in the evening. In fact most diners who visit Collectors Cafe based on a friend's recommendation are surprised to discover that they're eating in an art gallery, says the manager. They're here for the food, and no wonder. Although the prices are pretty steep for a family night out, the entrees (and ambience) are well worth the green for a special occasion, a romantic meal, or to treat yourselves for surviving another week at the beach with your kids.

McGregor's Mediterranean-inspired menu always features daily specials based on whatever seafood, vegetables, and fruits are in season. Favorite appetizers include grilled Maine lobster with a Thai hot pepper peanut sauce and cucumber-seaweed salad or jumbo ravioli filled with smoked chicken and served in a brown butter sauce with fresh asparagus. The entrees range from simply delicious vegetarian pasta to the decadent New Zealand lamb loin marinated in thyme, rosemary, and garlic served over macaroni with four cheeses, tomatoes, and roasted fennel. There's always a grilled fish of the day served with an artichoke, spinach, and linguine fritatta and tomato-marjoram sauce. Also, this wouldn't be the Carolina coast without the requisite jumbo crab cake; only, instead of French fries and tartar sauce on the side, this bad boy is served over roasted butternut squash with a white port mustard sauce and roasted sweet peppers.

For anyone starving for fine food and fine art, the Collectors Cafe is worth the drive from any vacation address an hour or two north or south of Myrtle Beach. Who knows? You may end up with that perfect oil painting you've been searching for to hang above the mantel back home or you may just discover "your place" to revisit each time you come to the coast.

Secret Information

Location: Myrtle Beach, South Carolina.
Address: 7726 N. Kings Highway
Phone: 843-449-9370.
Fax: 843-449-6129.
Hours: Coffee House and Art Gallery are open noon until midnight Monday through Saturday. Dining room is open 6 P.M. to 10 P.M., Monday to Thursday, and 6 P.M. to 10:30 P.M., Friday and Saturday.
Price: $15 to $30.
Reservations: Recommended.
Credit cards: American Express, Diners Club, Discover, MasterCard, Visa.
Details: The restaurant is sandwiched between other shops in a strip mall, so look carefully or you'll miss it.

TOP SECRET

For a more down and dirty kind of art than you'll see at the Collectors Cafe, make plans to attend the annual Sun Fun Festival held the first weekend of June along the beaches of Myrtle Beach, North Myrtle Beach, and the South Strand. The four-day fete includes more than fifty varied indoor and outdoor activities, including an amazing Sandcastle Building Contest where artistic sand sculptors create architectural masterpieces that are quickly erased by wind and water. For the less artistically gifted, there's always a Watermelon Eating Contest, Bubble Gum Blowing Contest, and a horseshoe pitching contest. For more information on exact dates and locations of events, contact the Myrtle Beach Chamber of Commerce at 843-626-7444 or write to them at P.O. Box 2115, Myrtle Beach, SC 29578.

Pawleys Island

63

Weather-beaten Wealth

Mom used to say that "old money wore old clothes." The nouveau riche were those who had gained their wealth in the last generation or two and felt the need to dress up, drive fancy cars, and build ostentatious homes in gated, manicured communities. But the truly wealthy, she reasoned, bought quality and stuck with it for years—old Volvos, worn chinos and oxford shirts from Abercrombie and Fitch, and bare-bones beach cottages that hadn't seen a renovation or paint job since great-grandfather bought the place in the 1920s. Well, if Mom was right (which she usually is), then there must be plenty of old money still floating around in the salt marshes of Pawleys Island, South Carolina. Pawleys (named for the family who owned the adjacent properties) is a timeless treasure, but a decidedly weather-beaten and sometimes shabby one. And that's just the way the island's full-time and fiercely devoted summer residents like it.

In fact, up until Hurricane Hugo cut a path through the 3.5-mile island back in 1989, little had changed here in generations. The same families had owned the elegantly shabby cottages and beach houses for years, and the summer residents were mainly regulars who rented the same house, the same week, year after year. Hugo didn't destroy this rustic, insiders' club completely, but his fury did smash beyond repair ninety rickety, old-timers' "Bird's Nest" cottages on the island's south end. The homes rebuilt (by the same long time island residents) in their place—half-million-dollar behemoths on lots valued at $300,000-plus—altered the look and feel of Pawleys, to the distaste of some. Bumper stickers on the cars of locals, which once read "Arrogantly Shabby" were replaced by ones created by the island's mayor, Julian Kelly, that had the word *shabby* crossed out.

Perhaps the greatest assault on the character of the island was the central air conditioning that accompanied these bright and shiny new structures. Before Hugo, open windows and ceiling fans were the only ways to cool the air on the island. With the introduction of new technology, some residents feared the end of Pawleys life as they'd known it was near. Fortunately, however, few island homeowners (most of whom live somewhere else in the winter) have followed the lead set by the new Bird's Nest builders. And the strict island zoning ordinances, prohibiting everything from soft drink machines to luxury condos, stand strong. Until another hurricane does any housecleaning on the island, it appears that the pace of Pawleys will continue on as before in traditional, timeless, and slightly tattered fashion.

The Pawleys Island tradition is one of solitude and sun, white sand and weather-worn cottages, and good fishing and few distractions. The only restaurants are across the North or South Causeways on U.S. Highway 17 and the only hotels on the island are two small beach inns, the Sea View Inn and The Pelican Inn Bed-and-Breakfast. Locals have been summering there since the 1800s, when rice plantation householders moved their families out here from May to November to escape malaria or "summer fever." Most pre-1822 homes were destroyed by hurricanes, but eight of the original Pawleys Island historic homes remain along Myrtle Avenue (named for the wax myrtle shrubs common to the island). A brochure available at the town hall offers a brief history of each home. All are privately owned, but if you're a guest of The Pelican Inn, you can visit the P. C. J. Weston House, which was built by the lieutenant governor of South Carolina—the house is now the inn. Another piece of Pawleys' past is the South Causeway, known as Allston's Bank back in 1846 when Gov. Robert F. W. Allston's family built it. Today, the causeway, which is the oldest one in continuous use in the state, gives island golfers quick access to the Pawleys Plantation Golf and Country Club. That's probably not what Gov. Allston had in mind when he built the causeway, but it comes in handy when you run out of milk or want to play a quick nine holes before the heat sets in.

While other beaches are developing every available inch of sand into luxurious villas and estate homes, Pawleys keeps 'em coming back with creaky doors, worn wood floors, and peeling paint. Although families still summer here year after year, there are rental homes and cottages readily available through Pawleys Island Realty (see Secret Information). Most houses feature a traditional Pawleys Island screened-in porch and plenty of ceiling fans.

Only about a hundred residents live on Pawleys Island all year round. That makes winter a perfect time to visit. It's still warm enough to golf, walk along the beach, and waste an afternoon snoozing in one of those famous Pawleys Island-made hammocks (see Top Secret). Plus, all those Suburbans and Volvos and Expeditions won't be back until May. Without the people, you can bike along the narrow paths and see a Pawleys Island that closely resembles the rice planters' summer colony of the 1800s. Oh, and bring your bikes to explore the narrow lanes that weave across the island and a bucket to collect all those shells kicked up after a winter storm. But be sure to leave the outside world behind, because that darn air conditioning is about all the modern convenience Pawleys Island can take, thank you very much. This is a place that has thrived for hundreds of years simply by staying the same. Stay there, and you'll understand why.

Secret Information

Location:	About twenty miles south of Myrtle Beach, South Carolina off U.S. Highway 17.
Address:	Pawleys Island Realty Company, 88 North Causeway Road, P.O. Box 306, Pawleys Island, SC 29585.
Phone:	800-937-7352 or 843-237-4257.
Fax:	843-237-1691.
E-mail:	pawleysco@aol.com.
Web site:	www.pawleysislandco.com.
Price:	Smaller cottages range from $600 to $800 per week, and oceanfront homes range from $2,000 to $3,000. Average beach homes fall somewhere in between, depending on location.
Reservations:	Required.
Credit cards:	None.
Details:	The above information is for Pawleys Island Realty Company, through which you can book a place to stay on the island. For general information, write to Pawleys Island Town Hall, Information Center, P.O. Box 181, Pawleys Island, SC 29585.

TOP SECRET

Although Pawleys Island rope hammocks set the standard for classic hammock design around the globe today, chances are that few people would own or even know about the comfy contraptions if the Great Depression hadn't struck the Lowcountry. A South Carolina riverboat pilot named Captain Joshua John Ward first made the rope hammocks in the late 1800s to create a cool sleeping spot for himself during hot, summer boat trips ferrying rice between local plantations and commercial centers like Georgetown and Waverly Mills. Ward wove his design without knots and created hammocks for family and friends. The "secret" hammock style was passed on by the captain's brother-in-law, A. H. "Doc" Lachiotte, who duplicated the design to make gift hammocks in the 1920s. When the Depression hit, Lachiotte sold the hammocks (and hence, the family recipe) to tourists in the Pawleys Island area to earn some much needed cash. Today, the best spot to buy an authentic old-time hammock is the Original Hammock Shop on U.S. Highway 17 (800-845-0311; www.hammockshop.com). The hammocks they sell for $90 to $150 are woven by skilled artisans recreating Captain Ward's design—each one takes about three and a half hours to craft.

What's the Buzz

64

What's the most populated city in South Carolina? Columbia? Myrtle Beach? Charleston? Nope. It's Bee City in Cottageville—home to about 1.4 million buzzing bodies. "Bee City is a little town made up of eighteen bee hives," explains Diane Biering, co-owner of one of the Palmetto State's most unusual attractions, which is about an hour inland from Charleston. The bee abodes include seven "streets" with names like Drone Avenue and Queen Street. There are eighteen bee hives decorated to look like small-town businesses with signs such as GLORY BEE CHURCH OF CHRIST, the BUZZ CUT BARBER SHOP, and B-52 AIRPORT.

The city is actually a working honey bee farm. Biering's husband, Archie, learned to raise bees from his father, and when the couple moved from Summerville (Secret 73) to the country more than a decade ago, they decided to start a bee-keeping business. The Bierings, though, had more than profit in mind; they also wanted to educate others about their favorite insects.

At Bee City, there's a screened observation area from which visitors can safely watch the swarms go about their daily bees-ness (sorry, couldn't resist the pun) of collecting pollen and generating beeswax and honey. The site often hosts school and church groups for programs on beekeeping basics held in a classroom with about eighteen thousand bees, including a queen, in a glass hive. Individual visitors can also watch a video on bees and sit in on a class, if one happens to be going on at the time.

The Honey and Gift Shop features (what else?) honey from Bee City hives as well as books on beekeeping, and candles and figurines made from beeswax. Along with the bunches of bees, the Bierings keep deer, llamas, chickens, goats, sheep, ducks, and rabbits, some of which children can feed and pet.

Life is always buzzing on the streets of Bee City. (COURTESY OF ARCHIE AND DIANE BIERING)

Secret Information

Location:	In Cottageville, South Carolina, on the alternate inland U.S. Highway 17 route, about 11 miles northeast of Walterboro.
Address:	1066 Holly Ridge Lane, Cottageville, SC 29435.
Phone:	843-835-5912.
Hours:	9 A.M. to 6 P.M. Monday to Saturday.
Price:	There's a $2 suggested donation to see Bee City. Scheduled groups of fifteen or more can pay $2.50 per person for a two-hour class and beeswax souvenir.
Reservations:	For educational programs for groups of fifteen or more.
Credit cards:	None.

TOP SECRET

Okay, what if you visit Bee City and think, *Wow, what a cool hobby. I'd like to have a hive of my own?* No problem. Owners Archie and Diane Biering hold in-depth, professional beekeeping classes twice a year in March and November. They cover such topics as the agricultural benefits bees bring through pollination, breeding bees, collecting honey, and beekeeping equipment. The cost is $25 per person or $30 per family. For more information, give Bee City a buzz (see Secret Information).

Bowens Island Restaurant

American Graffiti

65

You can't judge a book by its cover, and in the case of Bowens Island Restaurant just south of Charleston, you can't judge it by what it's covered with. Every surface of the simple block structure is covered with graffiti—names, dates, sayings, observations, drawings, you name it. When you first drive up the bumpy dirt road just off SC Highway 171 heading to Folly Beach (Secret 79), you come across a deserted building that looks like no human has entered in years. Inside, stuff is scattered along the walls and in the corners—old televisions, a sit-down beauty shop hair dryer, and a 1946 Seeburg jukebox.

Owner Robert Barber isn't sure how the clutter and the scrawls got started. He admits that he and his relatives are sort of pack rats; they never seem to throw anything out. He says that until the '70s the walls of the restaurant, which was opened by his grandmother May and grandfather Jimmy just after World War II, were unmarred. Sometime in the '70s patrons started leaving their marks on the place, and now it's become a tradition. The junk and scribbles don't seem to bother Barber much, nor does it disturb the mix of locals and tourists who soak up the deliberately easygoing atmosphere and gobble down the classic Lowcountry cooking.

Bowens Island is a fourteen-acre, unincorporated spot of county land that juts out into the coastal tidelands between Folly Island and the mainland. May and Jimmy bought the whole thing in 1946 and built a small dirt causeway to connect it with the main road. It started out as a fishing camp, but anglers kept asking May to cook what they caught, so eventually they started serving food. She ran it until 1990, working up until the week she died at age eighty-two. As a memorial, the side of the restaurant features portraits of her, Jimmy, and John Sanka, who came to work for the couple in the restaurant's early days and more or less never left. Barber, a lawyer who spends a lot of time lobbying in the state capital of Columbia, took it over, and it hasn't changed much. In

Feel free to write on the walls while you chow down on Carolina seafood at Bowens Island Restaurant.

fact, Citadel cadets and Charleston Medical College students of decades ago sometimes stop in and are astonished that time has pretty much stood still. Barber has done one thing to modernize, though. About five years ago he installed indoor restrooms, saving patrons from having to walk across the road to use the facilities.

The menu is almost pure Lowcountry seafood—fried shrimp, frogmore stew, lump crab cakes, fish, and grits. However, Bowens Island (locals hardly ever bother to add the word "Restaurant") is best known for oysters, all of which come fresh from the waters within three miles of the island (see Top Secret). The atmosphere isn't for the fussy. Diners eat inside at antique—to use the term generously—tables with mismatched chairs or outside on a deck. Some parents may prefer that the kids not see the sometimes explicit sentiments scribbled on the walls. The sights, sounds, and smells can sometimes be a bit raunchy. And though fresh-faced and friendly high-school and college-aged students make up the staff, don't expect the food always to come quickly.

It doesn't bother Barber if some people don't find Bowens Island to be their thing. "It can look a little imposing and sometimes people come in, look around, and leave, but 99 percent of the people love it. It doesn't bother me," he says. "The appeal of the place is to people like me, people who like to look for local color, something a little different with an aura of authenticity about it. When you come the half mile or so down that dirt road and see the restaurant and the water, you feel like you're in the Lowcountry. Bowens Island isn't just a restaurant, but a state of mind."

Secret Information

Location: Off SC Highway 171 (Folly Road) just before the bridge to Folly Beach, South Carolina.
Address: 1870 Bowens Island Road, Bowens Island, SC 29412.
Phone: 843-795-2757.
E-mail: bowensis@charleston.net.
Hours: 5 P.M. to 10 P.M. daily except Sundays.
Price: Dinners $8 to $16.
Reservations: Not accepted.
Credit cards: None.

TOP SECRET

We've never eaten oysters like this—by the shovel full. At Bowens Island Restaurant, oysters are steamed and served classic Carolina style. The oyster chefs, Goat and Henry, place large clumps of individual mollusks stuck together on a large sheet of metal heated by burning wood underneath. The oysters are covered with wet burlap cloth and left to slowly steam. (Sometimes when the weather is too hot or there are lots of customers, the oysters are cooked in a steamer out back.) Goat or Henry uses a shovel to pick up a load of piping hot oysters, then dump them on the table in front of diners in the Oyster Eater's Room, which has tables covered with newspapers. (In May Barber's time, people eating other kinds of food weren't allowed in the oyster room lest they scarf up seafood they hadn't paid for, and the rule still stands, although occasionally Robert Barber will make an exception for members of parties with different tastes who want to sit together.) Diners get melted butter, cocktail sauce, and saltines still in plastic wrapping. The only utensils are an oyster knife, a small fork, and a bucket in which to throw empty shells. With the all-you-can-eat option, shovelful after shovelful of sweet oysters just keep coming until you can't take any more. They're so much better than you can get in the fancier restaurants in Charleston because they come right from the outside. A sign says that Goat and Henry only work for the tips they get, but that isn't true. Barber does pay them but wants to encourage patrons to add a gratuity for all their hard work. To eat oysters you have to get to Bowens at the right time of year. They pretty much stick to the old rule of serving oysters only during months with *R*s in them, so they only have them in season, which generally runs from September 15 to May 15.

66

Middleton Inn

Secret Garden

Many visitors to Charleston, South Carolina, find their way up the meandering Ashley River to America's oldest landscaped gardens, Middleton Place. They stroll around the picturesque eighteenth-century plantation, visit the historic Middleton Place House that was built in 1755, and stop to watch the blacksmith, potter, carpenter, and weaver in the plantation stableyards re-create the daily activities of a self-sustaining Lowcountry plantation. Then, they climb back into their cars and drive back to their hotel or rental house for the night.

That's the usual way to see Middleton Place, but we prefer to take the road less traveled. Our favorite view of the lush plantation is through the floor-to-ceiling windows of the contemporary Middleton Inn, which is hidden among the towering pines and live oaks on a wooded bluff adjacent to Middleton Place. As a guest of the inn, the grounds that attract visitors from around the globe are your own secret garden. During daylight hours, you can roam freely through the plantation and even help milk the cows in the morning. And since the tourists leave at 5 P.M., that means you have plenty of time in the early evening to explore "your" garden and watch the shadows dance across the lagoons and quiet lanes in soul-soothing serenity.

With 110 acres of original plantation land surrounding the Middleton Inn and more than two hundred years of history supporting it, you'd probably imagine the inn as a white-columned, antebellum structure or maybe a sturdy, brick Federalist building. But this inn is as surprising as it is serene. At first glance, in fact, it seems out of place, like the misfit item on a first grader's worksheet where the instructions are to circle the thing that doesn't belong. Completed in 1987, the Middleton Inn's striking twentieth-century architecture serves as "an exciting counterpoint" to the eighteenth- and nineteenth-century architecture of Middleton Place, says Charles Duell, a direct descendant of the Middleton family and president of the Board of Trustees of Middleton Place. While the traditional Middleton Place was designated as a National Historical Landmark, the modern Middleton Inn earned the highest national honor award of the American Institute of Architects for its unique design. On the surface, the two are strange bedfellows, but after closer scrutiny, you can appreciate why this unusual union makes perfect sense.

The sleek, European lines of the four modular, cedar buildings that house the inn's guest rooms and lodge create a boundary between the forest in back and the lawn overlooking the river. Like giant Lego structures, the three-story cubes are clustered around tranquil, manicured courtyards. The bathroom walls and floors are covered with soothing marble and tile, while the bedroom spaces are welcoming and bright. Sand-blasted glass-block walls let the natural light stream over the oversized bathtubs (allow 30 minutes to fill them) and cypress wall paneling, and wood-burning fireplaces add a warm richness to the living spaces. And those dramatic floor-to-ceiling windows make the magnificent panoramic vistas of the pine forest and river an extension of the room; traditional pine plantation shutters are available to provide privacy.

The only nods to the past in the guest rooms are the braided floor rugs of early American design and the hand-crafted furniture. Even though the design and interior decoration of the inn itself is a modern marvel, the genteel southern hospitality of the staff and the sumptuous, traditional Lowcountry cuisine prepared in the Middleton Place Restaurant (a short walk along the river path from the inn) are direct descendants of the original plantation. Whether you're enjoying breakfast in the airy and contemporary glassed-in breakfast room or mingling with the cows and sheep that graze freely on the grounds in front of the historic Middleton Place House, you'll always feel as if you've traveled back in time.

The main purpose of Middleton Place, Duell says, is to "educate and preserve," and the presence of the inn nicely complements that mission. Guests of the inn learn about eighteenth-century plantation life and gain a greater appreciation of the need to preserve the natural treasures of the Lowcountry—all the while enjoying the pampering and amenities associated with a contemporary, upscale inn.

Secret Information

Location:	Fourteen miles northwest of Charleston, South Carolina, on the Ashley River Road.
Address:	4290 Ashley River Road, Charleston, SC 29414.
Phone:	800-543-4774 or 843-556-0500.
Fax:	843-556-0500.
E-mail:	middletoninn@mindspring.com.
Web site:	www.middletoninn.com.
Rates:	$109 to $169.
Reservations:	Required
Credit cards:	American Express, MasterCard, and Visa.
Details:	Various packages are available for two people that include one or two nights lodging at the inn, dinner at Middleton Place Restaurant, outdoor activities or flowers and champagne, and tour tickets for Middleton Place House.

TOP SECRET

With a 110-acre plantation in your own backyard while you're staying at the Middleton Inn, seize the opportunity to go out and play. The inn offers a range of eco-activities that show off the flora and fauna of Middleton Place. You can tour the property with an experienced Middleton Place naturalist, for example, either by foot, bicycle, or kayak (our favorite). During the winter months, while paddling flat-bottomed keowees (kayaks) through abandoned black-water rice fields under a canopy of cypress trees dripping with Spanish moss, you may encounter bald eagles, owls, white-tailed deer, feral hogs, alligators, and snakes. If you'd rather explore above water level, climb onto one of the gentle trail horses for an hour's ride through historic rice fields, woods, and wetlands. Check with the inn for more information about its eco-adventure programs (see Secret Information).

Romp Through the Swamp

Generally speaking, the places most worth seeing are usually the most out-of-the-way. That's the deal with Francis Beidler Forest in Four Holes Swamp, near Harleyville, South Carolina. It's about forty miles northwest of Charleston and accessible only from secondary roads off U.S. Highway 178. The final stretch into the site managed by the National Audubon Society—Sanctuary Road—is a narrow dirt lane befitting the entrance to a swamp forest more than a thousand years old. Take it slow and easy and you'll get yourself in the perfect mind-set for a visit to this eleven-thousand-acre sanctuary.

Although the Carolinas are home to endless miles of swamps, forests, and marshlands, most are accessible only by foot, bicycle, or canoe. Fortunately, the Francis Beidler Forest, the largest virgin cypress-tupelo swamp forest in the world, is available to everyone, including those in wheelchairs or kids in strollers, thanks to a barrier-free wooden boardwalk that weaves its way through 1.5 miles of ancient trees and eerie blackwater streams. The land was owned and protected by the family of Francis Beidler, a lumberman and early conservationist, until the 1960s when the Audubon Society and the Nature Conservancy purchased it.

Before you set off on your walk, spend a few minutes at the visitor's center, where you can enjoy the hands-on exhibits of turtle shells, animal pets, and even a bobcat skeleton. They also have displays on birds, wildflowers, and other flora and fauna you'll see outside. If you have a few minutes, ask to see the narrated slide show on the forest. You'll learn the difference between a swamp and a marsh—a swamp has trees, a marsh doesn't.

Although you'll pick up a pamphlet to guide you along the boardwalk, chat with the naturalist on duty for insight on what to look for that day. The swamp forest is home to 44 species of mammals, 140 different kinds of birds, 39 types of fish, 50 different reptiles, and 40 varieties of amphibians. He or she will know, for example, exactly where a particular corn snake has been hanging out or the best places to look for a slimy salamander or a yellow-bellied slider turtle—keep in mind, though, that this isn't a zoo where every creature is readily visible in a manmade habitat. If you're quiet, walk softly, and take your time, chances are you'll be rewarded with sweet bird songs and sightings of lizards, turtles, snakes, and frogs. Even if you don't spot a single Carolina pygmy rattlesnake or spadefoot toad, a peaceful stroll through Beidler is worth it for the trees.

The behemoth bald cypress and tupelo gum trees that tower above the black water swamp look like NBA players cooling off their feet in a kiddie pool. Even if you've stood beneath the mighty redwoods out West, you can't help but be awestruck by these beauties. And if you venture into the swamp in summer and fall (when water levels are at their lowest), you'll get the chance to crawl inside a hollowed out tree at the water's edge and look straight up at a patch of blue sky above. It turns out the eastern big-eared bat loves to nest in hollowed out trees in swamps, and the Beidler Forest is one of the few places around that still has any.

As you walk beneath the canopy of leaves and wildflowers, the black water backdrop adds an eerie element that sends younger kids reaching for a familiar hand to hold. Bigger kids (adults included) may take a moment to think back to the days when the Yemasee Indians paddled through this swamp to fish or when American Revolutionary War generals Nathaniel Green and Francis "The Swamp Fox" Marion camped out here with their men. There's history and magic in these trees, but mostly there's wonder.

Secret Information

Location: Off I-26 near Harleyville, South Carolina.
Address: 336 Sanctuary Road, Harleyville, South Carolina 29448.
Phone: 843-462-2150.
Fax: 843-462-2713.
E-mail: swamp@pride-net.com.
Web site: www.pride-net.com/swamp.
Hours: 9 A.M. to 5 P.M. Tuesday to Sunday.
Price: Admission to the boardwalk is $5 for adults ($4 for Audubon Society members) and $2.50 for children age six to eighteen.
Credit cards: No credit cards for admissions. MasterCard and Visa accepted in the Swamp Shop gift store.

TOP SECRET

During March, April, and May the tourist numbers are down and the swamp water is up at Francis Beidler Forest. That's the perfect time to take a guided canoe trip and get a turtle-level view of this mysterious swamp. Both two-hour and four-hour trips are offered, and the spots fill up fast so make your reservations a month or two in advance. No one under eight is allowed on the four-hour paddle and no one under six can participate in the two hour Saturday afternoon trip. Prices range from $5 for children on the two-hour paddle to $15 for adults on the four-hour trip. Some basic canoeing experience helps since you'll be maneuvering around cypress knees and through narrow creeks and be sure to bring along lunch, a drink, and an extra cookie for your guide (if you want to be led back out of the swamp). For more information on upcoming guided canoe trips, night walks, and other special programs, contact the sanctuary (see Secret Information).

68

Charleston

Grace and Beauty

The only way to see Charleston—the historic area at least—is to walk it. Sure, you can drive your car, ride a trolley, or take a guided carriage ride, but the beauty of Charleston lies in its small details—indigo growing along white wooden fences, women weaving sweetgrass baskets on the sidewalk, architectural treasures hidden high on the facades of homes, hidden gardens glimpsed only through closed wrought-iron gates. You can't get to know Charleston in a rush. You need to stroll through its streets and stop to study its gracefulness and beauty. You need to take the time to talk with those who have lived here all their lives and embody the conflicting character of the place—sometimes aristocratic and stand-offish but always perfectly well-mannered and extremely gracious.

The Charleston area stretches from Kiawah and Seabrook Islands in the south to around Summerville in the west and Mt. Pleasant and Isle of Palms in the north. The heart of the area is the historic district perched on a peninsula surrounded by the waters of the Ashley and Cooper Rivers. The city was founded on that spot in the late 1600s because it was a perfectly defensible port. Governed for years by eight Lord Proprietors designated by King Charles II, for whom the city was named, it was once even walled in, medieval style. Over the years, it thrived as a center of trade in commodities like indigo, rice, and slaves, with fully one-third of the Africans brought in chains to North America passing through Charleston. Its Old World flavor—the result of little space to expand, wealth washed away by the Civil War, and energetic preservation efforts—draws tourists to such sights as Rainbow Row, the East Bay Street run of homes painted in pastels, and a blocks-long public market housing dozens of small merchants.

To see all that downtown Charleston has to offer, we recommend walking as much as possible. If you want to take a few days to explore the area, choose a hotel or inn in the historic district and park the car

Charleston is famous for being one of the first cities to preserve its historic

until you leave. That's also the best way to experience the hospitality and attention to detail that are common to every kind of Charleston lodging, from private homes (Secret 75) to luxury hotels. To travel longer distances, take the DASH trolley system, which includes five routes that will get you close to most any sight you'd like to see. Also keep in mind that though Charleston looks quaint, it's a city and certain areas are prone to crime. The rule of thumb used to be that you should stay below Calhoun Street when visiting, but the area frequented by tourists has expanded with new hotels and shops, and now the area considered safe extends north to the Visitor and Transportation Center (see Secret Information).

Once you get out of downtown, the character of the Charleston area changes. To the south are James and Johns Islands, which have truer Lowcountry feel than the city itself. They are the gateways to the relatively new, decidedly exclusive Kiawah Island and Seabrook Island as well as the much more down-to-earth Folly Beach (Secret 79). If you are on the south side of Charleston, take time to see the Angel Oak, which lies off of Bohicket Road on Johns Island. The huge tree is estimated to be more than fourteen hundred years old, sprouting during the Dark Ages, and is sixty-five feet tall, twenty-five-and-a-half feet wide. It's in a public park open 9 A.M. to 5 P.M. daily.

Heading inland, our favorite drive is along Highway 61, the oldest highway in the state, which roughly parallels the Ashley River and passes by a string of plantations and historic sites such as Middleton Place (Secret 66). Further inland lie towns like Summerville, where wealthy Charlestonians built homes to escape the summer heat on the coast.

Over the bridges spanning the Cooper River to the north, which offer spectacular views but give those of us with a fear of heights the willies, lies Mt. Pleasant, a booming upscale suburban community packed with restaurants. Military buffs will want to head straight to Patriot's Point, home of the aircraft carrier *Yorktown* and gateway to Fort Sumter, the spot in Charleston Harbor where the Civil War started. Beyond it lies Sullivan's Island and the Isle of Palms. Sullivan's (Secret 80) is a long-time summer retreat that has a real residential feel. The Isle of Palms is home to Wild Dunes, a gated resort of multi-story condominiums, luxury beach houses, and expansive golf courses. It's our favorite place to stay to combine a spend-the-day-on-the-sand beach vacation with easy access to the walkable historic sites, great restaurants, and shopping opportunities of big city Charleston.

Secret Information

The place to start exploring the Charleston area is the Visitor and Transportation Center at 375 Meeting Street. There you'll find all the booklets, brochures, and advice you need to decide what to see in the city. The former railroad station stretches a full city block and features a twenty-minute movie, *Forever Charleston*, that captures the unique character of the city in the voices of its citizens. If you're not staying in the city, leave your car in the parking lot and catch one of the DASH trolleys that leaves from the stop outside—if you're going to be doing a lot of hopping on and off exploring, buy a one-day pass for $2 or a three-day pass for $5 at the center. The visitor center is open from 8:30 A.M. to 5 P.M. or 5:30 P.M., depending on the time of year. For more information, call the center at 843-853-8000. If you want to get information about Charleston before you arrive, check out the Charleston on-line visitor's center at www.charlestoncvb.com.

Handwoven sweetgrass baskets are on sale along the streets of Charleston's historic district.

TOP SECRET

While paying attention to Charleston's historic homes, tourists sometimes overlook the city's magnificent churches. St. Michael's Church, at the corner of Broad and Meeting Streets, for example, was built in 1752 and is the oldest church in Charleston. Stop by pew number forty-three in the Colonial Georgian building and you just might step on the same spot where the foot of George Washington or Robert E. Lee (both attended services at the church) tapped years ago during a long-forgotten preacher's sermon. The French Huguenot Church at 136 Church St. was rebuilt in 1845 after the original 1687 structure was destroyed in a fire. The house of worship is home to a rare Henry Erben pipe organ (c. 1845) that is still used in services today. Although the sound of all church bells ring sweet, none chime for Charlestonians quite as melodiously as the traveling bells of St. Michael's Episcopal Church at 80 Meeting Street. Originally imported from England with the church clock in 1764, the bells were taken back to England as booty during the American Revolution. They were returned years later, but during the Civil War, they were on the move yet again, to Columbia, South Carolina, to keep them out of harm's way. Later, they were damaged by fire and had to make the journey back to England for recasting. Once again they were returned to Charleston where, today, they remain ringing every quarter hour. When services aren't underway, most historic Charleston churches like these open their doors to reverent visitors. Since each church has its own rules and regulations about suggested donations, guided tours, photography, and visiting hours, call ahead before making plans to tour.

69

Stono River Stables

Horsing Around

"This used to be a cotton plantation," G. Marion Reid says while navigating his bare-bones Chevy Suburban through the lush sea island forest his family has owned for generations. "But we figured out that it's a lot easier to pick Yankees than to pick cotton."

The Yankees who keep Reid in business are the horse-loving tourists who flock to Kiawah, Seabrook, and the other Charleston-area resorts in the summer. The few, however, who are fortunate enough to find his Stono River Stables tucked away on a dirt road that runs past tidy mobile homes are far from fleeced. Anyone who can sit on a horse can take a guided trail ride through Reid's two hundred acres of forested Lowcountry paradise on rustic Johns Island. And if they're smart enough to stop and sit a spell under one of the massive shade trees, they can get the best deal of all—a chance to swap a tale or two with the man who, since 1969, has operated this low-key, low-tech stable hidden in the woods. Reid, a long, lean Charleston native with Marlboro Man rugged good looks and Rhett Butler style, is a charming and gracious host, and he knows his horses.

"I had a horse years ago, married a girl who had a horse, and my present wife married me because I had a horse," says Reid, who retired as Charleston Airport Director in 1979 to focus full-time on his four-hoofed passion. Currently, Reid is grooming one of his twenty-two horses to run for riches at Tampa Bay Downs. That thoroughbred's mom, Singer, was a former racehorse herself. The story of the breeding and foaling of her baby, "Blacknoch," is chronicled on the Stono River Web site at *members.tripod.com/stonoriverstable.*

If talk of thoroughbreds and the Internet gets you picturing a sleek equestrian facility with manicured lawns and computerized, climate-controlled stalls, it's time to refocus. This part of Johns Island is rural agricultural (lots of family fruit and vegetable stands), and what makes Stono River so special is that it blends right in. The small, black-and-white sign marking the turn for Stono River at narrow Hut Road is easy to miss if you're zooming down River Road just counting the minutes until you get to your oceanfront villa or beach house. But if you go slowly enough to check out the peaches and peanuts at the roadside stands and marvel at the majestic oak canopy above, you'll see the sign. Drive slowly past the mobile homes (there'll probably be kids playing outside) and when you reach the forest you're there. It's cool and green, and everything looks like it was transplanted from times past—right down to the tire swing hanging from a shady oak.

While trail rides through the cool, maritime forest where deer and turkey roam and otter and eagles are regularly spotted is enough to attract most recreational riders, Stono River Stable is also a serious equestrian training facility. For $15 per day, riders can trailer in their own horses to tackle the Cross Country course, which includes sixty-three jumps on a hundred acres. Although the course Reid spent fifteen years building is for serious riders, some of the obstacles could probably cause even a horse to chuckle. There are old buoys put out to pasture after years of marking fishing reefs and a sturdy Navy rescue boat Reid ended up buying in an attempt to speed along a snail-paced auction.

"I went to the auction to buy something else, and it was taking forever...five dollars, ten dollars...so I suggested they start the bidding at $200 just to move things along," recalls Reid. "So the next guy says $205! I said $250 to move it along again and the auctioneer says, 'Sold!' I didn't even want that boat."

Reid did want the old D-18 twin Beech airplane that now serves as lawn decoration outside his home. The house, which Reid terms a "contemporary farmhouse," looks more like a traffic control tower salvaged from his former career. Reid had an architect design his concrete block retreat back in 1967, and although various hurricanes have toppled several age-old trees around it, the fortress remains.

In addition to trail rides, conversation, and quirky structures, Stono River Stables offers stadium jumping courses, a 5/8-mile conditioning track, a lunging paddock, miles of trails, shaded pastures, barns, and a dressage arena. Boarding is available on a weekly basis or you can lease a horse by the month. There are also lessons for beginners to advanced riders taught by experienced riders, many of whom are extremely bright college students on break. Hey, we don't know about their classroom performance, but scoring a summer job in such an idyllic, out-of-the-way setting obviously shows some savvy on their part.

And if riding isn't your thing, you can still spend the day walking or jogging through the maritime forest on the property of Stono River Stables. It's an ideal spot for bird-watching, communing with nature, or just escaping. Bring a camera, bring a picnic lunch, and even if you're not a Yankee, bring $15 to pay for foot access to the Property for G. Marion Reid.

Secret Information

Location: Off River Road on Johns Island, South Carolina.
Address: 2962 Hut Road, Johns Island, SC 29455.
Phone: 843-559-0773 or toll free 877-777-8951.
Web site: www.members.tripod.com/stonoriverstable.
Hours: Daylight hours.
Price: $20 for a guided trail ride; $15 for foot access.
Reservations: Recommended.
Credit cards: None.
Details: No special equipment or clothing is required. There are safety stirrups on the saddles, so any shoes are okay.

TOP SECRET

Stono River Stables offers a Summer Riding Camp for kids ages six to sixteen. The weekly sessions run from the end of May until the middle of August and cost $160 per week or $40 per day. Young horse lovers of all riding levels who are on vacation—and who need a vacation from mom and dad—can sign up for a week, a month, the whole summer, or just for the day. Activities include grooming and tacking; riding lesson; trail and bareback riding; and routine horse care. The camp runs from 9 A.M. until 1 P.M. so if your family is staying at Kiawah, in Charleston, or on one of the area islands, there's still plenty of beach time left in the late afternoon. The camp is limited to 10 children per day; sign up when you're making your beach reservations to guarantee a spot. For more information and an application, visit the Stono River Web site or call the stable (see Secret Information).

Martha Lou's Kitchen

70

Good Food Cheap

It is sometimes important to return to your roots. It's too easy to grow up, get a little money in your pocket, and forget where you came from. In some ways that's happened to southern cuisine, which has become a bit uppity as practiced in the trendy restaurants by culinary school graduates. In some ways it's forgotten where it started, in small "meat-and-threes" where cooks who've never heard of *Le Cordon Bleu* serve up specials like fried chicken with your choice of three vegetables—nothing fancy, just hearty, home-style cooking. It might do some of the superstar chefs good to get reacquainted with the roots of their craft, and there's no better place for them to do it—or for you to taste classic southern cooking—than Martha Lou's Kitchen in Charleston, South Carolina.

Housed in a small pink and blue building opposite Berg's Paint Store, Martha Lou's is owned by Ruth Gadsden, but the soul of the place is her mother, Martha Lou. For more than sixteen years, they've been putting in twelve-hour days, dishing up breakfast, lunch, and dinner for a loyal clientele of locals who like good food cheap. The Hearty Man breakfast, for example, consists of sausage, corned beef hash, or fried bologna with grits, eggs, and toast for $4. The lunch and dinner menu usually includes a choice of fried chicken, whiting (or another kind of fish), or pork chops with such sides as lima beans, white rice, baked macaroni and cheese, collard greens, cabbage, corn bread, and bread pudding. The price of a plate of food doesn't get above $6. Matthew and Ted Lee, who have made a career out of being connoisseurs of traditional cuisine, (Secret 74), say that Martha Lou's serves "the best southern food we know of, all made-to-order. The fried pork chops and the whiting are sublime." When friends come to town, the Charleston natives tell them there are just two places they *must* go: Martha Lou's and The Wreck (Secret 78).

Martha Lou herself, however, isn't all that interested in talking about the craft of cooking or what makes her daughter's restaurant special. To her, turning out perfectly breaded and browned chicken or pork chops is just what she and the rest of the staff at the small sixteen-seat diner do every day; it's no big deal. She may not know it, but she's keeping the roots of southern cuisine alive.

Secret Information

Location: Charleston, South Carolina.
Address: 1068 Morrison Drive, Charleston, SC 29403.
Phone: 843-577-9583.
Hours: 7:30 A.M. to 7 P.M. Monday to Friday; 9 A.M. to 4 P.M. Saturday.
Price: $4 to $6 a plate.
Reservations: Not accepted.
Credit cards: None.

TOP SECRET

Though it doesn't include Martha Lou's Kitchen, the book *A Locals' Guide to South Carolina's Best Kept Dining Secrets* by Brian Katonak with Lynne Katonak ($12.95, Sandpiper Publishing Co.) offers a good compendium of reviews of restaurants throughout South Carolina, including other "meat-and-threes" like The Fork Restaurant (864-877-9544), which is upstate in Greer, and Grandma's Kitchen (843-448-2126) in Myrtle Beach. Pick it up if you'll be spending a lot of time traveling off the beaten track of the Palmetto State and want to taste the wide range of foods and flavors it has to offer.

Palmetto Islands County Park

Family Fun Park

71

We'll wager that most of the moms and dads who vacation with their children on the Isle of Palms, or elsewhere on the Mt. Pleasant side of the Charleston area, don't know that minutes away is one of the best places in the area to have some family fun—Palmetto Islands County Park. Just a few miles north of the Isle of Palms Connector, which ties U.S. Highway 17 to the island, the 943-acre recreation area is the perfect place to go when the kids are bored with the beach.

The park is part of the Charleston County Park and Recreation Commission system. Unlike other metropolitan areas where parks are merely preserved public lands in which to picnic, the Charleston parks are stuffed with active recreation options ranging from fishing piers (Secret 79) to climbing walls (see Top Secret). We haven't encountered a city that does a better job of providing fun, low-cost places for the public to play.

Palmetto Islands, land surrounded by marsh, is designed to be a spot for families and groups to spend the day.The park center is built above a two-acre pond you can explore via rental paddle boats. The balance of the park is a tropical maze of picnic areas, bike trails, boardwalks, nature paths, and fishing and crabbing spots. The Big Toy Playground is the spot to let the kids slide and swing. For a bird's-eye view of the surrounding marsh and tidal areas, climb to the top of the fifty-foot observation tower. The centerpiece of the park is Splash Island, a waterpark featuring a two-hundred-foot slide and the swirling Cyclone water ride. It's not as large as a commercial water park, but there's plenty of space for the kids and adults alike to swim, slide, and splash. It's clean and cute, as well as a great bargain.

Splash Island at Palmetto Islands County Park is a cool alternative to the beach for families vacationing on nearby Isle of Palms.

Secret Information

Location: Off Highway 17 near Isle of Palms, South Carolina.
Address: 444 Needlerush Parkway, Mt. Pleasant, SC 29464.
Phone: 843-884-0832 or 843-762-2172.
Fax: 843-884-0254.
Web site: www.ccprc.com.
Hours: Park open 9 A.M. to 7 P.M. May to August; 9 A.M. to 6 P.M. March, April, September, and October; 10 A.M. to 5 P.M. November to February.
Season: The Splash Island waterpark is open daily from the end of May through August; weekends only in May and late August/early September.
Price: $1 per person to enter the park. For Splash Island it's $6.55 for adults, $4.95 for children under forty-eight inches, and children two and under are free.
Reservations: For picnic shelters and groups only.
Credit cards: Discover, MasterCard, Visa for park concessions, but not for the gate fee.

TOP SECRET

If you're staying on the opposite side of Charleston from Palmetto Islands County Park, say at Kiawah or Seabrook, check out another great part of the city's park system: James Island County Park. Like Palmetto Park, the 643-acre area includes a water park—Splash Zone. It also has two unique ways you can test your mind and body—a climbing wall and a challenge course. The fifty-foot climbing wall can handle up to sixteen people at a time as they try not to slip off the artificial handholds peppering the vertical plane. People ages four and up can tackle the wall for $10 a session; groups of five to ten people pay $15 a head for four hours of climbing time, harnesses, and belayers (people to hold the rope attached to the harness to prevent falling). The Challenge Course is a team-building and personally challenging program that involves games, traversing cables, and climbing a fifty-foot tower. The program is set up for groups of eight to fifty people and prices vary. For more information, call the park at 843-795-7275.

72

Seewee Restaurant

See Food

Once you get the past the junction with the Isle of Palms Connector on U.S. Highway 17 traveling north from Charleston, things get rural real fast. One minute you're on the edges of upscale Mt. Pleasant, a suburb of Charleston with all the requisite superstores anchoring miles of malls, and the next you're in the countryside of the South Carolina coast. The highway cuts into miles of low-slung flora, bordered largely on the inland side by the Frances Marion National Forest and on the waterside by the Cape Romain National Wildlife Refuge. The roadside is scattered with occasional farms (including plenty of places to pick your own strawberries in the late spring), ramshackle stands where women weave and sell sweetgrass baskets, and the occasional convenience store. You get the sense that not much has changed around here in the last, say, fifty years, and that the local folks are just fine with it.

The Seewee Restaurant fits right in with this sense of life lived at a slower pace. It was built as a general store in the early 1920s and, despite having been converted to a restaurant, retains the feel of a community gathering place. It's housed in a simple building with a red tin roof and screen doors that slap shut as you push open a heavy red door to enter. The floors are worn tongue-and-groove wood, and the shelves—from the original store—are stacked with huge containers of green beans, whole tomatoes, and mayonnaise. The gleeful chatter among customers seated at unsteady tables in mis-matched straight-backed chairs along with the friendly staff makes it seem like a family reunion.

Often at the center of the hubbub is owner Mary Rancourt, who bought the general store in the '60s, shut it down when her son died in an accident in 1974, then reopened it as a restaurant in 1993 because, as she says, she "needed the income and to occupy my mind." The recipes for all the food served at the Seewee are hers, and

The Seewee Restaurant is a throwback to the simple life of old-time South Carolina.

she still makes the she-crab soup and some of the sweets, such as the pecan pie herself. Her sister and sister-in-law make the other desserts, including pound cake, caramel cake, and New York-style cheesecake. Tok Makis is the chef, and he is supported by local cooks who add authentic local flavor to the menu, including Barbara Young, who specializes in fried chicken. "It's the best fried chicken I've ever eaten," confides Rancourt, "and I've eaten a lot of fried chicken." All the seafood is fresh and can be served fried, grilled with Jamaican jerk spice, blackened, or Seewee style—cooked with Old Bay seasoning, garlic, lemon, and sherry. There's also hearty fare such as roast pork loin and country-fried steak. Entrees come with three sides such as fried green tomatoes, sweet potato casserole, and fried okra. And the desserts? Well, we can feel our ourselves putting on weight just thinking about them.

"What draws people here is first of all the food," says Rancourt, "but the ambience of the place is what makes it interesting. It's all original from the general store, and we've kept it the same as it was. People here grew up with these things. People feel they are back in time."

Secret Information

Location: On U.S. Highway 17 North between Charleston and Georgetown, South Carolina.
Address: 4808 Highway 17 North, Awendaw, SC 29429.
Phone: 843-928-3609.
Fax: 843-928-3139.
E-mail: mranc14555@aol.com.
Hours: 11 A.M. to 9 P.M. Monday to Thursday; 11 A.M. to 10 P.M. Friday; 8 A.M. to 10 P.M. Saturday; 11 A.M. to 3 P.M. Sunday.
Price: Lunches $4.25 to $11; Dinners $9 to $16.
Reservations: Not accepted.
Credit cards: Discover, MasterCard, Visa.

TOP SECRET

The Seewee Restaurant gets its moniker from the name of a local Indian tribe that lived in the area. "Seewee" is thought to mean "island" or "island people." No one knows for sure, though, because the tribe was largely wiped out, according to the restaurant's owners, when they tried to canoe to England to sell deer skins to the King and were caught in a huge storm. Survivors picked up by passing ships were sold into slavery, and the Seewees who had remained on shore slowly disappeared. Their home is now largely the Francis Marion National Forest and the Cape Romain National Wildlife Refuge. Before or after having a meal at the restaurant, you can learn more about the history and ecology of these wilderness areas by stopping by the Sewee (yes, they spell it differently than the restaurant) Visitor and Environmental Center just up the road on U.S. Highway 17. It features a live red wolf display and education area, a live bird-of-prey display, and an auditorium with an orientation film. The center is open Tuesday to Sunday 9 A.M. to 5 P.M.; call 843-928-3368 for more information.

Woodlands Resort and Inn

Great Estate

73

Sometimes in life you just have to indulge yourself—spend more money than you should, let other people do things you could do perfectly well yourself, eat lavishly prepared and presented food, surround yourself in ridiculous luxury. Shedding any sense of the practical and wallowing in the good life is just the appeal of the Woodlands Resort and Inn in Summerville, South Carolina. The forty-two-acre wooded estate tucked in an upscale residential neighborhood is an oasis from common sense and all the "have-tos" and "must-dos" and "I-don't-wannas" that most of us go through in the grind of our daily lives.

The inn itself looks something like the classic southern plantation home, with stone pillars flanking the imposing grand entrance. Part of the ultra-upscale Relais and Châteaux consortium of more than four hundred châteaux, country houses and restaurants around the globe, it features just nineteen guest rooms (priced at around $300 and up a night) equipped with such amenities as fireplaces, whirlpools, and heated towel racks. The rooms and the rest of the inn were decorated by New York designer David Eskell-Briggs (his name is hyphenated so he must be good), and feels classic, yet not claustrophobic and stuffy the way some expensive accommodations do. The grounds are equally inviting—filled with gardens of flowers, a swimming pool, croquet lawn, wedding garden, two clay tennis courts, and walking trails. There's also an on-site spa that offers facials, manicures, pedicures, massages, and other indulgences.

The house was built in 1906 on a hundred-acre site by Robert W. Parsons, one of the rich Charlestonians who flocked to Summerville to avoid the summer heat along the coast. After changing hands a couple of times and resisting being completely eaten up by the surrounding development, the private estate had fallen into disrepair by the 1990s. It was reborn as an inn after an eighteen-month restoration and has drawn raves from such reviewers as *In Style* magazine and *Andrew Harper's Hideaway Report.* Since opening in 1995, however, it is still relatively undiscovered.

Besides nineteen indulgent guest rooms, the Woodlands Inn houses the only five-star restaurant in South Carolina.

Even if you can't afford to stay there, at least treat yourself to lunch or dinner at the inn's dining room, the only AAA five-diamond restaurant in all of South Carolina (take that, Charleston!). Executive chef Ken Vedrinski serves up a fusion of Carolina and continental cooking, accompanied by a wine list that's won the *Wine Spectator* Award of Excellence. A typical dinner "Tasting Menu" ($89) includes wine and features chilled English pea soup with lemon and grilled day boat scallops; seared New York state *foie gras* and crispy savory French toast with warm apple cider soup; Alaskan rock fish with fresh porcini mushrooms and fifty-year-old balsamic vinegar; Summerfield Farms grilled lamb tenderloin with truffled Yukon gold potato puree; cippolline onion and Barolo wine reduction; all topped off with toasted pistachio semifreddo with blood orange caramel. Whew! Less expensive are the four-course meals offering a range of choices ($56). If the dinners are too expensive, have lunch at the inn and choose among offerings such as a Caesar salad with grilled chicken or tempura shrimp for $9.50 or rigatoni pasta with pancetta bacon, fresh shrimp, and roasted peppers for $14.

Sure, you could fill your stomach at Shoney's or put a roof over your head at Motel 6 for much less, but the Woodlands Resort and Inn isn't about saving money. It's about spending it while you've got it on the best you can get. Sometimes that's just what you've got to do.

Secret Information

Location: Summerville, South Carolina.
Address: 125 Parsons Road, Summerville, SC 29483.
Phone: 843-875-2600 (main number) or 800-774-9999 (reservations).
Fax: 843-875-2603.
E-mail: reservations@woodlandsinn.com.
Web site: www.woodlandsinn.com.
Hours: Restaurant open daily for breakfast from 8 A.M. to 10 A.M., for lunch 11 A.M. to 2 P.M., and Monday to Saturday for dinner 6 P.M. to 9 P.M.
Price: \$50 to \$100 per person for dinner and \$10 to \$20 per person for lunch.
Rates: \$300 per night and up.
Reservations: Recommended.
Credit cards: American Express, Diner's Club, MasterCard, and Visa.
Details: The restaurant serves special Thanksgiving and Christmas dinners, hosts an annual Dream Victorian Tea in early December, and has monthly wine-tasting dinners at which a special wine is featured with prices starting at \$66 per person, depending on the cost of the featured wine.

TOP SECRET

The Woodlands Resort and Inn's hometown, Summerville, is known as Flowertown. It's an ideal day trip as a break from burning to a crisp on the beach, especially during the spring when hordes of flowering trees and shrubs explode with color. The best spot to see them in big numbers is Azalea Park, which is the site of the annual Flowertown Festival, but pretty much everywhere you'll spot azaleas, dogwoods, wisteria, redbud, and other blooms. Any time of the year, Summerville is worth a stop to shop, eat, or sightsee. The town square area has dozens of shops to poke about, including People, Places, and Quilts (843-871-8872), one of several spots in town to hunt for antiques, and In High Cotton (843-875-7922), which features cotton clothing at discount prices. For a bite to eat, check out the Reminisce Tea House and Restaurant (843-821-4388), which is housed in an 1888 Victorian home, or Time Well Spent (843-875-2408), a Victorian tea room popular with the locals. Architecture lovers should take the six-block walking tour that showcases homes dating back to the 1820s. For more information, stop by the tiny Greater Summerville/Dorchester County Chamber of Commerce just off Main Street on Doty Avenue.

74

The Lee Bros. Boiled Peanuts Catalogue

Southern Comfort Food

Okay, we admit we're pushing it a bit to include the Lee Bros. Boiled Peanuts Catalogue among secret "Places to Eat" in the Carolinas. There's no one place you can go to sit down and sample such southern fare as Old South Pickled Okra, Mrs. Sassard's Fig Preserves, Real 100 Percent Tennessee Sorghum, Allen's Poke Salet, Carolina Gold Rice, and Mrs. Fearnow's Brunswick Stew (made with chicken, not the traditional squirrel)—all washed down with Wink or Cheerwine. No, you can only get all that and much more by ordering it from Ted and Matthew Lee. They are siblings who've built a business selling the southern comfort foods that can only be found at roadside farm stands, rapidly disappearing general stores, and county fairs. With a little planning, though, you can include their products in your vacation—maybe as part of a picnic on the beach or with Sunday brunch in your villa overlooking the eighth hole fairway, we'll leave it to you. The truth is, savoring boiled, pickled, jellied, and otherwise-prepared southern fare isn't about eating at a single place, but about a state of mind—a state of mind by which the Lee brothers live their lives.

Ted and Matthew, you see, grew up in Charleston, but left to attend college in New England (Harvard and University of Massachusetts at Amherst; these guys are no dummies). "We quickly realized that a lot of things we grew up with and loved we couldn't get at any price," recalls older brother Matthew, "boiled peanuts in particular." For themselves and as a service to other expatriate southerners, they began boiling their own peanuts in their dormitory, apparently they didn't burn the place down because they graduated and went to New York. They ended up in frustrating publishing jobs and art history-related stuff. "In desperation," says Matthew, "we said to ourselves, 'Why not fall back on what anyone in the South falls back on in a tough place? We can always boil up peanuts and sell them by the side of the road.' We decided not to sell them by the side of the road, though, although it might have gone over well on Broadway."

Boiled peanuts are a southern delicacy that bear little resemblance to roasted peanuts. Raw peanuts, which are legumes that grow underground, giving them an earthy quality, are plunged into hot salted water and cooked, then served still warm and soaked, usually in wet, brown paper bags. "People think they know what peanuts taste like, but they aren't comparable to anything else. You either love them or hate them," says Matthew, who adds that they taste and have a texture more like chickpeas or truffles than their dry, salty cousins consumed at baseball games. "They are unique in that they are a cultural phenomenon that's only associated with stands by the side of the road, not something made or sold in restaurants, grocery stores, or even the home. As kids we'd drive out to Folly Beach about twenty minutes away from Charleston and see a whole run of stands selling boiled peanuts. We'd always stop for some at Randy's Rolling Goobers. Goobers is a slang word for peanuts that came from a West African word." As a tribute to the idea of stopping by the roadside for a treat, the Lees sell bumper stickers that read: I BRAKE FOR BOILED PEANUTS.

In New York, the brothers started boiling peanuts in their tenement and tried to hawk them to local restaurants. The Yankees weren't that interested, "so we decided to try to sell them to people who already knew what they were and loved them. It was less dispiriting," says Matthew. Using Ted's 1952 sewing machine they stitched brown paper pages into the first Lee Bros. Boiled Peanuts Catalogue and started sending it out. Some timely publicity in the *New York Times* caused the business to take off, and over time, they've added a slew of items, from Cheese Straws to Pickled Peaches, to their selection of mail-order southern comfort foods.

"We're selling a southern sensibility," says Matthew. "The real distinction is that the products we sell are homemade-style as opposed to grocery-store style. Fig preserves, for example, are big sellers, especially during the winter. They're put up by a company that's been doing it since the 1920s, and we're always sold out by Christmas. Figs may be one of the secrets of the South. It seems like every other backyard has a tree that putters along silently all year, then for a brief five days at the end of July and beginning of August issues forth fruit with a beautifully cool velvety softness as subtle as under-ripe melon. Tasting fig preserves is like remembering childhood. The fact that it touches very specific nerve endings in the brain means that our people who buy from us will put up with our crude customer service methods." The Lees have just started accepting credit cards, but they aren't totally behind the times; they have a Web site that lists all the products they sell.

Now employing several people and operating out of Charleston, the Lee brothers' mail-order business has also opened a second career for them as writers specializing in regional foods. The pair are working on a book, tentatively titled *Endangered Foods*, which will spotlight traditional homemade delicacies that are disappearing from the American scene.

If you're on vacation in South Carolina and don't have time to order from them, the Lees recommend heading to the local Piggly Wiggly supermarket to find the kind of true southern fare they sell. "We hope that with more people shopping there they won't get hip and pass them over for '90s-type products," says Matthew. "They still sell traditional items like Cheerwine soda, Moon Pies, Duke Mayonnaise. We sell Piggly Wiggly T-shirts in our catalog because they have a certain spirit of simplicity and loyalty to foods that don't exist in other places. Piggly Wiggly has shown us the way."

Secret Information

Location: Charleston, South Carolina.
Address: P.O. Box 315, Charleston, SC 29402.
Phone: 843-720-8890.
Web site: www.boiledpeanuts.com.
Price: Varies.
Credit cards: American Express, Diner's Club, MasterCard, Visa.
Details: Send $1 to start receiving a catalog every six months.

TOP SECRET

The Lee Bros. Boiled Peanuts Catalogue got its name from Ted and Matthew Lee's craving for one of their home region's oddest delicacies after they headed to college up north—unshelled peanuts cooked in salt water and consumed while still hot and soggy. Now back home, their favorite spot for sampling what they think of as an icon for true southern culture is Harry's Hot Boiled Peanuts, a classic roadside stand at the junction of River Road and Maybank Highway on Johns Island, south of Charleston. Stop by and tell Harry and his wife, Helen, that the Lee boys say, "Hey."

Historic Charleston Bed-and-Breakfast

75

Home and History

Don't try to use a travel agent to book a place to stay through Historic Charleston Bed-and-Breakfast. The folks representing the owners of more than sixty historic homes in the downtown Charleston area who rent rooms to visitors want to talk directly to you to make sure they match you up with just the right room. "We have nothing against travel agents, secretaries, or family members," says Jo Bacon, the reservation service's manager, "but we do ask the people who will be staying in one of the homes to book directly so we can give them time to decide exactly what they want. We describe the properties in detail—for example, one has steep outside stairs that may not suit everyone. One time a booking was from a brother who gave it as a wedding gift but didn't give the couple all the details. When they got here, they were looking for an inn with a sign outside and couldn't find the house. It was a disaster. We like to give guests the personal touch and attention."

Charleston is known for its architectural and historical treasures—elegant, gated homes with beautiful courtyard gardens representing a range of styles starting with eighteenth-century Georgian and Regency, Greek Revival, and Queen Anne. Most tourists only get to see the outside of these buildings on walking tours or carriage rides, but those who book through Historic Charleston Bed-and-Breakfast get to spend a day or more living inside them, chatting with the owners, and pretending they, too, are part of the Charleston upper crust.

The reservation service was started by a local woman who started renting rooms in her home, but she got more requests for reservations than she could fill. She started arranging for people to stay with her neighbors, and the service grew into a business that now employs one full-time and six part-time reservationists. The properties it represents don't advertise, so you're not likely to find them on your own. They are all licensed by the City of Charleston and inspected each year by Historic Charleston Bed-and-Breakfast staff. Each property is unique

The best way to get inside the walls of Charleston's private homes is by booking a room through Historic Charleston Bed & Breakfast. (COURTESY OF HISTORIC CHARLESTON BED-AND-BREAKFAST)

and reflects the personality of the owner. All have either a private entrance or keys to the front door for guests, so you don't need to feel like your comings and goings will be monitored. Rooms range from single bedrooms with private baths in homes in the downtown historic district to an entire Victorian house outside the city in Summerville (Secret 73).

Manager Jo Bacon is very protective of the owners of the properties Historic Charleston Bed-and-Breakfast represents, and she won't reveal their names or exact locations except to visitors who make bookings through the service. She says the reason is that, "when we have, in the past, published an owner's name or the address of a home, people begin calling directly to the property, and the owners don't want that. The reason they have retained our service is to not have to make the reservations themselves." But she gladly describes examples of properties representative of what Historic Charleston Bed-and-Breakfast offers.

One example of the service's offerings is a one bedroom/sitting room combination accommodation with its own private entrance, a small kitchen, full bath, queen four-poster bed, love seat, and cable television located within walking distance of "everything." The owners live in the main house, which is a perfect example of the Charleston Single House, a unique architectural style favored in the city dating from the 1700s. Furnishings include antiques, or reproductions, and there is a lovely garden. In this property, the guests do not go into the main house. Per night rates are $115 in low season and $135 in high season.

Another type of rental is represented by a home in which the owners rent a queen suite and a king suite, each with its own bath. Guests share the owners' elegant mahogany dining room for a full served breakfast, and they have access to the living room, study, and music room. This home dates from the early 1700s. Because the owners are away during low season, this property is available only during high season at $225 for the queen suite and $250 for the king. Bacon adds that many of their properties are detached carriage houses with one, two, or three bedrooms. These were built originally as separate "kitchen houses" to prevent the danger of fire in the main house.

Secret Information

Location: Charleston, South Carolina.
Address: 57 Broad Street, Charleston, SC 29401.
Phone: 800-743-3583 or 843-722-6606.
Fax: 843-722-9589.
Web site: www.charleston.net/com/bedandbreakfast.
Hours: 9 A.M. to 5 P.M. Monday through Friday.
Rates: Vary widely.
Reservations: Required.
Credit cards: MasterCard, Visa accepted for deposits; cash or check required for payment.

TOP SECRET

Charleston has a plethora of great inns and bed-and-breakfasts beyond those represented by the Historic Bed-and-Breakfast Association, one of the most famous of which is Two Meeting Street Inn (843-723-7322). The nine-guest-room, 1892 Queen Anne home is right on the edge of the Whitepoint Gardens at the South Battery on the Charleston waterfront. Several blocks away, at No. 173, across from the City Market, is the Meeting Street Inn (800-842-8022 or 843-723-1882), a 140-year-old building that's a true inn, not a home, with fifty-six guest rooms, a Jacuzzi in the garden courtyard, and a lobby bar. The problem is that people sometimes get the two confused and end up booking Two Meeting Street Inn when they want more of a hotel-atmosphere or booking Meeting Street Inn when they really want to stay in a romantic bed-and-breakfast by the waterfront. We're not recommending one over the other, but when someone suggests you stay at the "Meeting Street Inn," make sure you know which one they mean.

76

South Carolina Artisans Center

Heart Gallery

A small Victorian cottage in Walterboro, South Carolina, is the heart of art in the Palmetto State. The house is the home of the South Carolina Artisans Center, a showroom for the state's best artists and craftspeople, and is about an hour inland from Charleston. Only paintings, sculptures, and other works selected by a jury of experts go on sale there, so you can be assured that anything you buy—from a twenty-dollar piece of handmade jewelry to a ninety-five-thousand-dollar hand-blown glass and wrought-iron lamp—is an example of creativity at its finest. The staff takes time to talk to visitors about each of the pieces, and each purchase comes with a "bio card" that introduces the artist, the medium in which he or she works, and his or her philosophy. The artists get 60 percent of the selling price; the center keeps the balance to support its activities. Most of the artists represented aren't getting rich from their efforts—they're doing what they love and hoping that the public will appreciate the passion they put into their work.

The twenty-four-hundred-square-foot, six-room center was opened in the early '90s as an outlet for South Carolina artists to market their work. So far it has featured creations by about two hundred artisans who come from the Piedmont to the Lowcountry. Works include wood carvings, pottery jewelry, fiber art, hand-blown glass, jewelry, paintings, and sculpture. There's something for everyone's taste—waterfowl decoys, jugs and mugs, tapestries, lamps, hand-painted and etched tiles, stained glass, decorated gourds, paintings, and prints. Although some of the art is modern, the bulk is folk art and crafts, work that represents the often raw and rural crafts such as weaving baskets from sweetgrass. One of the craftsmen whose work is often on display, Ronnie Riddle, who lives just south of Charleston in Meggett, sculpts and paints the boats and birds of the marsh country that surrounds his home. His home and studio overlook Wadmalaw Sound on the Intracoastal Waterway, and Riddle's art reflects his love of nature. "This location gives me wonderful inspiration and much of the subject matter I portray in my sculpture, carvings, and paintings," he says. Using the "creative energy that God has given" him, Riddle creates interpretive sculptures of birds and people using cedar driftwood. Some pieces are primitive in style while others are quite sophisticated. Known as "the barefoot craftsman," he says of his art, "My design goal when doing these sculptures is to subtract as much detail as possible and still capture the essential form of the subject. "

The center doesn't exist just to sell art, but emphasizes that it is there to educate the public about traditional Carolina art forms and keep them alive. To that end, it features a variety of educational programs, classes, and special events during the year. The Handmade Series—held on the first three Saturdays of the months of March, April, May, September, October, and November—for example, draws artists and craftspeople from around the state to show off art forms such as woodworking, crocheting, decoy carving, broom making, embroidery, and wheat weaving. "The single biggest thing we do as part of our educational mission is the Handmade Series. It provides the only opportunity a lot of people have to interact with an artist and to see fine work being created," says Denise Simmons, the center's director. Those who visit during the Saturday sessions, which begin with the artists' arrival at 10 A.M. and continue until 3 P.M., will be able to learn something about working with clay, painting on silk, or making handmade paper, for example. Visitors may participate for whatever time they wish—an hour or less to all day, and there is no charge; everything is supplied. The center also offers courses for aspiring artists such as stained glass making, basket weaving, and jewelery making.

Secret Information

Location: Walterboro, South Carolina.
Address: 334 Wichman St., Walterboro, SC 29488.
Phone: 843-549-0011.
Fax: 843-549-7433.
E-mail: artisan@lowcountry.com.
Hours: 9 A.M. to 6 P.M. Monday to Saturday; 1 P.M. to 6 P.M. Sunday.
Price: Ranges from $25 to $50 per class per person depending on supplies required.
Reservations: Required for classes.
Credit cards: American Express, Discover, MasterCard, Visa.

TOP SECRET

A self-guided tour of the historic town of Walterboro, which was founded by brothers Paul and Jacob Walter in 1784, begins and ends at the South Carolina Artisans Center. Pick up a brochure, or purchase a tape, at the center or the Chamber of Commerce office on Benson Street (843-549-9595). Then set out for a three-mile loop to see historic homes like the 1800s Dent-Lining-McDaniel-Hiott House and the 1910 Savage-Salter-Bridge House; landmarks including the Old Jail, which looks like a small castle, and the Walterboro town clock; and spots to shop such as Novit's Antique Mall and Thompson's five-cents-to-one-dollar store, a rare surviving example of the classic small town five-and-dime store. For more information about things to do and see in Walterboro and its home county of Colleton, call 843-549-9595.

Charleston Tea Plantation

Tea Time

77

Iced tea is the ice water of the South. Servers refill tall glasses for free at nearly every restaurant, and some places don't even charge you for a glass with a meal because, well, it's tea. Tea is an essential part of life down here. In fact, it almost seems as if, in the South, iced tea must come straight from the tap in every kitchen.

Of course, it doesn't, but where does the tea come from? Well, it turns out that true southern tea is grown right on the Carolina coast at the nation's only commercial tea-growing operation, which also happens to be a visitors-welcome farm—The Charleston Tea Plantation on Wadmalaw Island, South Carolina.

"This is the only place in the whole United States that you're ever going to see tea growing," says Sarah McLester, the daughter of owner Mack Fleming. "If you want to see tea plants and where your iced tea comes from, this is the place."

The place—a 127-acre spread located "at the end of the world," according to McLester—is about thirty-five minutes south of Charleston. Even if you hate tea, the drive down to rustic Wadmalaw Island is worth the gas. Few tourists find their way near the end of the Maybank Highway, so you're in for a treat. Free from fast food joints and traffic, you can savor the rural country scenery, ease up on the accelerator, and take life at a slower pace. Drive to the end of the road, about a mile past the plantation, and you'll discover another jewel of Wadmalaw, the charming fishing village of Rockville, home of The Hall—the Rockville Yacht Club—which has been continually operating regattas for more than a hundred years.

If you are a tea lover, though, then the pilgrimage to the plantation is a must. Fleming, a horticulturist who has grown tea on three continents, and his partner, Bill Hall, raise 320 varieties of tea here. They allow visitors to walk into the fields of waist-high tea plants unaccompanied and sample sweetened and unsweetened teas and iced teas (they also provide the requisite cookies) for free. Various animals belonging to Mack's wife roam the property, including two Katachin sheep named Mollie M and Tess; a pair of Top Knot geese; three horses; and "innumerable dogs and cats," a couple of which live in the open-air, gazebo-style gift shop designed and built by Fleming.

"This is a farm experience—a nice place for families and for a picnic," says McLester, who advises visitors to "pack a lunch" since the plantation is located pretty much in the middle of nowhere. "Children don't need to be quiet here. They can come and stretch out and enjoy the relaxed setting."

McLester says her dad enjoys giving the group tours and sharing his wealth of knowledge of tea growing and tea history with church groups, teachers, school groups, and tour groups. Self-guided wanderers can also learn about the tea production process and get a little history lesson watching the plantation's video show.

Tea was first planted on the farm in 1962, reintroducing the plant to the United States. Those plants were taken from a turn-of-the-century plantation about forty miles away that had operated from 1888 until the owner's death in 1950. Back then the Charleston Tea Plantation was owned by Thomas J. Lipton. Mack Fleming came on board in 1978 as the head of the research station, where he later met partner Bill Hall. The pair bought the plantation in 1987 and have been growing tea and an international family-based business ever since. The Charleston Tea Plantation's trademark American Classic brand includes different varieties of black teas.

The lush, working plantation is also home to the two owners and their families, so although visitors are warmly welcomed during the week, the weekends are reserved for the hands-on farmers' well-deserved rest and relaxation. And although the plantation includes a unique gift shop offering a variety of tea and tea-related products, ornaments, accessories, and jewelry, plus locally produced sweet grass baskets and photography and paintings by local artists, this is still a real farm—not a comfy tourist attraction. When you visit, wear sturdy shoes and bring a jacket if it's cool outside. "Since we're open all year, the open air part gets a little more open air in the winter," jokes McLester. "We get a little rugged out here."

If you've ever wondered where the tea on your table comes from, check out the Charleston Tea Plantation. (COURTESY OF CHARLESTON TEA PLANTATION, INC.)

Secret Information

Location: On Wadmalaw Island, South Carolina.
Address: 6617 Maybank Highway, Wadmalaw, SC 29487.
Phone: 800-443-5987 or 843-559-0383.
Fax: 843-559-3049.
E-mail: chastea@awod.com.
Hours: 10 A.M. to 4 P.M. Monday to Friday.
Season: Open April to January.
Price: FREE (there are group tours for $5 per person with a minimum of ten and a maximum of forty-five).
Reservations: Required for groups tours.
Credit cards: Gift shop accepts MasterCard and Visa.
Details: This is a working farm, so individual tours are self-guided.

TOP SECRET

The first Saturday in May each year, the Charleston Tea Plantation hosts a Tea Festival from 10 A.M. to 4 P.M. In addition to tea samples and owner-led tours and lectures, there are classic car shows, food and craft vendors, and entertainment. Best of all, it's all free and open to the public. For more information, call the plantation (see Secret Information).

78

The Wreck of the *Richard and Charlene*

Castaway Your Cares

The Shem Creek area of Mt. Pleasant, South Carolina, is lined with seafood restaurants angling for your business. You can't miss the signs for R. B.'s Seafood Restaurant and Raw Bar, Ronnie's, and the Shem Creek Bar and Grill—all of which are good, but not the best place in the area to get fresh fish and shellfish. No, that honor goes to a spot that doesn't even have a sign and is a bit difficult to find—The Wreck of the *Richard and Charlene*.

The Wreck, as everybody calls it, is run by reluctant restaurateurs Fred and Patricia Scott (Pat is actually the owner). It's not that they dislike serving people, it's just that they want to attract people who are really looking for "seafood like Charlestonians want it," as Fred, a lawyer who likes to hang around the restaurant and mix with the crowd more than his spouse does, puts it. "We're just *into* seafood."

The only-come-if-you're-sure-we're-what-you-want attitude may be the reason that The Wreck, which looks like an old ice-storage building, is unmarked except by two flags and a stylized wooden sculpture of a fish out front. To find it you have to drive to the end of Haddrell Street on the farthest point of Shem Creek from the main road. The restaurant is wedged between the Magwood and Wando seafood companies—if you're in doubt about whether you've found the place, look for the boat wreck off to the left side. Around back is the dining room, which overlooks the scenic waters of the creek and the fleet of fishing boats that bring in the fresh catches served nightly. The place is far from elegant and is oriented more to those who want to go out and have a casual good time rather than a formal meal.

The name of the restaurant tells the story of how it got started. The property on which it is located is owned by Patricia and had been leased to shrimpers as a place to bring in their catch. "Then hurricane Hugo came along in 1989," explains Fred, "and blew in a big Atlantic-style trawler named the *Richard and Charlene*, which smashed into the dock.

The only sign for the Wreck of the Richard and Charlene *is the stylized fish affixed out front.* (Courtesy of Fred Scott)

The shrimp business was over. We tried to sell the land or develop it, but couldn't." The property was zoned to allow a restaurant so they opened a breakfast place serving dishes like shrimp and grits and whiting and eggs, despite not knowing anything about the food business. After a while they added lunch to the menu, then dinner, eventually dropping service during the day to focus on evening meals. "Pat named the place The Wreck of the *Richard and Charlene*," Scott says. "It was woman's intuition."

The Wreck's menu is kept simple—just seafood. No steaks. No chicken. No barbecue. No portobello mushroom sandwiches. The fare includes such fresh catches as grouper, flounder, mahimahi, shark, shrimp, oysters, and scallops, primarily fried to perfection in light peanut oil (for the low cholesterol).

The Wreck doesn't advertise and instead has built a busy business through word-of-mouth. "The patrons are local and from other places—they find us," says Scott. "The restaurant is for people who like seafood and is not a great place for people who don't like seafood." It offers the *best* classic Carolina seafood on Shem Creek, or pretty much anywhere, may we add.

Around back, it's just a short walk from the dining room of the Wreck, as locals call it, to the docks of Shem Creek.

Secret Information

Location: On Shem Creek in Mt. Pleasant, South Carolina.
Address: 106 Haddrell Pt., Mt. Pleasant, SC 29464.
Phone: 843-884-0052.
Hours: 5:30 P.M. to 9 P.M. Sunday to Thursday; 5:30 P.M. to 10 P.M. Friday and Saturday.
Price: Dinners average $16.50.
Reservations: Not accepted.
Credit cards: None.
Details: The Wreck has no sign. It's the building between the Magwood and Wando seafood companies; look for two flags at the dead-end of Haddrell Street.

TOP SECRET

The Wreck of the *Richard and Charlene* makes especially great crab cakes. They are prepared by long-time restaurateur, Henry Shaffer. He owned the Charleston landmark Henry's restaurant, which opened just after the Depression and was famous for the crab cakes his mother would prepare using a recipe that had been handed down through the family for generations. She'd make them at home and then take them to her son's eatery for his customers to gobble up. When The Wreck opened, Shaffer, now retired and around age seventy, offered to make his mother's crab cakes to sell there. He comes in about twice a week to create them and they keep a supply refrigerated so you can order his family's special-recipe crab cakes any time.

Folly Fishing Pier

Cast About

79

Driving into Folly Beach you get the sense that if you're not at the end of the world, you'll probably be able to see it from here. The locals have dubbed Folly the "Edge of America," a title pretty much any coastal community could claim, but somehow here it does seem to fit perfectly.

Unlike Kiawah, Isle of Palms, and Charleston's other area gated- and green-resort communities, Folly is a true old-time beach vacation spot complete with hot dogs, sno-cones, pinball machines, and a narrow stretch of sand. There's a sea- and wind-battered charm to Folly that borders on seediness near the six-mile island's mid point and elevates into a California-beach-bungalow style on the eastern and western edges. In between sits an eclectic collection of tidy to teetering cottages that have managed to survive the fires and hurricanes that have ravaged the area over the years. But the whole part about seeing the end of the world (or the edge of America, depending on where you're coming from) comes from Folly Beach's crown jewel, the Edwin S. Taylor Fishing Pier. This wooden beauty, constructed in 1995 in the style of old-time beach pavilions, stretches 1,045 feet into the Atlantic Ocean, twenty-three feet above sea level. And if you drive all the way down to Folly Beach from Charleston, you owe it to yourself to pay the four bucks to park, walk out way past where you could ever hope to swim, and take in the scenery.

The Taylor or Folly Beach Pier is new, clean, well-maintained, and actually attractive. If you're familiar with fishing piers you'll understand why this description seems so amazing. Folly Beach Pier is the Cadillac of area fishing piers. That means no graffiti, no trash, and no chance a strong wave might knock the whole structure into the Atlantic (after being battered by enough hurricanes, some other piers look one storm shy of total destruction).

Although the pier's 7,500-square-foot, diamond-shaped platform and 1,400-square-foot, two-story, green-roofed shelter look more fancy

Cast away your cares and spend a few hours fishing from the pier at Folly Beach.

than functional, this is a serious fishing pier. There's a Gangplank Gift and Tackle Shop that sells supplies, bait, and fishing passes and features a running list of all the prize catches hauled in from the pier. They have fifty to sixty sets of gear, so they rarely run out, which is why reservations aren't required. The gift shop also sells apparel, beach towels, sunglasses, toys, and gifts and has a snack bar.

Folly's new pier and pavilion is a marvel. However, it will probably never match the storied history of its predecessor, Folly's Atlantic Boardwalk of the 1930s. Guy Lombardo, Tommy Dorsey, and other big band stars took to the stage at Folly, bringing with them hordes of fans. Today, young people still flock to the pier, but instead of dancing shoes, they carry wet suits and fiberglass boards. The area around the pier is a surfer favorite, and it's fun to watch the water walkers bob up and down on their boards like giant penguins waiting for the perfect wave.

If you are an angler, no one has to sell you on a well-equipped twenty-five-foot wide fishing pier that stretches over water where king mackerel roam. But the non-bait-and-hook crowd still might pass by the chance to take a stroll out to the end of the Folly Beach Pier. Big mistake. If nothing else, the pier is a place to bird- and people-watch both on the platform and off the sides. There are surfers, ocean kayakers, and gulls and pelicans to your left and right; fishermen and their families of every shape and size hang on the railings; and with a good pair of binoculars you can see up and down the whole length of Folly Beach, plus probably the end of the world, from pier's end. And if you did want to try your hand at fishing, there's no easier or cleaner place to try. The staff at the tackle shop will set you up with rod and bait, then all you have to do is plop your line over the side and wait. If you feel a pull on your line you'll get plenty of free advice as to what to do next because over here at the Edge of America the folks are friendly and they know how to fish.

Secret Information

Location: Folly Beach, South Carolina.
Address: 101 E. Arctic, Folly Beach, South Carolina 29439.
Phone: 843-588-FISH (3474).
Fax: 843-588-2406.
Web site: www.ccprc.com/pier.htm.
Hours: 6 A.M. to 11 P.M. April to October; 8 A.M. to 5 P.M. December to February; 7 A.M. to 7 P.M. March and November.
Price: FREE.
Credit cards: Discover, MasterCard, Visa.
Details: It costs $4 after 9 A.M.to use the parking garage, but if you purchase a fishing pass ($4 for county residents, $6 for others) or buy an entree at the Starfish Grill, the on-pier restaurant, you'll get credit for the parking charge. Fishing gear rents for $5 for a half-day and $8 for all day, plus a deposit of $25.

TOP SECRET

There's a great swimming beach at the southwestern end of the island called Folly Beach County Park. For $4 per car you can spend the day under the watchful eye of a lifeguard, use the restrooms, buy snacks, grill out, and even rent beach chairs and umbrellas. It's a fun family beach, and if you have kids in tow, head there early to get a parking space. If you're the kidless kind and are up for a bit more adventure and a lot less company, however, then there's also the favorite local sunning spot on the opposite end of the island. Going this route requires more guts and ingenuity, since there's no parking and a big NO TRESPASSING sign (which everyone ignores). Take a left at the center of town and follow the beach road northeast as far as you can. When you hit the NO TRESPASSING sign you're almost there. This is the path to the Old Coast Guard station. The long forgotten trail is lined with thick hedges of beach roses and leads to the north point of the island. When you get a great view of the Morris Island Lighthouse, which was once on dry land but is now surrounded by water, and, in the distance, Charleston Harbor, you're there. Locals, wildflower lovers, and birders love to sneak back here to sun, swim, and savor the scenery. Occasionally, however, the serenity is broken by the whir of chopper blades and the splash of sailors and Marines on training exercises. This is still government property, so a friendly invasion isn't out of the question. But don't worry, those guns aren't loaded with real ammunition. At least we hope not.

Restaurant Row

80

Station 22 on Sullivan's Island, South Carolina, has a small-town Saturday night sort of spirit. You can park along the street and stroll with the kids, checking out the various menus posted in the windows of the several restaurants within walking distance of the intersection of the island's two main streets—Ben Sawyer Boulevard and Middle Street. Everyone's laid-back and many are locals who walk or pedal over for dinner. On the sidewalk in front of some restaurants there's likely to be a yellow Labrador with a bowl of fresh water waiting patiently for his owner to finish dessert. It's just that kind of place.

As you cross the bridge from Mount Pleasant, stay to the left on SC Highway 703 toward the Isle of Palms. Rather than taking the turn toward the gated resort of Wild Dunes, keep going straight when you come to Sullivan's Island, and you'll discover the mini-restaurant row at Station 22. It's called that because it's built up around the old Station 22 trolley stop. In the island's early days, you see, a trolley used to cart passengers from Station 9 at the Charleston Harbor end of Sullivan's all the way to Station 32 at the Breach Inlet end, just west of Isle of Palms. Today, the cross streets on Sullivan's Island still bear the names of those station stops. Although houses on Sullivan's Island are pricey, it's been a summer retreat for Charlestonians since the 1800s and has a residential, real-folks-live-here feel compared to newer and more manicured area developments such as Wild Dunes or Kiawah Island.

The heart and soul of Station 22's eclectic array of eateries is Dunleavy's Pub. Bill Dunleavy and his sister Patty fashioned their family-friendly eatery after Dublin's best watering holes. In Ireland, Ma, Da, Grandma, and the kids all gather together in the pubs to eat, drink, laugh, and swap stories with friends and neighbors. That's Dunleavy's. When the air is warm, the windows and doors are flung open and the laughter and chatter spills into the street. And if there's no live music playing, there are always sports channels beaming on the three televi-

The lighthouse on Sullivan's Island towers over nearby attractions such as the restaurant row at Station 22 and historic Fort Moultrie.

sion sets. Whether you need to cool off with a pint of Guinness or are looking for a casual spot to bring the family for sandwiches and burgers, Dunleavy's (843-883-9646) is the place.

Across the street from the pub, lies one of Sullivan's newest spots to eat and one of our favorite finds, The Dog House Grille (843-883-5600), established in 1998. Located in a white clapboard cottage with an open-air front dining porch, it's a casual spot decorated with whimsical dog-fancier touches. There are dog bowls on the walls, which are trimmed in vibrant lime green, blue, and pink, and the menu features the Puppydog Corner for kids. The small bar with red chili lights strung above is more intimate than Dunleavy's, but there's a pool table in the back if you're looking for a little more action. The menu features grilled hot dogs and polish sausage dogs, of course, but most of the items are far more inventive—and don't taste a bit like dog food—like the Teriyaki Salmon Caesar salad served with grilled foccacia bread and the Thai Spring Rolls (an appetizer that makes a great light lunch or supper).

If it's fun rather than food you're after, check out Bert's Bar (843-883-3924) just up the block from Dunleavy's Pub. The building used to house the local pharmacy and soda fountain, but the only prescription being dispensed these days fits in a frosted mug. There's a cover charge for live blues and rock 'n' roll, and you can order burgers and lighter fare.

Next door, Station 22 (843-883-3355)—a restaurant that shares its

The beaches of Sullivan's Island have been a summer escape for generations of Charlestonians.

name with the area, so don't get the two confused—features a welcoming bar where locals gather to listen to tunes on the jukebox and the occasional blast of the train whistle, courtesy of the bartender. A model train chugs around the bar and old photos on the walls tell the story of days past on Sullivan's Island and the community's love affair with the rails. Station 22 is also a well-respected restaurant, featuring seafood, beef, and pasta in a "let's dress nice for dinner" sort of atmosphere.

A bit farther down Middle Street is Sullivan's Restaurant (843-883-3222) located in the former Moma's Tea Room (a local favorite), where you can fill up for the week on Monday nights at the all-you-can-eat calabash shrimp event. Sullivan's, the nearby Atlanticville Cafe (843-883-9452), and Sully's Restaurant (843-883-9777) all feature fresh seafood and are favorites with locals and out-of-towners alike who are looking for a little ocean breeze and neighborhood atmosphere with their dinner.

Secret Information

Location: Sullivan's Island, South Carolina.
Phone: See above for phone numbers of restaurants.
Hours: Call restaurants.
Season: Call restaurants.
Price: Varies.
Reservations: Call restaurants.
Credit cards: Call restaurants.

TOP SECRET

For one of the best views of Charleston and Fort Sumter drive out to Fort Moultrie located on the western end of Middle Street on Sullivan's Island. The fort, which is operated by the National Park Service, was strategically built at the mouth of Charleston Harbor and is named for its first commander, William Moultrie. From 1776 to 1947, it served Charleston residents well, defending the city first from the British and then from relentless Union attacks. Today, the restored compound is open to visitors (call 843-883-3123 for seasonal hours) and offers a glimpse of Charleston's rich military heritage (kids love exploring the tunnels). It also offers a panoramic view of its harbor. Bring along a pair of binoculars and climb up the observation post. On a clear day, you'll see windsurfers, private and military sailing vessels of all shapes and sizes, Fort Sumter, James Island, and the historic Charleston skyline. If you have some extra time and are into curiosities, also take a few minutes to visit the tiny Sullivan's Island public library on I'on Street, which is next to the local elementary school. It's the only library we've ever seen that's inside an old fort—it's tucked under the bastions of another part of the former Fort Moultrie, which actually consisted not just of the restored site mentioned above but of various embankments all along the edge of the island.

Linda Page's Thieves Market

Junque Shop

81

Linda Page says she started selling antiques while she was still in diapers. The forty-something owner of Linda Page's Thieves Market now runs the business started by her father in 1959 and says she took it over because, "This is not work. If I didn't do this, I'd have to get a real job."

The market is actually a big red barn that looks out of place among the mostly more modern businesses in upscale Mt. Pleasant, South Carolina. Inside, it's literally stuffed to the rafters with stuff. "We like to call it 'junque,'" says Page. "We have a real mix of items you would expect to find in an older person's house. A lot of it could be called kitsch, which is in right now in decorating. We're finally cool."

Prowl among the aisles and you'll find everything from old farm tools to posters for the *Andy Griffith Show*. There are chairs, tables, sofas, headboards, and other furniture that looks like it came straight from Beaver Cleaver's home. "We have a lot of great kitchen pieces like Hoosier baking cabinets," says Page. "They were made in Indiana and have a porcelain top to put hot pans on and flour bins and spice racks." Looking for an old bathtub, a snow sleigh, or a statue of Neptune? Head to Page's.

Page's business is named Thieves Market because, she says, "items are priced so cheap it's like the customers are stealing them." She admits that she likes what she does as much for the chance to meet and work with people as collecting cast-off possessions. She only buys complete estates, so she meets lots of folks who are grieving for a loved one and often forms close friendships with them as they go through tough times. Her business has even gotten her into the movies, in a way. She's been called upon to provide props for films made in the Charleston area, such as Mel Gibson's *The Patriot*. She enjoys visiting with people who walk into her unheated, un-air-conditioned barn just for the nostalgia of seeing something like an

You may find a steal at Linda Page's Thieves Market.

old Glenn Miller album. "This is a fun place to be," she says. "Cats, chickens, geese walk through. There's no telling what stray will be here tomorrow."

So what kind of antiques does Page herself collect? "I'm drawn to 1950s glassware, utilitarian stuff from suburban households" she reveals. "I collect keys from old motels, you know, the ones with the big plastic tags. And I collect 'mourning' pictures, photographs of people in caskets at funerals, a typically southern thing."

Page says she can ship anything you buy on vacation at the Thieves Market back home for you, so don't worry about whether that oak armoire will fit in the back of the minivan. And even if you don't buy anything, she says, "The interesting thing about travel is that you can always take home memories. Come here, or to another antique store, and give your children a hands-on history lesson. Kids come in here and look at a rotary telephone and say, 'What's that?' Exploring a store like ours is an interesting way to teach kids about the past."

Secret Information

Location: Mt. Pleasant, South Carolina.
Address: 1460 Ben Sawyer Boulevard, Mount Pleasant, SC 29464.
Phone: 843-884-9672.
Fax: 843-881-6749.
E-mail: thievesmkt@aol.com.
Hours: 9 A.M. to 6 P.M. Monday thru Saturday. Noon to 5 P.M. Sunday, April to Christmas.
Price: Varies widely.
Credit cards: American Express, Discover, MasterCard, Visa.

TOP SECRET

Linda Page, owner of Linda Page's Thieves Market, is a licensed and bonded auctioneer. For some fun, and maybe to pick up a bargain antique or two, stop by her business when she's having an auction, which happens about once a month. "We buy complete estates and a lot of times not everything is suitable for selling in the store, because it's better or different than our typical inventory, so we offer it at auction," Page explains. Treasures up for sale, which are usually available for inspection in a back building on Page's property well before the auction date, may include fine furniture, sterling silver, crystal, oriental rugs, and pretty much any other kind of valuable antique. Page went to school to learn the tongue-twisting art of bid calling and says she "practices a lot in the shower." She's often called upon to use her talent at local charity auctions. If you've never been to an auction before, it's fascinating to watch instantaneous supply-and-demand capitalism in action. For information about upcoming auctions, give Page a call at the Thieves Market (see Secret Information).

82

Why Kids Love the Beach

FYI

An Open Letter to Parents

Sometimes what's going on in your children's minds is the biggest secret of all for parents. We asked our oldest daughter, Katharine, an aspiring writer, to consult with her two younger sisters, Mary and Cassidy, to tell us—and you—what kids are really thinking when they're on a family vacation at a place like the Carolina coast. This may not reflect the hormone-addled-older-teen or can't-sit-still-boy perspective, but here's her take, in her own words, of what kids like her really want out of time at the beach with Mom and Dad.

Dear Parents,

No one has to tell you that kids' lives are extremely busy. Between homework, sports, and school, we really don't get a chance to sit down and relax. And when we do get a little free time, we usually spend it watching television, playing on the computer, or talking to friends. Most weeks, the only time we get a chance to talk to our parents is at the dinner table, where everyone is worn out from a long and exhausting day. The generic question, "How was school?" doesn't really cover all the issues in a kid's life. So most of the time, you parents and we kids live in totally different worlds, having no idea of what's going on in each other's busy lives. We know you love us. We know you're working so hard to give us a wonderful life. But what we'd like to know is more about you, and we'd like you to know more about us.

That's what makes a week at the beach so special for us, because we have you—our parents—to ourselves for seven whole days. Spending time with parents may seem dorky when we're home with our friends, but on vacation it's okay because we're in a different place, away from our friends, and we can really be ourselves. Unfortunately, when you parents think of what kids must want on vacation it usually involves spending the day on a crowded beach, playing miniature golf, or dragging us to some other tourist attraction. Don't get me wrong, these are all fun things to do (especially water parks and go-carts), but some-

times everyone (kids and parents included) needs a chance to relax and relate. So here's the secret: My sisters and I—I'm thirteen and they're eleven and nine—think the absolute best part of our annual beach vacation is the daily early morning walk on the beach. Take my real-kid word for it, this is the perfect chance to really get to know your children without being rushed for time.

It's so cool being up "before the chickens," as my Nana would say (seeing her for a week is another great part of going to the beach) and watching the sunrise. But it's especially great to walk and talk with your parents. There are very few people on the beach early in the morning, so you'll probably have the place mostly to yourselves. This is a special time where you can find out more about your babies: about their fears, their friends, and their hopes for the future. And they can find out more about you. I love hearing stories about when my mom was a kid, like her misconception about orange juice coming from horses—it seemed logical because she knew that milk came from cows, and juice and milk came in cartons, and horses also live on farms.

Another great thing about an early morning stroll on the beach is that it's free, and you and your kids can learn more about nature and the environment. During the day, the beach is so crowded with umbrellas and towels that you can hardly see the sand. But in the quiet of the early morning, you can see far out into the ocean and hear the cries of many birds. When my family walks along the beach, we often see dolphins leaping out of the ocean, their slim gray bodies glistening with salt water. In the distance, you can sometimes see small islands or even cities. At my favorite little beach where we usually walk, South Beach in Sea Pines Plantation on Hilton Head Island, South Carolina, we can see Savannah's tall buildings rising out of the mist. There are also always shells to be found along the shore (the best shell hunting is always in the morning), but don't forget that some are homes to creatures. I remember when my younger sister, Cassidy, found a huge shell on the beach and didn't understand why she couldn't bring it home. Mom tried to explain that there was something living in there, but Cassidy didn't fully grasp what she was saying until the creature popped its head out of the shell. Yikes!

What I'm trying to say is that even though we love movies, restaurants, and games, we kids don't have to be entertained all the time. We would really like to get to know you, and we hope you'll enjoy a chance to get to know us, too. Please leave the laptop, the beeper, the cell phone, and the Palm Pilot at home, and take advantage of this golden opportunity to really spend time with us and learn about our hopes, fears, and how cool we really think you are.

Secret Information

If your kids have secret insights about what makes a great beach vacation they would like to share with other parents in a future edition of *100 Secrets of the Carolina Coast*, e-mail them to Katharine—our kids' correspondent for the book—at *Katharine@100Secrets.com.*

TOP SECRET

This is Katharine Duckett with some more secret advice to you parents: You know books, television shows, and movies like The Brady Bunch *often show kids walking to friends houses or riding their bike to the store. Unfortunately, our world today really isn't safe enough for most of us kids to do that anymore. But if you're spending your vacation in a small island community like the place we go almost every year, South Beach on Hilton Head Island, you can give your kids a little more room to roam. After our morning walk on the beach, for instance, my sisters and I usually go by ourselves to buy a paper and some candy from a nearby general store at South Beach. Over the week, the lady who works there gets to know us, and we have time to stop to look at the boats and the fishermen. Then we walk back to our condo and sing and talk along the way. We don't have to cross any roads, and because it's so early, we usually don't run into many cars or people. Of course we always stay together, we never talk to strangers, and our Mom is usually on the porch watching us walk home, so we're really not alone or doing anything dangerous. But that little bit of independence and freedom feels great, and we look forward to it all year. I think that when you're looking for a place to stay at the beach, for your kids' sake, try to find somewhere where they can safely walk to a store, ride a bike, and experience (at least a little bit) what it was like to be a kid when the world was a safer, friendlier place.*

Poogan's Porch

Classic Cookin'

83

According to local lore, Poogan's Porch in Charleston, South Carolina, was built as a family home in 1891. Eventually, the area developed from residential to commercial, and the previous owners moved away, but they forgot one important thing: their dog Poogan. Now, the story doesn't say whether they were just forgetful or downright mean, but it does mention that in 1976, when the restaurant opened, Poogan was there to greet customers. Being a "good ol' down South porch dog," Poogan was embraced by the restaurant's owners as a mascot, and he remained the porch greeter until his death in 1979. Though he's gone to that great kennel in the sky, (and this might sound cliche, but it's true), his memory is very much alive at his home.

It's not just a sentimental story that makes Poogan's Porch a find. To our tastes, it's one of the best examples of old-style southern food and atmosphere to be found anywhere. While Charleston is filled with world-class eateries, we think Poogan's has just the right mix of comfortable charm, friendly service, and delicious down-home food to make it the best place in the city to get a taste of classic country cuisine.

When you walk through the door you're met with the smell of spicy cooking and aged wood. Architectural aficionados will be struck by the building's nineteenth-century heart-pine floors, dual staircases, ceiling fans, fireplaces, and ornate woodwork. The menu is equally satisfying. Specializing in Creole foods such as jambalaya, gumbo, she-crab soup, seafood, quail, alligator, and other "very southern" things, Poogan's Porch has been featured in magazines such as *Gourmet, Bon Appetit,* and *Cuisine.* Standout dishes include the Carolina crab cake appetizer, the she-crab soup, the apple-glazed pork tenderloin, and the incredibly fluffy biscuits. For dessert, try the decadent peanut butter pie.

Poogan the pooch has passed on, but the restaurant to which he lent his name continues to serve some of the best classic southern food in Charleston. (COURTESY OF POOGAN'S PORCH RESTAURANT)

Secret Information

Location: Charleston, South Carolina.
Address: 72 Queen Street Charleston, SC 29401.
Phone: 843-577-2337.
Fax: 843-577-2493.
Web site: www2.discovernet.com/rest/poogans/index.html.
Hours: 11:30 A.M. to 2:30 P.M. for lunch; 5:30 P.M. to 10 P.M. for dinner; seasonal Sunday brunch 10:30 A.M. to 2:30 P.M.
Price: Lunch about $8, dinner about $16 to $17.
Reservations: Recommended.
Credit cards: American Express, MasterCard, Visa.

TOP SECRET

Besides classic southern food, Poogan's Porch is noted as the home of a ghost. Though we've never seen her ourselves, it's said that the apparition of the late Zoe St. Amand sometimes shows up to harass staff and customers with her paranormal pranks. In fact, the entire city of Charleston is famous for its spirits. To see several of its ghostly haunts and hear spooky stories, including more about the Poogan's Porch poltergeist, sign up for the Ghosts of Charleston tour. TourCharleston offers the guided walking trip that starts on the waterfront three times every evening at a cost of $14 for adults and $8 for kids. To make reservations or for more information, call 800-854-1670 or 843-723-1670 or visit their Web site at www.tourcharleston.com.

Spoleto Sibling

84

The internationally acclaimed Spoleto Festival USA attracts hordes of performing arts aficionados and people who love a party to the Charleston, South Carolina, historic waterfront district each spring. During the seventeen-day-long feast for the senses (which usually launches on Memorial Day weekend), more than a hundred performances by gifted dancers, musicians, actors, and singers are offered. There's ballet and chamber music, opera and orchestra, theater and dance, and more. Some of the most interesting and offbeat experiences occurring during Spoleto don't require a festival ticket (which range from $10 to $75 per event) but are part of a lesser-known, but just as fun and fabulous, local event called the Piccolo Spoleto Festival.

The Spoleto Festival USA was a 1977 spin-off of the original Spoleto Festival held in Italy, which was created in the late '50s by Pulitzer Prize winning composer Gian Carlo Menotti because he wanted to establish a European venue for the best young American artists. The Charleston version inspired Ellen Dressler Moryl, director of Charleston's Office of Cultural Affairs, to create a sibling celebration in 1985: Piccolo Spoleto ("piccolo" is Italian for smaller than ordinary size). The idea was to complement the internationally-focused and sometimes pricey main festival with one that featured work by regional and local artists. Each year, more than four hundred Piccolo Spoleto events are scheduled throughout the city, most free or a lot cheaper than those at the more formal, big-brother festival.

The Piccolo Spoleto schedule is published in May (usually a few weeks before the festival), but most locals take a pretty free-form approach to planning their Piccolo routine. Since the event is concentrated in the compact historic waterfront district and performances take place morning, noon, and night, the strolling and sampling approach allows you to savor all of the sights and sounds without racing around to make specific performance times. Some of the most amazing performers—like Atlanta's Seed and Feed Marching Abominable (a 120-member guerrilla band that parades around in pajamas by day and clown costumes after dark)—make whatever street they happen to be on their stage. Impromptu parades, lightning-fingered fiddlers and magicians, and amazing one-man bands provide an endless array of free arts experiences on every street corner. Using this buffet arts-as-you-go approach, you'll also probably stumble upon a Spoleto Festival USA event or two you'd like to attend. Although some performances are sold out weeks in advance, plenty of them have tickets (especially singles) available at the last minute, so if you're interested just ask at the box office.

Two of the favorite (and free) Piccolo Spoleto events are the Children's Festival and the Sand Sculpting Competition. The children's affair (usually held on the opening Saturday of Piccolo Spoleto at Marion Square) features clowns, comedy, magic, music, and storytelling by professional entertainers and talented children from across South Carolina. There are plenty of hands-on activities for kids of all ages, including an arts and crafts tent, a joke and poem wall, and a participant-painted mural. The sand sculpting event is usually held the same day across the bridge at Isle of Palms County Park. Individuals or teams of two to four persons pay $5 apiece to compete, but spectators can come see the phenomenal sand art for free (parking is $4 per car). If your kids love to build sand castles and cities (or enjoy burying your torso while you snooze on the beach), you might want to funnel all that creativity into the Children's Team category for sand sculptors age fourteen and younger.

The Piccolo Spoleto events requiring tickets celebrate performing, literary, and visual arts, so there's bound to be something you'd enjoy. Recent line-ups have included the Charleston Symphony Orchestra, Jazz and Blues Harbor Cruises, Cabaret at the Midtown Theatre, and the inspirational Festival of Churches, featuring local and regional church choirs, choral groups, and music ensembles performing in some of Charleston's beautiful and historic churches and synagogues.

Although the Piccolo Spoleto and Spoleto USA performances wrap up each evening by 11 P.M. or so, the street performances and partying lasts well into the wee hours. Jazz clubs, bars, and restaurants stay open to accommodate revelers and festival performers (easily identified by those bulky instrument cases they lug around) and some of the best street acts can be seen after-hours at the city's open-air marketplace.

Secret Information

Location: In the historic waterfront district of Charleston, South Carolina.
Address: Piccolo Spoleto, Charleston Office of Cultural Affairs, 133 Church Street, Charleston, SC 29401.
Phone: 843-724-7305.
Web site: www.charleston.net/piccolo.
Dates: Piccolo Spoleto is held concurrently with the Spoleto Festival USA for 17 days, usually starting Memorial Day weekend.
Price: Most events are FREE. The ones that cost range from $10 to $15.
Reservations: Order Piccolo Spoleto tickets in advance through SCAT (South Carolina Automated Ticketing) at 843-577-4500; mailing in the order form from the Web site; or by visiting the box office at Gaillard Municipal Auditorium, 77 Calhoun St., Charleston, SC 29401.
Credit cards: Discover, MasterCard, Visa.
Details: Call or write the Charleston Office of Cultural Affairs (address above) for a Piccolo Spoleto brochure. For information on the Spoleto Festival USA call 843-723-0402; write to Spoleto Festival USA, P.O. Box 704, Charleston, SC 29402; or visit their Web site at www.spoletousa.org.

TOP SECRET

One of the best events of Piccolo Spoleto's bigger sibling, Spoleto Festival USA, is also the last. The Festival Finale, held on the lush grounds of Middleton Place (Secret 66), features an exuberant concert by the acclaimed Spoleto Festival Orchestra followed by a spectacular fireworks show. Gates open at 2:30 P.M. for the 8:30 P.M. event, and locals arrive early with blankets (a limited number of lawn chairs are permitted) to stake out a spot. Plan to arrive early and pack a supper picnic. Be sure to include plenty of extra food to share with the local media celebrities who judge the Finale Picnic Contest. Registration for the contest takes place between 3 P.M. and 4 P.M. and the judging is from 5 P.M. to 6 P.M. Participation in the picnic competition is free, but tickets to the Festival Finale are $25 per person. For more information, contact the Spoleto Festival USA organizers (see "Details" in Secret Information.)

85

Old Post Office Restaurant

Go Postal

The Old Post Office on Edisto Island, South Carolina, isn't old and the building it's located in never was a post office. When chef and co-proprietor Philip Bardin and his partner, operator, and main proprietor David Gressette, bought the site to open a restaurant in the late '80s, there was a dilapidated, termite-infested post office there that had also doubled as Bailey's General Store. The building had been a gathering place for locals long ago and seemed a natural spot to create a different sort of meeting place for the residents and tourists of today. Before tearing the old structure down, the pair salvaged all the old post office boxes and related postal memorabilia from the place. Then, they built their new Old Post Office in the same architectural style of the original building. The exterior features a bright red trim and an authentic tin roof, and the interior is decorated with the treasures from the original old post office, including the window where stamps were sold.

Bardin is the son of an abstract oil painter and a Radio City Music Hall ballerina who were both from small towns in South Carolina. He also comes from a "long line of restaurant people," he says. "My family had the small Bardin Hotel and dining room that was passed down to me. It was in Elloree, South Carolina, a tiny dot of a town, and a lot of the foods and recipes I use came from there. Some of our recipes are over a hundred years old." Gressette was "practically raised on Edisto" at his grandfather's pavilion and has a close relationship with local sport fisherman and farmers from whom he buys the restaurant's food. Gressette says, "The seafood and vegetable places know to call me when they get something especially nice."

The Old Post Office isn't much of a kids' place, though well-behaved children won't be turned away. It caters more to adults who want to sample true Lowcountry food made from the freshest local ingredients. In addition to the traditional favorites like deviled crab cakes, shrimp and grits, and fried quail with Aunt Min's duck-stock gravy, the restaurant also features updated southern dishes. Recently Bardin hired Sous Chef Bill Twaler, a member of the United States Culinary Olympic Team, who specializes in the modern cuisine. "Bill is going to be famous and won't be around for long," says Bardin, "so visit us now to taste his cooking. He does modern dishes, and we split it into the best of both worlds from the traditional items that I cook to the updated creations he comes up with. Bill really lets his imagination run wild."

Each night Bardin inserts a special menu inside the regular one that features a dozen dishes—half created by Bardin and half created by Twaler. Although each dish is unique—for instance, the pork tenderloin medallions are marinated in mustard, herbs, honey, and served with a Jack Daniels whiskey cream sauce; or the chicken is coated with pecans and topped with blueberry sauce—"there's not a plate that goes out of the kitchen that doesn't have grits on it," says Bardin. In fact the grits are so popular that the restaurant now sells the finely milled, whole-grain grits in two-pound bags under the Old Post Office label. Pick up a bag or two for $5.30 each including tax and try the recipe on the bag when you get home.

Years ago, the Edisto Island postmaster used to leave the post office on horseback (he later used a Model A, says Bardin) to deliver mail on the island. Although the restaurant's link to the past, architecture, and memorabilia are what catch visitors' attention at first, it's the cuisine that captivates the senses and transforms accidental tourists into devoted regulars. "The food is the most important thing," adds Bardin. "The bread is fresh-baked every day, and all the desserts are made fresh on the premises. You'll have to come taste it all for yourself."

Secret Information

Location: On Edisto Island, South Carolina.
Address: 1442 Highway 174, Edisto Island, SC 29438.
Phone: 843-869-2339.
Fax: 843-869-2372.
Hours: 6 P.M. to 10 P.M. Monday to Saturday May to August; 6 P.M. to 10 P.M. Tuesday to Saturday September to April. Lounge opens at 5 P.M.
Season: Closed the first two weeks in January.
Price: $17 to $20.
Reservations: Required.
Credit cards: MasterCard, Visa.

The Old Post Office Restaurant now occupies the site where Edisto Island residents had collected their mail since the 1880s. (COURTESY OF THE OLD POST OFFICE RESTAURANT)

TOP SECRET

For a fun and filling breakfast or lunch head across the salt marsh from Edisto Island where the Old Post Office Restaurant is located to the small oceanfront community of Edisto Beach. Just before you hit the sea on Jungle Road you'll see a whimsical sign featuring a cow in snorkeling gear. That's the logo of a funky little take-out or eat-in spot called The Sea Cow Eatery (843-869-3222) and consuming one meal there makes you an official "Moo Maniac." The neon pink paper menu includes Moo La La French Toast, The Sea Cow (garlic grilled shrimp on a bed of spinach with ranch dressing), and our personal favorite to order (it makes our kids giggle), The Stuffed Pig (marinated pork tenderloin strips sautéed with carrots and onions on crispy pita bread with sour cream cucumber sauce). Breakfast runs from 7 A.M. until 11 A.M. Tuesday through Saturday, and lunch is served from 11 A.M. until 3 P.M. The Cow serves only breakfast on Sunday, from 8 A.M. until noon, and is closed on Monday.

Hunting Island State Park

Good Time Hunting

86

Hunting Island is slowly washing away. Foot by foot the beach is eroding and the water is encroaching on the trees along the shore. There's talk of the government undertaking the challenging task of stopping the receding sand, but for now the experts have decided to let nature take its course. The result is something like a scene out of *Jurassic Park.* Along the beach lie toppled palm trees, looking as though a T-Rex knocked them over on his way to terrorizing some scientists who toyed with Mother Nature. Especially when the beach is deserted during the winter, it's an eerie, but extremely cool, sight.

Hunting Island State Park is safe for the moment, though, and offers one of the most diverse mixes of recreation and attractions we've ever seen. The most prominent feature of the park is the Hunting Island Lighthouse, which was built in 1875 and is the only historic lighthouse on the South Carolina coast that is open to the public. For 50¢ you can climb its 167 steps and see a panorama of woods, ocean, and beaches. Surrounding the tower are outbuildings from the original lighthouse keepers' complex, which feature exhibits on lighthouse history and what it was like for keepers to man a lonely sentinel keeping sailors safe from running ashore. Today the lighthouse is about 1.25 miles away from its original location. Unlike the stone Cape Hatteras Lighthouse, which took a massive effort to transport away from the approaching sea (Secret 7), its Hunting Island cousin is constructed of cast iron plates intended to be easily taken apart and moved when erosion threatens; it was shifted to its current home in 1889.

The balance of the five-thousand-acre park is devoted to camping and outdoor recreation. For those who want to stay overnight, there are two hundred campsites, most with water and electric hookups. About forty can be reserved in advance, but the bulk are first-come, first-serve. If you plan ahead—way ahead—you may be able to snag what park ranger Mike Walker calls "the most popular cabins in the state." The

The uprooted palms and windswept dunes give the beach at Hunting Island State Park the look and feel of a deserted tropical island.

park has fifteen two- or three-bedroom cabins just steps from the beach, each with heating, air conditioning, linens, television, microwave, and kitchen supplies. The park takes reservations for the cabins, which sleep six to ten people, only one calendar year at a time, and phones start ringing the first workday after New Year's.

Recreation options include sunning and swimming along the three-mile long beach; fishing for trout, bass, and drum off the pier or the shore of the shady lagoon; and exploring nature trails, including a three-tenths of a mile boardwalk into a salt marsh that's home to shrimp, fiddler crabs, and other creatures. The park is also one of the few we know that allows mountain biking—check at the visitor's center for information about what trails are open to cyclers. Ask, as well, about special programs the park rangers put on, such as kayaking trips (Secret 89), crabbing clinics, and barrier island backpacking.

The panoramic views are spectacular from atop the Hunting Island Lighthouse, but hold on to your hat and sunglasses—the island's stiff winds make a trek to the observation deck a true adventure.

Secret Information

Location: On U.S. Highway 21 east of Beaufort, South Carolina.
Address: 2555 Sea Island Parkway, Hunting Island, SC 29920.
Phone: 843-838-2011.
Fax: 843-838-4263.
E-mail: hunting_island_sp@prt.state.sc.us.
Web site: www.huntingisland.com.
Hours: 6 A.M. to 9 P.M. April to September; 6 A.M. to 6 P.M. October to March.
Price: Admission is $2 per person (South Carolina residents, senior citizens, disabled persons, and kids fifteen and under are free). It's 50¢ to climb the lighthouse. The cabins rent for $66 to $105 a night.
Reservations: Make reservations well in advance for cabins; some campsites can be reserved and some are first-come, first-serve.
Credit cards: Discover, MasterCard, Visa.
Details: There is a gift shop in the park store at the campground open all year and one located next to the lighthouse that is open seasonally.

TOP SECRET

Hunting Island State Park is one of the best places to see loggerhead turtles hatch. Because of the severe beach erosion at the park, the eggs that mama turtles lay in the sand are carefully moved to a higher-ground hatchery. This creates a safe, controlled environment in which the young hatchlings can slowly fight their way out of their first homes, and park visitors can watch without endangering them. The experience is enhanced by educational programs and talks on the endangered loggerheads by park rangers. There are late-night tours with a guide, and occasionally, you can see a mother turtle coming ashore. Loggerheads lay their eggs in the summer and the young hatch from mid- July through early September, with August being the best month for viewing. For specific information about when and where to catch the tiny terrapins making their entrance into the world, contact the park at 843-838-2011.

Daufuskie Island Club and Resort

Fantasy Island

87

Staying on an island is a bit like being snowbound by a blizzard. As long as you have food, supplies, and power, you can hunker down and enjoy your family and your surroundings without worrying about meeting a deadline or making an appointment. You're stuck. You're not expected to do anything productive. You can read and nap and eat lots of junk food until the snow lets up, the roads are cleared, and real life resumes. It's wonderful.

Unfortunately, there are few places left on the Carolina coast where you can experience that delightful sense of being cut off from the world and all of its distractions. Most of the islands hugging the coast are connected to the mainland by bridges, providing easy access for tourists, developers, and sightseers. There are some islands left that are unconnected and inaccessible, but many of them are private or are preserves with either no overnight facilities or only primitive campsites. Finding a secluded island hideaway to call your own—at least for a week—takes a little searching and some serious cash. If you're willing and able, you can have that fantasy island you've always dreamed about. Just cross Calibogue Sound from Hilton Head, South Carolina, and stay at the Daufuskie Island Club and Resort on unspoiled Daufuskie Island.

According to locals, Daufuskie Island today looks pretty much like its manicured-greens-and-gated-community neighbor, Hilton Head, did fifty years ago. That was before Charles Fraser started developing the place, and before the Army Corps of Engineers built the bridge that would make Hilton Head Island easily accessible. True, Daufuskie now features a few high-end golf resorts and its own exclusive neighborhood, Haig Point, but roughly half of the island remains undeveloped wilderness. The preserved oceanfront beaches are lined with driftwood (you're not allowed to take any with you) and shaded by vine-twisted oaks that are hundreds of years old. Deer freely roam through the thick pine forests. Most of the roads are unpaved (which makes things pretty dusty when golf carts and service trucks pass by), and the tangled undergrowth is a haven for snakes, alligators, and other creatures. Up until the 1980s there was also still quite a presence on the island of Gullah descendants of freed slaves who farmed and lumbered the coastal areas of South Carolina, Georgia, and northeastern Florida. The name of the island reportedly comes from the locals identifying land as "the first key" in Gullah dialect, but we've also heard it's a variation of a Native American word. Today, most of the natives have moved to nearby St. Helena Island, but some of their historic buildings, including the 140-year-old Union Baptist Church and the one-room schoolhouse, where author Pat Conroy taught for a year (Secret 61), remain.

The place to bed down on this lush, Lowcountry paradise is the up-up-upscale Daufuskie Island Club and Resort. The resort's rambling, two-story, antebellum-styled oceanfront inn was built back in the 1980s when developers turned the former Melrose Plantation into a golf resort. The fifty oversized and ocean-view rooms, each featuring a sitting room, large dressing area, and elegant furnishings, were designed to house resort members who had paid $35,000 to $50,000 in initiation fees to be able to golf on the secluded island. When the resort (actually the present property includes two former resorts) was sold to Club Resorts, owners of Pinehurst and the Homestead, and renamed Daufuskie Island Club in 1996, the members only access was lifted. Today, members still are ferried out to the island where they are pampered and treated to every luxury imaginable—alongside those who didn't have to pay a Mercedes-priced tab for the same boat ride and room.

The inn, which sits at the end of a grand plantation avenue lined with Spanish moss-draped live oaks, is hugged by wide plantation porches, perfect for dolphin watching or daydreaming. There are also 35 two-bedroom and 2 four-bedroom cottages (most of which were completely renovated recently—the completion date for all renovations is spring 2001) with either ocean or salt marsh views. There are no Piggly Wiggly or other supermarkets on the island (a path over the lagoon leads to a small general store), but you won't go hungry. Breakfast and dinner add-ons to the room rate are available for $155 per person, so you can choose your meal based on your appetite rather than your wallet. The dining options at the resort range from a sandwich shop to a jacket-required four-course dinner at the elegant Stoddard Room, located in the main inn. There's also a comfortable sportsman's lodge at

Originally the vacation property that became the Daufuskie Island Club & Resort was accessible only to members paying up to $50,000 to join, but it has recently been opened to anyone seeking an island hideaway. (COURTESY OF PRINGLE, DIXON, PRINGLE ADVERSTISING)

the Equestrian Center where you can play pool, darts, or watch a ball game on the big screen television, and Jack's Place, located in the resort's clubhouse serves lunch and a casual dinner.

Daufuskie Island Club and Resort is definitely a fantasy island for any golfer. The championship Melrose Course was designed by Jack Nicklaus and the other championship course, Bloody Point, was laid out by Jay Morrish and Tom Weiskopf (major improvements were completed on both courses in 1999). But even if your golf game is restricted to carpeted courses featuring spinning windmills and big plastic animals, there's still plenty to do at the resort. Most of the options are focused on the great outdoors (the room televisions are intentionally tiny to encourage guests to explore the surrounding forest, marshes, and beach) and include tennis, bicycling, croquet, lawn bowling, volleyball, fishing, crabbing, horseback riding, swimming, and a year-round outdoor-theme program for kids ages four to twelve called Camp Calibogue. But remember, perhaps the best part about being on an island is that no one expects you to do anything. And at Daufuskie Island Club and Resort, you can do it in style.

Secret Information

Location: Off the coast of Hilton Head Island.
Address: P.O. Box 23285, Hilton Head, SC 29925.
Phone: 800-648-6778 or 843-842-2000.
Fax: 843-686-3755.
Web site: www.daufuskieclub.com.
Rates: $120 to $195 depending on the season.
Reservations: Required.
Credit cards: American Express, Diners Club, Discover, MasterCard, and Visa.

TOP SECRET

If you just want to visit Daufuskie Island for the day rather than stay at the Daufuskie Island Club and Resort, there are plenty of private charter boats that will take you there from marinas in Hilton Head, or you can dock your own vessel at the public landing on the southwest side of the island. Unless you're prepared to bike or walk once you land, though, the best way to both get to Daufuskie and tour the island is to sign on with Adventure Cruises, which leaves out of Shelter Cove Harbour on Hilton Head. Owner Mark Maurer has been taking visitors on the one hour-fifteen minute boat ride out to Daufuskie since 1979. His narrated tours ($17 for adults and $8 for kids three to twelve), which include round-trip transportation on the sixty-five-foot double-deck boat *Adventurer*, can be combined with an informative bus tour of the island ($10) operated by local islanders who share their wealth of knowledge of Daufuskie history. During the summer, the cruise departs every day except Sunday at 12:15 P.M. and returns at 4:45 P.M. Maurer shuts down his business between December and mid-February, and cruises are limited during the rest of the off-season. For more information, call Adventure Cruises at 843-785-4558.

88

Going to Carolina in Your Mind

When we think of the Lowcountry, the image of Spanish moss always comes to mind. A pale bluish-green with small soft spikes almost without weight, it drifts on the wind and drapes wherever it falls on what seems like every oak and other kind of tree in coastal South Carolina. Neither Spanish nor moss—it only grows in the tropics and is part of the same family of plants as the pineapple—it seems to us the perfect symbol of the take-life-as-it-comes feel of the area. It's hard to get worked up about much of anything when you're on the beach gazing out at the endless ocean or driving along roads so overarched by old oaks that they feel like tunnels. Every time we go there, we're snapped back into the realization that the secret to staying sane in today's world is remembering not to sweat the small stuff—the essence of the Lowcountry lifestyle.

The Lowcountry refers to the coastal plain of the Palmetto State, in contrast to the Upcountry of the Piedmont and above. If you've never been there before, it may give you a strong sense of deja vu once you finally visit—you've seen it before in dozens of movies shot in the area, including *The Big Chill*, *Prince of Tides*, *Glory*, *The Great Santini*, and *Forrest Gump*. It's probably a film director favorite because of the sunlight, which ranges from a dewy golden glow in the early hours of the morning to a sharp orange that melds slowly into a soft coral as the sun sets.

The Lowcountry includes Charleston, but for the purposes of this secret we're using it to refer to the area—and attitude—stretching from the Georgia border north to the Edisto River. (For the lay of the land around Charleston, see Secret 68). While there are pockets of rushed activity and upscale development, most of the countryside consists of rural backroads lined with simple homes in which people of modest means live life much as their parents did. You don't get the impression that they care much that Intel lost eight points in the market that day or that Iraq is acting up again. Instead, there's fishing to be done, pick-up trucks to repair, and supper to cook.

The major vacation areas of the Lowcountry are a study in contrasts. On the one hand, there is the newer resort Mecca of Hilton Head Island, which only started to be developed after it was connected by a bridge to the mainland in the '50s. Shaped like a huge foot—parts of the island are sometimes referred to as the heel, arch, and toe—it owes its billboard-free, manicured atmosphere to Charles Fraser, who created the gated and regulated Sea Pines Plantation on the island's tip, a site that includes the red-and-white lighthouse that's become the symbol of the island. The restricted-access, "plantation" model has spread across the island in the form of about a dozen plantations and throughout the rest of the Carolina coast. We admit we were a bit intimidated the first time we drove up to a guard shack to get into a plantation, but we've gotten used to nodding at the guy in the Smoky Bear hat as he checks out our pass and waves us through the gate. Perhaps because it's so new, Hilton Head often feels like a suburb of the Northeast or Midwest (you're likely to see as many license plates from Michigan or Ohio there as from South Carolina). Maybe that's one of the reasons it so appeals to outsiders, because since no one is from there—except for a small local black population that's been largely shut out of the island's prosperity—everyone who visits feels like it's his or her own special place.

On the other hand, the Beaufort area of the Lowcountry has more true southern tradition and pace. The waterfront area running along Bay Street has a small-town feel with restaurants, antique shops, art galleries, and historic homes all within walking distance of one another. Surrounding the town is a maze of waterways and bridges that link lesser-known vacation havens like St. Helena Island, Hunting Island (Secret 86), and Fripp Island. Beaufort is also the center of Gullah or Geechee culture (Secret 99), which gives parts of it an almost foreign air. Overall, the Beaufort area is among the coziest communities we've encountered along the coast and is relatively undiscovered by travelers when compared to Hilton Head, Charleston, and Myrtle Beach.

As you travel between Beaufort and Charleston on U.S. Highway 17 another contrast occurs. The area is primarily wild and dominated by the confluence of the three rivers that meet to form the ACE Basin (Secret 89). This gives Edisto Island and Edisto Beach, which lie at the end of SC Highway 174 along the way, the feeling of being cut off from everything else. Unlike most of the other major beach communities in the state, Edisto takes a relatively long time to reach from a major thoroughfare. That means that the island hasn't been scarred by major development and is still the classic, family-friendly beach community at which you rent a house, cook your own meals, let the kids run around, and don't get into the car for a week. It's one of our favorite spots to really retreat to the beach.

To us, the entire Lowcountry is not just a place, but a sensibility. It's not only Spanish moss, but the Zen of seeing flocks of egrets soaring through the sky, alligators sunning themselves on the banks of canals, and miles and miles of unbroken tall-grass marsh. It's sand as far as the eye can see and warm ocean water that has none of the chill that you'll find further north. When life gets too stressful, if there's no way we can take a break to get our bodies there, you can be sure that we are, to paraphrase James Taylor, goin' to the Carolina Lowcountry in our minds.

Secret Information

For more information about the Lowcountry, contact these organizations:

- Hilton Head Island Chamber of Commerce Visitor and Convention Bureau, P.O. Box 5647, Hilton Head Island, SC 29938; 843.785.3673; info@hiltonheadisland.org; www.hiltonheadisland.org.
- Greater Beaufort Chamber of Commerce, P.O. Box 910 Beaufort, SC 29901-0910; 843-524-3163; comments@beaufortonline.com; www.beaufortonline.com.
- Edisto Chamber of Commerce, P.O. Box 206, Edisto Beach, South Carolina 29438; 843-869-3867; eichamber@aol.com; www.edistochamber.com.

TOP SECRET

If you haven't been to Hilton Head Island in the Lowcountry for awhile, you may not know about the Cross Island Connector, which was completed just a couple of years ago. The toll road ($1 per car), which is not on many maps or included in many guidebooks still in circulation, cuts about thirty minutes off the old time it took to travel through the congestion of U.S. Highway 278 to the Sea Pines Circle area at the end of the island. It makes getting to and from the mainland a breeze and relieves the island of what was becoming a traffic nightmare, turning off more and more regular visitors.

89

The Kayak Farm

Paddling Last Great Places

"We work hard, but our work is playful by nature—and fun," says Will Gibbons, who is the co-owner and operator of The Kayak Farm on St. Helena's Island, South Carolina, with his brother Eric, who has a degree in environmental education and is an American Canoe Association instructor. From a five-acre former tomato farm, the siblings offer trips that take travelers into wilderness areas such as the nearby ACE Basin. A maze of tidal waterways and islands formed by the merging of the Ashepoo, Combahee, and Edisto Rivers as they meet the Atlantic, the basin is among the biggest undeveloped areas on the coast and has been named one of the thirty-five World's Last Great Places by the Nature Conservancy. You can explore coastal wetlands like the ACE Basin on land, but you won't really *experience* them until you get on the water with Will or Eric on a kayaking or canoeing adventure.

The Kayak Farm's property lies next to St. Helena's Village Creek. It includes a barn for storing kayaks and equipment, and a one-acre fresh water pond that Will describes as "the gem of the property." The brothers use the water to give kayaking lessons, conduct demonstrations, and most importantly, check out guests' paddling skills before they take them out on sometimes choppy river and ocean waters. Will describes the business as a "grassroots, good-old-feeling place—a bright and friendly place. We do things in an old-fashioned way, trying to keep it real."

Beginners are more than welcome, and it doesn't take long for even those with no experience to get into the rhythm of pumping the paddle on one side of the boat, then the other, to propel a kayak along. You may end up a bit sore from working your arms and shoulders and sitting straight legged in the boat, on your rump, but it's the excitement of the adventure that will last, not the ache.

"We do full-bodied, local paddling throughout the sea islands," says Will, describing the trips he and Eric offer. On an excursion into the amazing ACE Basin, for example, paddlers can see untold numbers of

Guides from the Kayak Farm take travelers deep into the dark waters of the ACE Basin.

birds: egrets, heron, Canada geese, wood ducks, osprey, wild turkeys, quail, eagles, and wild storks. Dolphins roam the salt water on the edge of the ocean and inland alligators thrive in the fresh waters of the rivers. Bobcats, raccoons, mink, deer, and sea otters, which play in the waters plied by paddlers, also populate the shoreline. The area is rich in sea life—crabs, shrimp, and countless varieties of fish. The plant life is no less diverse or stunning, ranging from endless stands of sea grass that shimmer at sunset to dark forests of cypress jutting out of the black waters through miles of swampland. Much of the basin was formerly used to grow Carolina Gold Rice and for hunting, but has now been left for nature to reclaim.

The Kayak Farm also has an arrangement with Hunting Island State Park (Secret 86) to offer outings into the two-mile-long park lagoon guided by park naturalist Mike Walker, who was born and raised in the area. Don't call The Kayak Farm to reserve a place on the Hunting Island tour; that's booked through the park office at 843-838-4868.

For Eric and Will Gibbons, kayaking is more of a lifestyle than a profession. They're on duty seven days a week, around the clock, all year long. They treat kayakers to sunrise and sunset trips, overnight and weekend adventures, half- and full-day lessons, and custom tours—whatever a guest wants. "We encourage winter kayaking and canoeing, too," says Will, "because the weather is so beautiful that time of year."

Secret Information

Location: On U.S. Highway 21 east of Beaufort, South Carolina.
Address: 1289 Sea Island Parkway, St. Helena Island, SC 29920
Phone: 843-838-2008.
Fax: 843-838-9766.
E-mail: thekayakfarm@islc.net.
Web site: www.thekayakfarm.com.
Hours: No set hours; call ahead to make sure someone will be on the property when you come by.
Price: $25 per hour of lessons; $35 1/2 day tour; $65 full day tour; $90 one day overnighter.
Reservations: Recommended.
Credit cards: None.
Details: Children are welcome as long as they are big enough and strong enough to fit into and propel a kayak—generally about ten years old, though they have taken some as young as six. The kids are given lessons on the farm's pond. Experienced paddlers can also rent kayaks from the Kayak Farm and set off on their own.

TOP SECRET

Covering 250 miles from near Aiken, South Carolina, to the coast, the Edisto River is the longest of the three rivers that come together to form the ACE Basin. It's also believed to be the longest blackwater stream in the world, so called because of its slow-moving, tannin-stained waters. For passionate paddlers, it's a paradise, especially the sixty-six-mile-long Edisto River Canoe and Kayak Trail, which is something like a soggy version of a hiking trail. It starts near Walterboro and wanders through the Lowcountry among forests of oak, maple, cypress, tupelo, and pines populated with all manner of land, air, and water wildlife. The Edisto River Canoe and Kayak Trail Commission runs trips covering different parts of the trail and can provide more information, such as the location of put-in and take-out places if you want to paddle the trail on your own. For more information, give them a call at 843-549-5591.

Old Fort Pub

Guarded Secret

90

Although it shares its name with an island that depends on attracting tourists for its economic prosperity, Hilton Head Plantation prides itself on being more of a quiet, residential neighborhood than a vacation spot. There are golf courses and a few restaurants, but mainly the development is home to year-round residents whose homes are hidden in the pines and whose kids play soccer on the neatly groomed fields. To get past the guard at the main entrance off U.S. Highway 278 or the more convenient, lesser known back entrance (Cypress Gate off Squire Pope Road) you need to justify why you're there. Fortunately, there's a great reason to give the guard to get you in—you're on your way to the Old Fort Pub Restaurant.

The Old Fort Pub in Hilton Head, South Carolina, gets its name from its historic neighbor, Fort Mitchell, a Civil War gun battery. All that remains of Mitchell are several dirt mounds and moats constructed by the Union Army after it captured the island in 1861. A circuitous trail under the oaks, dotted with historical markers and some cannons, delights the children and helps pass the time if you're waiting for a table at the pub. The restaurant itself looks old, but like most things on Hilton Head it's yet to reach middle age. It was built in traditional Lowcountry-plantation-style in 1973 and started serving up sandwiches even before the Hilton Head Plantation opened its sales office or started developing the area. Today, a more upscale menu focuses on specialties like the creamy Lowcountry oyster stew baked in a pastry bowl and triggerfish and lemon herbed crabmeat served in a sweet potato crepe. There are still plenty of sandwiches at lunch, with the crab cake and fried oyster varieties topping the list of local favorites, and of course, the requisite plump and juicy pub burger.

The food is divine and well worth the drive from anywhere in the Lowcountry. Okay, there are plenty of great restaurants along the coast, but few can match the setting of the Old Fort. Shaded by sprawling live

The Old Fort Pub looks like a historic Lowcountry landmark, but it was actually built in the 1970s. (COURTESY OF OLD FORT PUB)

oaks and practically hanging out over Skull Creek, the building is so much a part of its natural surroundings that it looks as if it must have grown on that spot from some charmed restaurant-producing seed. The subtle pale gray exterior accented with blue shutters blends in perfectly with the Spanish moss hanging from the finger-like branches outside. There are swings on the wooden boardwalk out front and a few rocking chairs on the covered porch. The back is a wall of windows, which provide panoramic views of Skull Creek and the Intracostal Waterway and the best views of the sunset on all of Hilton Head.

In the evening, candlelight dances off the glass. The walls in the cozy lobby are filled with Civil War-era photos and letters and an autographed photograph of actor John Travolta, who dined at the Old Fort while filming the movie *A Civil Action*. Take the center spiral staircase up through the second floor Sunset Room (a secluded dining spot seating only thirty guests) to the rooftop widow's walk where you can stargaze or toast the sunset. Call a few days in advance (especially during the summer) to reserve a table by the window in the airy first floor dining room. If you're not up for an elegant dinner by candlelight but still want the view, stop in at the intimate yet casual bar or sip gin and tonics on the spacious outdoor deck overlooking Fort Mitchell and the water.

Since its early days, the Old Fort Pub has done quite nicely without much advertising. You won't find it featured in the stacks of local restaurant guides that seem to be available outside every eatery, shop, and hotel on the island. "Plenty of people know about us, especially the locals," says the genial General Manager Tom Trice. "We probably see just as many locals as tourists."

With no campaign to attract the typical coupon-carrying crowds found at most tourist spots, you'll really get the sense that you've discovered a secret in the Old Fort Pub. The other diners probably figure that if you know about the place you must live here or summer here every year, so you're instantly treated like an insider. It's relaxing; it's friendly; and the views and Lowcountry specialties are spectacular. Who knows? Once you've gotten in the gates of the Hilton Head Plantation and have savored the food and sunset view at the Old Fort Pub, the guards may have to come and throw you out to get you to leave.

Secret Information

Location: In Hilton Head Plantation on Hilton Head Island, South Carolina.
Address: 65 Skull Creek Drive, Hilton Head, SC 29926.
Phone: 843-681-2386.
Fax: 843-681-9287.
E-mail: oldfortpub@aol.com.
Web site: www.celebrationusa.com.
Hours: Noon to 10 P.M. Monday through Saturday; 11 A.M. to 10 P.M. Sunday; closes one hour earlier during daylight saving time.
Price: Lunches range from $7 to $10; Dinners range from $16 to $24.
Reservations: Recommended.
Credit cards: American Express, Diner's Club, Discover, MasterCard, Visa.

TOP SECRET

The Old Fort Pub is part of Pierce and Bonnie Lowrey's collection of Hilton Head Island restaurants, appropriately named The Lowrey Group, which was established in 1990. The Pub's sister restaurants are the understated CQ's Restaurant, located in Harbor Town in Sea Pines Plantation (843-671-2778); the waterfront Boathouse II Restaurant (843-681-3663) just down Squire Pope Road from the Old Fort; and Antonio's Fine Italian Restaurant in the Village at Wexford (843-842-5505). Each restaurant is distinctive, yet exudes the casual, insider's feel of the Old Fort and mirrors its top-notch food. The best way to sample all four restaurants, which generally don't do any other advertising, is to sign up for a Celebration! card (applications are available at the restaurants and on-line at www.celebrationusa.com). As a cardholder, you'll receive $25 in restaurant certificates to help celebrate your birthday and anniversary; a monthly newsletter on restaurant and island-wide promotions and events; the chance to enter monthly drawings for dining certificates and bottles of wine; and the opportunity to earn additional gift certificates and prizes through the Frequent Fare program. Spend a total of $250 at any or all of the Lowrey restaurants, for example, and you receive a $25 gift certificate. The Celebration! card is free for island residents and $15 per year for everyone else. For more information, call 843-686-9900 or send a query by e-mail to info@celebrationusa.com.

Parris Island Museum

Marine Land

91

Ask any man over age seventy about the South Carolina Lowcountry and chances are "vacation spot" won't be the initial image that comes to mind. For many seniors (even plenty who today call the Carolinas home), their first visit may have involved a buzzcut, a hard bunk, and maybe even a war. Up and down the Carolina coast, military bases, forts, and history abound. Of all the sites associated with this rich military heritage, no place can stir up the emotions and memories like Parris Island, South Carolina.

Parris Island's history dates back to 1562 when the French Huguenots set up shop here. But the history with which most Americans are familiar is the World War II era, when Parris Island served as the training site for 204,000 marines. Ask around at the next family reunion and you're bound to turn up someone who passed through Parris Island (or knew someone who did) on his or her way to Europe or the South Pacific during World War II or later to Korea, Vietnam, or the Middle East.

Today, Parris Island is still a training depot for new marine recruits. Each year drill instructors train more than eighteen thousand men and fifteen hundred women to enter the corps. Unlike many military bases where you can't get on base unless you are ready for the haircut and the hard bunk, Parris Island welcomes visitors "on board." Your access is restricted to certain areas, of course, but as long as you show a valid picture ID and your vehicle registration to the MP on duty at the front gate, you can see Parris Island for yourself (or show your kids or grandkids where you spent the most memorable thirteen weeks of your life) from 6 A.M. until 6 P.M. on most days.

Stop by the Douglas Visitors Center, which is named for Paul H. Douglas, the oldest marine recruit, who was fifty years old when he entered basic training in 1942. (He later went on to become a U.S. senator from Illinois). Here you can pick up a map to lead you to the hidden treasure of Parris Island—the Parris Island Museum. Located in the War

Memorial Building, the museum (one of the largest in the southeast) tells the Parris Island and Port Royal area story through exhibits, a study collection, research facilities, and an archival collection focused on regional military and Marine Corps history. Out front, there is the Iron Mike monument (the museum's symbol), a memorial to the Parris Island-trained marines who died during World War I. Inside, there are displays dedicated to the island's Revolutionary War and plantation-era histories, plus artifacts from the Civil War. But the strongest emphasis is on the Parris Island of our grandfathers, fathers, husbands, and sons—as the Marine Corps recruit training center of the twentieth century.

There are real bunks, uniforms, guns, and mess kits used in life-size dioramas staffed by mannequin marines, so children of all ages can see the tools of their fathers' and grandfathers' trade during wars throughout U.S. history. The colorful medals and flags will hold even the tiniest tourist's attention, while detailed placards depicting specific battles and time periods will captivate adult visitors. With more than ten thousand square feet of exhibits highlighting marine history, heroism, and pride, even if the only marines you've ever seen are the ones on "the few, the proud, the marines" commercials, you're sure to walk out of here with a lump in your throat or a tear in your eye.

After touring the museum, be sure to consult your trusty map for the location of some other special monuments located on Parris Island. The newest addition is the "Known Marine," which was dedicated on April 24, 1999, to the past and future drill instructors of the U.S. Marine Corps on Parris Island. Look closely for the brass footprints at the center of the monument's base. These represent the yellow footprints where all new marine recruits put their feet when getting off the bus on arrival day. One of the most famous sights on the base is the "Iwo Jima Monument," which served as the prototype for the granddaddy Iwo Jima monument in Washington, D.C. This model was sculpted by the same Felix del Weldon and, of course, depicts the raising of the American flag on Mt. Suribachi in 1945.

An hour at the museum and a visit to the monuments will satisfy any appetite for Marine history. But if you really want an up-close-and-personal view of Parris Island, call the Douglas Visitors Center (843-228-3550 or 843-228-3297) at least one day in advance to make reservations for a free, narrated bus tour of the training depot. The tours are offered every Saturday through Wednesday at 1 P.M. and focus on the making of U.S. Marines and Parris Island history. If you'd rather get an earlier start

Discover the true meaning of the U.S. Marines' motto, Semper Fidelis, *at the Parris Island Museum.* (COURTESY OF PARRIS ISLAND MUSEUM)

on your visit, then plan to see Parris Island on a Friday morning for the 7:50 A.M. Morning Colors Ceremony (that's the raising of the flag for us non-military types). It's quite a moving ceremony with the stirring accompaniment provided by the Parris Island Marine Band. Stick around until 9:15 A.M. on most Fridays and you can cheer the newest Marines at their graduation ceremony. Graduation is held at the Depot's Peatross Parade Deck and lasts until around 10:15 A.M. Check at the visitor's center for directions and the most updated graduation schedule.

Secret Information

Location: South of Beaufort, South Carolina.
Address: Bldg. #111, Marine Corps Recruit Depot, Parris Island, SC 29905.
Phone: 843-228-2951.
Fax: 843-228-3065.
Web site: www.parrisisland.com
Hours: 10 A.M. to 4:30 P.M. daily. Open until 7 P.M. on Thursdays before graduations.
Price: Free.

TOP SECRET

There are plenty of military secrets hidden in the Carolinas besides the Parris Island Museum. One of the more colorful is the weekly Corps of Cadets Parade held at the Citadel in Charleston. Most Fridays during the school year—roughly the beginning of September through the beginning of April—the castle-like fortress that is the Citadel campus opens its doors to visitors and cadet family and friends for a glimpse of life inside the "Military College of the South." There's stirring fife and drum music, plenty of saluting and swords, and precision stepping by fresh-faced cadets all decked out in their dress white pants, gray jackets, and black hats. Most parades begin at 3:45 P.M. or 4:20 P.M. on Fridays at the parade ground—Summerall Field. Call the Citadel at 843-943-5000 to check the schedule. If you get on campus an hour before the parade, you'll have time to check out the Citadel Museum, located on the third floor of the Daniel Library (that's the first building on the right just inside the main gate). With exhibits celebrating life at the Citadel since 1842, you're bound to learn something more about the place than the fact that it wouldn't admit women until 1996. The Citadel is located at 171 Moultrie Street, and visitor parking is available along the Avenue of Remembrance.

Edisto Beach State Park

92

Outdoors with Insiders

Rob Achenberg, superintendent of Edisto Beach State Park (located at the end of Edisto Island, South Carolina) and president of the local Edisto Beach Chamber of Commerce, doesn't consider his remote, oceanfront park much of a secret. "The secret is out about this park," says Achenberg. "It has the highest occupancy of any campground in the state."

It's true, but most of those campers and daytrippers are South Carolina residents or natives who came to rustic Edisto Island and Edisto Beach as kids and return today with their own families from whatever state they now call home. Lots of folks know and love Edisto Beach State Park, but it's one of those insider secrets—like back in high school when all the cool kids were invited to a party but everyone else was clueless. Today, all the cool kids know a special spot where you can camp on or near the beach under a canopy of stars, live oaks draped with Spanish moss, and the tallest palmetto trees in the state. Now you do too.

"The park is relaxing. People come here to recharge. You can be as busy or as lazy as you want to be," says Achenberg of the 1,255-acre sea island paradise, seven hundred acres of which is maritime forest. "Some people come just to hang a hammock between two trees and relax or to go shelling. People find all kinds of stuff—sharks' teeth, mastodon teeth, horse teeth, bones, and fossilized material from extinct creatures. Sharks' teeth are the most common, but people do find whale vertebrae and different bone fragments of creatures long gone."

That link to the past is what makes the entire Edisto Island area such a treasure. The Edisto Indians roamed this forest as early as four thousand years ago, and the park is rich in Native American history. For those who came here as children, little has changed over the years in this sleepy barrier island community. The tiny haven of Edisto Beach still has a fleet of working shrimp trawlers, and there are no motels or hotels on either the island or the beach. Instead, there is one small condo complex, some fairway villas at the Fairfield Ocean Ridge golf course in Edisto Beach, and local realtors rent basic beach cottages for summer tourists. The favored place to stay, however, is over at the remote oceanfront state park.

There are 103 developed campsites located in two separate and distinctly different campgrounds. The most popular is the beachfront location, but the most private is the campground at the forested spot behind the salt marshes. There are also 5 two-bedroom, one-bath cabins located in the woods overlooking the salt marsh and Scott Creek, about one-and-a-half miles from the beach. The coveted cabins (make reservations up to a year or more in advance) let room-service regulars pretend they're roughing it. Each fully furnished cabin can sleep six and features heat and air conditioning, bed and bath linens, appliances, television, and an outdoor grill and picnic table. There's also a screened porch, which comes in handy during the summer insect season.

Those pesky bugs, Lowcountry heat, and the sometimes equally irritating in-season crowds, make summer our least favorite time to visit Edisto Beach State Park. Instead, make plans to pitch a tent or park an RV (about half the sites support recreational vehicles) at the park in the spring, fall, or winter. Or if you'd rather, pay a few dollars to park in the day-use area and simply enjoy the natural wonders and secluded beach access for the day. There are picnic shelters available on a first-come, first-served basis (you can also reserve one for $20 per day), and the heated restrooms come in handy, especially during the winter.

Whether you visit for the day, night, or your whole vacation, there's plenty of natural fun to fill your days at Edisto Beach State Park. Swim, hike, or unwind at the playground. Try your hand at surf fishing for spottail bass, sea trout, whiting, drum and sheepshead, or go shrimping with a cast net. Bring along a kayak and explore the protected estuaries on the sound side of the park. If you're an experienced paddler, surf the shore along the beachfront and look for dolphins. Or, if you'd rather take Superintendent Achenberg's advice, just spend your time hanging out in a hammock strung between two trees. With the sea oats gently waving in the salty breeze and the graceful egrets wading near the shore, there's really no better place to spend an afternoon. But let's keep that our little secret, okay?

Secret Information

Location: On Edisto Island, South Carolina, about fifty miles southwest of Charleston, South Carolina.
Address: 8377 State Cabin Road, Edisto Island, SC 29438.
Phone: 843-869-2756 (park office; shelter and cabin reservations); 843-869-2156 (camping information and reservations).
Fax: 843-869-3023.
Web site: www.southcarolinaparks.com or www.travelsc.com.
Hours: 6 A.M. to 10 P.M. April to October; 8 A.M. to 6 P.M. November to March; Park office hours are 9 A.M. to 5 P.M.
Price: Developed campsites $22 in season and $17 off season. Cabins are $60 per night.
Reservations: Cabins and a limited number of campsites can be reserved; other sites are first-come, first-served.
Credit cards: Discover, MasterCard, Visa.

TOP SECRET

Edisto Beach State Park is home to Spanish Mount, a large Native American shell mound dated to around 2000 B.C. The self-interpretive, four-mile loop Indian Mound Trail leads to cliffs overlooking Scott Creek, where the shell mound is located. You could easily hike the distance, but it's much more fun to bike. The single-track trail is one of the most picturesque biking paths on the South Carolina coast. You'll pass through the maritime forest, duck under Spanish moss hanging from ancient oaks, and bump over a wooden boardwalk to cross the salt marsh. If the Indian Mound Trail whets your appetite for a longer trek, head out of the park to the five-mile (ten-mile total out and back) Edisto Island Bike Trail. The route begins near the marina, winds around Fairfield Plantation, and is the perfect way for first-time visitors to get a feel for this laid-back and tropically lush island. The trail is flat and in pretty good repair, so don't fret if you haven't pedaled since your last vacation. For the tour de Edisto, you don't have to be Lance Armstrong or even work up much of a sweat.

93

Shrimp Shack

In the Rough

There aren't any beaches on St. Helena Island, South Carolina, (pronounced "S'int Helena" by those fortunate enough to live there), which is probably a good thing. Beaches tend to bring tourists and development and change, and St. Helena is all about heritage and history. Cotton and shrimp share the throne on this, the largest of Beaufort County's sixty-five islands. The former made plenty of local plantation owners rich in the eighteenth and early nineteenth century and the latter provides the name and the main course for the best little lunch place in the Sea Islands.

The Shrimp Shack, located on the east end of St. Helena Island just before you cross Johnson Creek and head on over to Hunting Island (Secret 86), looks at first glance like it could be an upscale bistro transplanted from Beaufort. There's a bright blue awning out front that covers both the front steps and the walkways leading to a detached screen porch. Delicate white Christmas lights trim the front entrance and adjacent light poles. And the gray, weathered wood sign on the road, coupled with the fishing nets artfully strung along the front wall, give the place the air of rustic elegance those pricey seafood places in Hilton Head love. Even the gravel parking strip out front has its share of foreign luxury sedans. But relax, all is not as it seems. Find a place to park (if you can), and you'll quickly figure out that the awning isn't fashionable, it's functional. This is a clean, old-fashioned paper plate take-out or dine-in place, and the blue canvas protects diners from the elements when they're walking to the screen porch or sitting on the front stoop waiting for their order.

"We're what you'd call 'rustic,'" chuckles owner Hilda Upton, who built the Shrimp Shack back in July 1978 and is part owner of the dock across the street. "This is a family place. My daughters are an important part of the business—they each put in a shift; my husband helps out; and one of the women who cooks with me has been here since we opened."

Upton takes the family focus to heart. Each year she gives everyone on her staff a few days off in August, so they can buy back-to-school supplies for their kids. And each day, whether the busiest, hottest day in July or the coldest in January, she's behind the counter at her Shrimp Shack making sure every local and traveler who passes her way can have a hot, fresh, homemade meal.

"I tell people to call in the off-season from October to March to check when we're open, but, except for the real cold days, we try to be open for lunch every day except Sunday," says Upton, who allowed herself an extended vacation in 1999 so she and her husband could take a land-and-sea trip tour of Alaska for their fortieth wedding anniversary. "The first few years we closed in the winter. But then we discovered that there were a lot of people around here who'd like to stop in for lunch."

Before you can even pull open the Shrimp Shack's front screen door, the comforting aroma of crisp-fried something makes your stomach growl. Most of the time it turns out to be the specialty of the house—the shrimp burger. Upton doesn't advertise it as the specialty. She really doesn't have to advertise at all ("people out driving from Hilton Head, Charleston, and other places will come all the way over here for lunch," she says). But if you sit on one of the wooden benches in the shack's "dining room," you get the idea that most people in the place came for the shrimp burger. Upton estimates she probably shells and deveins about fifty pounds of shrimp a day in the high season, all of it straight from the Upton family's own boat, aptly named *Miss Hilda*. To make a burger, the shrimp are gently pressed into a patty, covered lightly in batter, and freshly fried to golden deliciousness. Be sure to order one with a side of hush puppies, which are huge and fluffy with a crisp exterior that crunches loudly. Oh, and they taste good too.

The most expensive item on the dinner menu is the bountiful fried seafood dinner for $12.55, and at lunch you can easily fill up for around five bucks. For the kids, and less adventurous sorts, there are hamburgers, chili dogs, and of course, french fries, but when you're on the island where shrimping is king, well, it would be a crime to eat anything else.

Step into the Shrimp Shack for fresh fried seafood served in a rustic setting.

Secret Information

Location: St. Helena Island, South Carolina.
Address: 1925 Sea Island Parkway, St. Helena Island, South Carolina 29920.
Phone: 843-838-2962.
Hours: 11 A.M. to 8 P.M., Monday through Saturday (call first for hours October through April).
Price: From $5 for lunch to $15 for dinner.
Credit cards: None.

TOP SECRET

The Shrimp Shack dishes all the Carolina seafood classics—shrimp burgers, fried shrimp, boiled shrimp, fried fish fillets, accompanied, of course, with french fries, cole slaw, and hush puppies. But they also have a treat we've never encountered anywhere else—fried sweet-potato fingers. Yams are sliced into thick oblong chunks, breaded, and cooked in oil. Their creamy orange centers melt in your mouth (honest) and slide down best with a big cup of sweet iced tea.

Old Point Inn

94

The Wedding Gift House

Beaufort, South Carolina (pronounced Bew-fert, not Bo-fort like its North Carolina cousin) is a largely ignored gem in the Lowcountry. It's got the historic atmosphere of Charleston to the north and Savannah to the south without the surrounding sprawl. While smaller than those two classic southern cities, Beaufort shares their feel—a walkable waterfront, oak-shaded streets rich with historic homes, and small shops and eateries in which to wile away an afternoon and evening. In and around the downtown area are nearly a hundred historic homes dating from as far back as 1717. By comparison the Old Point Inn, which was built in 1898, is practically brand new, yet it's the perfect place to stay and savor Beaufort's southern style.

Locals call the inn "The Wedding Gift House" because it was built just before the turn of the century by William Waterhouse as a present for his bride, Isabelle Richmond, on the city's east point on the Beaufort River. A late-Victorian-style home with first- and second-floor wraparound porches, it was one of the first bed-and-breakfasts in Beaufort and has had among the most stable ownership in longtime innkeepers Joe and Joan Carpentiere. The Carpentieres are gracious hosts, serving wine and soft drinks in the afternoon as guests relax and browse in the library or head outside to stretch out on the hammock. They particularly pride themselves on serving great breakfasts, which Joan describes as "gourmet, but recognizable"—rich French toast, scones with wild blueberries, or a "breakfast sundae" of peaches, pineapple, and yogurt, for example.

The Old Point Inn is filled with antiques but has a comfortable grandma's-house feel, with woven rugs, china cabinets, family pictures, and patterned wallpaper. There are just four guest rooms, each named after a different literary figure. The most popular is the Jane Austen Room, which features a romantic raspberry and rose decor and the only "eyelash" (referring to the curved shape) window in town. Rates are

Peeking out from the peak of the Old Point Inn is the only "eyelash" window in Beaufort.

reasonable, and the inn tends to draw couples who want time away with each other.

The inn shows its age in a good way through small details that you would never find in a more modern bed-and-breakfast. To get onto the second floor verandah, for example, you step through a full floor-to-ceiling Gib window, which is constructed to be opened upward into the ceiling like a pocket door rather than a real door. At the time the home was built, property owners were taxed on the number of exterior doors in a house; by substituting an oversized window, though, they created a loophole that saved them money.

Secret Information

Location: Beaufort, South Carolina.
Address: 212 New Street, Beaufort, SC 29902.
Phone: 843-524-3177.
Fax: 843-525-6544.
Web site: www.oldpointinn.com.
Rates: $65 to $110.
Reservations: Recommended.
Credit cards: American Express, MasterCard, Visa.

TOP SECRET

To help her guests get a feel for the scenic town of Beaufort, Old Point Inn co-owner Joan Carpentiere has put together a brochure and map giving the location and background of twenty-three of the downtown area's historic sites. If you're not staying at the bed-and-breakfast, see the area on horse-drawn carriage tours that leave from the visitor's center. An alternative for the fit and the frugal, though, is to unobtrusively follow the slow-moving carriages around on foot and eavesdrop for free on the narration provided by guides. Plum's Cafe (843-525-1946) is the place to eat a casual meal on the waterfront, and Hemmingway's Bistro (843-521-4480), tucked on the backside and under the buildings on Bay Street, is the spot locals go to drink beer and contemplate life. For fancier fare, dine at Bistro DeJong and Patisserie (Secret 97), and, if you have kids, let them get a taste of the terrific toys at Boombears (843-524-2525).

95

Red Piano Too Gallery

Funky Folk Art For Sale

Yes, there is a red piano. It sits just inside the front door of this funky, folk art gallery located in a former general store/boarding house on rustic St. Helena Island, South Carolina. The gallery, however, wasn't named for the piano. The original owner already owned a Red Piano Gallery in Hilton Head and added the "Too" to the name of her second studio. In 1991 when the gallery opened, an eighty-four-year-old piano was discovered upstairs in the living quarters of the family that formerly owned the building. Dusted off, carried down, and painted red, it now serves as the welcoming mascot of this most unusual and refreshingly unpretentious art gallery.

In most shops and art galleries, a red piano would probably be the most colorful piece around. But this is Lowcountry, South Carolina, where the influences of the Gullah, southern, and Native American cultures add vibrancy and energy to fabric, food, art, and architecture. The interior of the Red Piano is a tapestry of shades, shapes, and styles. There's a monumental shrine to Elvis, twinkling red Christmas lights, brightly painted jewelry and furniture, and a back room devoted entirely to African and African-American art, including traditional masks and sculpture.

Each piece focuses on the fun and fanciful, and best of all, this playful spirit extends toward all visitors who enter. Although Red Piano Too is a serious gallery, owner Elayne Scott and her staff actually smile when families stroll in off the creaky, fern-filled front porch. Instead of the hushed tones one would expect, the Red Piano Too is filled with laughter, chatter, and the joyful noise of people responding to incredible, yet accessible, art. Here parents and kids can actually spend time exploring and discussing art together without fear of being followed around by some secret, snobby gallery police.

"We're different from most other galleries," says the Red Piano Too's Suzanne Riley. "It's neat that parents can bring their children in. And teachers bring students here to show them all the different kinds of art and to show them that this is something they could do too. For example,

Elvis has become a favorite subject of folk artists who exhibit at the Red Piano Too Gallery.

teachers like to show children how some things in here are made out of gourds or how an artist chose to paint on cardboard or plywood instead of something more traditional. We have all these different things that you don't see at other art galleries. There's so much imagination in here."

Riley says the gallery specializes in southern folk artists: some locals (she estimates that works by South Carolina artists fill approximately half the gallery) and others from Alabama, Florida, Georgia, and Mississippi. Many of them favor Elvis-oriented themes, and a lot are self-taught, untrained artists, she adds. The result is pure magic for the eyes and the spirit. For example, artist Maggie Phipps transforms everyday gourds into fantastical tall dragonflies, praying manti, and herons while local artist Sabre Wolfe paints on pieces of an old tin roof to create whimsical works, depicting flowers in a vase or alligators. The Red Piano Too also has the more familiar prints and paintings ready for framing, of course, but the canvases are more likely to be the unexpected, like a vegetable, a pair of shoes, or a piece of furniture.

Although the Red Piano Too is a bit off the beaten path, folk art lovers from around the country call there regularly looking for pieces by particular artists who are featured in the gallery. Granted, tracking down a favorite folk artist over the phone saves time and travel, but somehow it seems there should be a rule that anyone who buys a work of art from the gallery should have to come in person to pick it up. The Red Piano Too isn't simply about promoting artists and giving them a place to display; it's an interactive experience for all the senses that can't be translated via phone or even the printed page. And although there's absolutely zero pressure from the gallery staff to purchase anything, the wide variety of shapes, sizes, and mediums means that there's likely something available in your price range.

"Our prints start at $10 to $15, and then we have a few pieces in here that are in the thousands of dollars range. Everything else falls somewhere in between," says Riley. "We try to keep our prices down so that everybody who comes in could afford to take something home with them."

Secret Information

Location: St. Helena Island, South Carolina.
Address: 853 Sea Island Parkway, St. Helena Island, SC 29920.
Phone: 843-838-2241.
Fax: 843-838-5638.
Hours: 10 A.M. until 5 P.M. daily.
Price: Varies widely.
Credit cards: American Express, MasterCard, Visa.

TOP SECRET

If you think a trip to an art gallery will be a tough sell on your kids, tell them about the bead table at the Red Piano Too Gallery. Kids of all ages can easily spend an hour or two selecting beads to make earrings, key chains, or bracelets. Every bead artist is given a clipboard to keep a running tally of the beads they've selected (it's wise to set a limit of $5 or so since individual beads on the table can range from a nickel up to a few dollars each). Gallery staff will help cut the leather, string, or wire used to string the beads and attach appropriate clasps. The beads themselves are tiny works of art ranging from funky peace sign patterns and polished stones to alphabet blocks and dog bone shapes. Staffer Suzanne Riley says one woman regularly comes in and buys beads in bulk to string on chicken wire and then shapes the art into pocketbooks. Other customers have been known to buy beads to make hippie curtains. Both of those projects would probably bust your vacation budget, but a simple bracelet or pair of earrings will only set you back the price of a pizza. And if your kids are like ours, they'll be begging you to stay at the Red Piano Too "just five more minutes" so they can finish their bead masterpieces. Now when was the last time your kids pleaded to stay in an art gallery?

96

Accessible Adventure

Up and down the Carolina coast there are acres of woods and rivers and marshes available to explore on foot, bike, canoe, or kayak. But for those who can't readily strap on a backpack and take to the wilds, the access to those out-of-the-way places is limited. Cars and nature just don't mix, so families with small kids, the disabled, seniors, and others who aren't physically able to trek into the backcountry often miss out on the chance to see nature at its best. That's what's so special about the Savannah National Wildlife Refuge.

Although the Savannah National Wildlife Refuge shares its name with the Georgia city, it lies on the South Carolina side of the state border. About half of its 26,349 acres of freshwater marshes, tidal rivers and creeks, and bottomland hardwood can only be reached by boat. But that still leaves plenty of nature for car-bound visitors who drive through the refuge on Laurel Hill Wildlife Drive. This route winds along earthen dikes that were built by plantation owners back in the mid or late 1700s and passes by freshwater pools, which were actually the plantation rice fields, and hardwood islands known as "hammocks." There are walking and biking trails too. You can hike along the dikes and get an up-close view of the alligators, otters, and other wildlife who live there. But if you have to stay in your car, the Savannah National Wildlife Refuge is ideal. From the comfort of your vehicle you can see the wading birds and waterfowl feeding in the freshwater pools; watch the alligators sunning themselves on the banks of the dikes; scan the thick woods for white-tailed deer, feral hogs, and wild turkey; and search the blue sky for hawks, and if you're lucky, an endangered southern bald eagle. There's even hunting access for the disabled (see Top Secret.)

Driving through the refuge is a bit like going on safari. On a spring or winter day, your car may be the only one meandering under the lazy cypress trees and across the open rice fields. Go slow. Roll down the

Keep your eyes peeled or you may miss the alligators because they blend in with the landscape of the Savannah National Wildlife Refuge.

windows. Pull off to the side and watch the river otters playing in the pools. It's hard to believe that such solitude and wonder can be found only nine miles from downtown Savannah.

Unfortunately, that close proximity to civilization has harmed the refuge over the years. Although located in South Carolina, the refuge sits on the river directly opposite Savannah's seaport facilities and industrial plants. As you start the drive, you can see the huge tankers and smoke stacks from the Laurel Hill Wildlife Drive entrance, although the view becomes uncluttered further into the refuge. Pollution and salt water intrusion from development along the coast is slowly killing the vast marsh, and the state of South Carolina is currently working to preserve and protect this natural jewel. So visit the refuge now while it's still brimming with wildlife and wonder.

The collection of birds assembled here makes the place a birder's dream. In the tidal pools and mudflats you'll see egrets, ibises, and herons, while the swamps attract birds like swallow-tailed kites, prothonotary warblers, and pileated woodpeckers. In late December and early January, more than a dozen types of ducks numbering a thousand or more invade the refuge and fill the air with their calls. Kids enjoy scanning the woods for owls but have even more fun keeping a gator count, especially in March, April, and October—prime sunbathing time for the long, leatherbacked green guys.

Secret Information

Location: On the South Carolina/Georgia border near Savannah, Georgia.
Address: Savannah Coast Refuges, Parkway Business Center, Suite 10, 1000 Business Center Drive, Savannah, Georgia 31405.
Phone: 912-652-4415.
Fax: 912-652-4385.
E-mail: r4rw_ga.scr@fws.gov.
Web site: www.fws.gov/r4eao/wildlife/nwrscr.html.
Hours: Open daily sunrise to sunset; closed on federal holidays.
Price: FREE.

TOP SECRET

Although the Savannah National Wildlife Refuge has been set aside to protect its animal inhabitants, controlled hunting and fishing are permitted at certain times. Bank fishing from the Laurel Hill Wildlife Drive is allowed year-round—a South Carolina fishing license is required. Bream, crappie, and largemouth bass make their homes here, but local fishermen prefer to cast a line on the Savannah River along the boundary of the refuge. There you'll need a Georgia license to fish. Hunting the surplus of feral hogs, turkey, deer, and squirrel is one tool used to manage the wildlife population and provide recreational opportunities. If you want to hunt—or want to avoid it—it's important to know that deer/hog hunting season is the month of November; squirrel and deer archery hunting season is October; and turkey hunting takes place for a week near the end of April. There's also a Disabled Persons' Deer/Hog Hunt usually held on the fourth weekend of November for hunters dependent on wheelchairs for mobility. For specifics on hunting and fishing regulations and the Disabled Persons' Deer/Hog Hunt contact the refuge office at 912-652-4415.

97

Bistro DeJong and Patisserie

Chef's Choice

You never quite know what will be on the menu at Bistro DeJong and Patisserie in Beaufort, South Carolina—it changes four or five times a year. "That's so that we don't get bored in the kitchen," explains the owner and head chef, Peter DeJong. "I get bored with things once I do them so many times. I've got to change to stay good, and it makes it interesting for customers to come back here because there's always something new."

DeJong is a third generation chef who grew up in Amsterdam, Holland, and started cooking at age twelve. He studied in his home country and in Belgium, and he later became a certified culinary instructor. He moved to the United States more than fifteen years ago and opened a bakery and restaurant in New York. He and his wife started looking for a good place to raise their family—they now have a school-age boy and girl—and settled in Beaufort, where his wife's grandmother lived. He opened the restaurant at the Beaufort Inn and worked there for four-and-a-half years before going out on his own.

"It was just time to open my own place," he says. "What I love best about having my own restaurant is that you get to make all the decisions. You don't have to listen to anyone else."

His restaurant is something of an oddity in the Lowcountry—a gourmet bistro in an area better known for heaping platters of fried seafood. The international flavor at his seventy-five-seat place a half-block from the waterfront reflects the diverse influences that come from living in the heart of Europe. "Dutch cooking by itself is not that interesting; it's lots of one-pot meals," he says. "But Holland is surrounded by countries like France and Italy, and a lot of neat flavors come through." DeJong's creations are also heavily influenced by the lively cuisine of the Dutch colonies in Indonesia. To keep the selections surprising, he constantly experiments with new dishes. "Sometimes I get inspired by another restaurant or chef, but I always do my own thing with the idea. I never just copy it."

The nightly menu is hard to predict. Appetizers may include sushi or perhaps a Cajun blue crab roll (crab with avocado), she-crab sherry soup, even tempura frogs' legs. DeJong always offers a mix of creatively prepared entrees—tenderloin of beef with a red stroganoff sauce (with a dash of Russian vodka), pecan-crusted grouper over spinach pesto fettuccine, and jalapeño grits with shrimp served in a cream sauce, for example. He also works wonders with veal, chicken, duck, pork, and fresh-off-the-local-docks seafood such as scallops and tuna. The "patisserie" part of the place's name refers to the bakery, which produces such desserts as a pecan meringue filled with coffee butter creme finished off with whipped cream or a flourless chocolate torte. The wine list is extensive and high quality, featuring about 140 selections.

As for the atmosphere, "it's designed so that everybody can pretty much feel relaxed," says DeJong. "It's very art-infused." That refers to its four archways painted with murals of historic Beaufort by local artists Eric and Suzanne Longo, which complement intimate tables set with white linen and fine china and glassware and stucco walls with areas of exposed brick. On Fridays the casual yet classy feel is further enriched by live jazz.

"I want customers to experience an evening where they enjoy their friends and, once they are served, food they can talk about," says DeJong. He targets locals as his core clientele but has an ulterior motive of attracting out-of-towners as well. "A lot of local people will get stopped on the street by visitors and asked, 'Where's the best place to eat?' I want them to point this way."

Secret Information

Location: Beaufort, South Carolina.
Address: 205 West Street, Beaufort, SC 29902.
Phone: 843-524-4994.
Fax: 843-524-0586.
E-mail: debistroarts@iscl.com.
Hours: Lunch 11:30 A.M. to 2:30 P.M. Tuesday through Saturday; Dinner 5:30 P.M. to 10 P.M. Monday through Saturday.
Price: Dinners average $28.
Reservations: Recommended.
Credit cards: American Express, Discover, MasterCard, Visa.

TOP SECRET

Besides serving delicious gourmet dinners nightly, Bistro DeJong hosts several special events that make it worth traveling to Beaufort. Every Wednesday is International Night, which features the authentic fare of a country such as Italy, France, or Mexico. All the international dishes are a la carte except Dutch Indonesian Night, which features a thirty-item buffet of sometimes unfamiliar vegetable, meat, and fish dishes. "We explain to people how to eat things and what to eat together," says DeJong. The restaurant also hosts monthly wine tasting dinners, for which DeJong makes five-course meals with five different wines and invites wine makers to come and talk about their craft. Reservations for the dinners are required, and they are always sold out. For those who want to hone their culinary skills, DeJong hosts cooking classes on Saturdays in the spring and fall. For more information about any of these events, contact the Bistro DeJong (see Secret Information)—the afternoon is the best time to call.

Beaulieu House

98

The Water is Wide

If you've ever read a Pat Conroy novel or watched the Barbra Streisand and Nick Nolte movie *The Prince of Tides*, you've pictured this place in your mind. There's the private fishing pier stretching out into the marshy river and the wide Pawleys Island hammocks designed for late afternoon naps hanging from the broad back porches. While savoring your morning coffee on the verandah you may half expect Nolte, ah, make that his character, Tom Wingo, to stroll in and ask for some cream. It's all you imagined and more because according to the owner Diann Corsaro, the land of the Beaulieu House Bed-and-Breakfast once actually did belong to the Trasks, the family Conroy loosely profiled in his *Prince of Tides* saga. Okay, so maybe a movie star won't show up for breakfast, but if you take your steaming cup of aromatic coffee to the end of the dock, chances are that a dolphin or two will stop by to say hello.

The surrounding land and marsh are rich with history, but the Beaulieu House itself was completed only in 1999. After her husband died suddenly, Corsaro decided to create a new life for herself and her spry eighty-plus-year-old mother, Wanda Dierks, on secluded Cat Island, a short drive from historic Beaufort, South Carolina.

"After I lost my husband I knew I needed something to keep me busy, and about the same time Mom needed to find another direction," says Corsaro, a comfortably elegant Renaissance woman who can talk as easily about international travel and art as she can about the price of roofing shingles. "I did the project to keep busy and regroup my life. We found Beaufort quite by accident and ended up loving the Lowcountry. Living in the Sea Islands is like being on vacation every day."

Corsaro's dream was not only to run a bed-and-breakfast but to transform the corner lot on this tiny strip of land just beyond the prestigious South Carolina National Golf Course into an architectural jewel featuring top-of-the-line materials and craftsmanship. For any one this would be a challenge, but for two northern women with few local connections, it

The back porches of the Beaulieu House overlook a peaceful waterway.

proved nearly insurmountable. Contractors and workmen didn't know what to make of the mother-daughter team and their grand vision. Corsaro persevered against still alive and healthy southern sexism, plowed ahead, and learned more than she ever wanted to know about construction. The result is a storybook, three-story salmon-hued inn with mother Wanda's smaller twin guest home attached via a covered breezeway.

"The feel is casual and friendly," says Corsaro, who utilized soft beach tones and lots of windows to welcome guests and the surrounding sun, sky, and blooming gardens into her distinctive inn. There are eight spacious guest rooms, including a family suite situated over the detached carriage house, with gleaming hardwood floors, French doors leading to wide porches with lazy ceiling fans, interior shutters, and private baths with Jacuzzi tubs and antique fixtures, hardware, and mirrors. Original art adorns the walls and books and magazines covering art, world affairs, and travel are available in the River Room for guests to peruse.

Although Beaulieu House is an elegant, romantic place, it is also one of the few bed-and-breakfasts we've encountered that welcomes families. Of course any mom would be on edge trying to keep toddlers from playing with Corsaro's extensive collection of dolls and antique tin wind-up toys, toy airplanes, and cars displayed on lighted shelves throughout the foyer and upstairs hall, but seasoned travelers of school age will be right at home. Upon arrival, kids are introduced to Corsaro's own "children"—two Bedlington Terriers brought over from England as pups, which she now breeds professionally. (She also has adult children who live out-of-state.) Child guests can walk Jezabelle and Daisey Belle up and down the sidewalk of the picket-fenced Sheffield Court, where the Beaulieu House is one of a dozen or so new "old" homes built to exacting historical standards. The kids can also venture along the golf course, but Corsaro warns all dog walkers to keep her babies on a short leash. "A neighbor's dog was eaten by an alligator over there," she warns. That one line is enough to keep dogs and kids close to the house and well behaved.

At the time this book was published a new sports complex was being built near the Beaulieu House and was planned to include a huge swimming pool, waterfall and bridge, lighted tennis courts, spa, kids' pool, and covered picnic area, all in a garden setting. In addition, directly across the street from Beaulieu House, the country club was expanding its dining room and pro shop and opening a large exercise room. Corsaro planned to join both facilities, so her guests can use them. Such hospitality is typical of Corsaro and her mother. They are the kind of people who will mix up a pitcher of lemonade and share it with you on the porch or simply smile, nod, and pass on by if they sense you want to stare out at the river in silence. Both have traveled the world, led rich and interesting lives, and will swap a story or two. Corsaro's mother prepares blintzes, freshly squeezed juices, and homemade marmalade and jams for breakfast. Her bountiful gourmet spread, prepared fresh each morning, will fuel your body for a day's worth of Lowcountry adventures. If you're short on ideas of what to do, Corsaro personally knows most of the area artists and entrepreneurs and can steer you toward the interesting and offbeat.

At least one morning during your stay we encourage you to stake out your spot in the hammock and let the gentle breeze and hypnotic lapping of the water against the dock lull you to sleep. Okay, so it's only 10:30 A.M., but this is your vacation and this is the Beaulieu House, where Corsaro and her mother will both readily attest that dreams can, and do, come true.

Secret Information

Location: On Cat Island near Beaufort, South Carolina.
Address: 3 Sheffield Court, Cat Island, Beaufort, SC 29902.
Phone: 843-770-0303.
Fax: 843-770-0303.
E-mail: beaulieubb@aol.com.
Rates: $125 to $150.
Reservations: Recommended.
Credit cards: None at the time of publication. Plans are to accept them starting in 2000, but, before arrival, call to check which are accepted.

TOP SECRET

Since moving to the Beaufort area to build the Beaulieu House, Diann Corsaro has quickly formed close friendships with people in the thriving local arts community. One of her closest friends is Del Holt, an artist and illustrator who specializes in painting animal portraits, often with a whimsical twist. Drop by his Pale Horse Studio (843-522-0611) at 1103 Paris Avenue, in nearby Port Royal, to see his series of Carolina cows. Look closely and you'll recognize that the bovines are mottled with spots in the exact shape of a map of the barrier islands around Beaufort and other parts of the coast. Younger guests will enjoy the inspirational children's book Holt illustrated, *The Throwaway Cat* by Steven and Judy Brantley ($16.95, Spring House Books, 1998). Check local book stores in Beaufort for a copy (Holt will autograph it for you when you stop by) or order one before you visit by calling the publisher at 877-559-4759.

99

Gullah Gullah Island

There are places in America that every citizen should be required to visit before they can vote. They are those special links to our past that evoke pride and pain and a real sense of how this country came to be. The Vietnam War Memorial in Washington, D.C., is one of those places along with the battlefield at Gettsyburg, Pennsylvania and the Freedom Trail in Boston, Massachusetts. Another place you've probably never heard about but shouldn't miss is the Penn Center on tiny St. Helena Island, South Carolina.

The Penn Center is the only National Historic Landmark District in the nation that focuses on African-Americans. It is on a list of the hundred most significant archeological sites in South Carolina. Here in 1862, the first school for newly freed black slaves was established in the back room of what was then the Oaks Plantation House. After a brief move to the Brick Baptist Church, an actual school building was erected across from the church two years later. This was the first Penn School (named to recognize the Freedmen's Association of Philadelphia, which provided the first prefabricated building in 1864).

The purpose of the original Penn School was to "foster the self-reliance, productivity, self-discipline, and intellectual growth of Americans of African descent." Although the school closed in 1948 when Beaufort County opened public education to St. Helena Island, the mission of the Penn Center (the name was changed to reflect the institution's new role as a community center and public resource), remained the same. Unfortunately the condition of the simple white clapboard buildings that make up the heart of the center did not fare as well. As recently as 1990, the Penn Center was one of eleven places on the endangered list of historic sites because of its deteriorated condition. A fundraising and renovation effort led by South Carolina Senator Ernest F. Hollings helped saved this national treasure, which Hollings termed, "the commencement of black history in this hemisphere."

The Museum at the Penn Center features exhibits chronicling African-American Gullah culture.

Today, Penn Center and its recently refurbished fifteen buildings and shaded grounds are alive with the sounds of schoolchildren, scholars, and sightseers of all cultures and colors who stroll under the massive sea oaks to hear the stories and music and see the photographs, films, and artifacts that tell the tale of this relatively secret slice of American history.

What sets Penn Center apart from any other historic site in the world is its link to the disappearing Gullah or Geechee (thought to derive from either place names like "Angola" or from the names of specific tribes like "Kissi" or "Gola") culture and language unique to the South Carolina Lowcountry. The Gullah language, a Creole blend of Elizabethan English and African languages, was created out of necessity in the slave coast holding pens where West Africans from Sierra Leone, Senegal, Gambia, Guinea-Bissau, and Liberia and others from the Caribbean found themselves thrown together. Living on isolated plantations on even more isolated Sea Islands, the language and culture developed and flourished. Because of the remoteness of the area, they were the only places in America where a large portion of African culture survived, rather than being stamped out as it was among slaves elsewhere.

Reading about the culture won't cut it. You have to experience it firsthand. It's a language of cadence and intonations. The Gullah "shout," rhythms translated from forbidden drums and old plantation melodies, is pure music magic—haunting, sacred, and addictive. (When you're at the Penn Center, pick up a tape of the local Hallelujah Singers, a Gullah group formed by sacred music vocalist Marlena McGhee Smalls, who played Bubba's mama in the movie *Forrest Gump,* at the bookstore. After you've toured the center, pop the music in your car stereo and let it soak into your soul as you drive around St. Helena Island.) In Charleston, you can watch the women on the sidewalks weave the traditional Gullah sweetgrass baskets, and even tony Hilton Head holds an annual Gullah Festival, but the true Gullah Gullah Island (yes many segments of the Nickelodeon children's television series of the same name were filmed on location in the area) is St. Helena Island. And its headquarters and heart is the Penn Center.

Penn Center is a living history site in the true sense of the word. There aren't tour guides dressed in period costumes like in Williamsburg or Plymouth Plantation; instead there are living ancestors of the freed slaves who live, work, and play in the place where an estimated 65 percent of the land is still owned by African-Americans. The Penn Center has always been the center of their island community. So instead of being a stodgy museum, it is an active meeting place where festivals, classes, workshops, and concerts are held regularly. (Dr. Martin Luther King, Jr. held annual meetings for his Southern Christian Leadership Conference here.) The granddaddy of them all is the Penn Center Heritage Days held every November. There's storytelling, a parade and fashion show, prayer meetings, dancing, demonstrations of Gullah skills and crafts, and of course, delicious Gullah dishes like Frogmore Stew (no frogs, just shrimp, blue crabs, sausage, potatoes, and corn simmered in crab-boil or beer), stewed okra and tomatoes and tater (sweet potato) pone.

You could make a quick trip to Penn Center's York W. Bailey Cultural Museum and get an overview of the history of the place. But to truly begin to understand why the Gullah culture came to be, why what was accomplished at Penn School was so extraordinary, and why it is so crucial now that this culture and this center be preserved, you need to spend a day on St. Helena Island. Take the time to stroll the grounds of Penn Center and browse through the books on Gullah, African-American, and Sea Island history in the bookstore. Taste, hear, smell, and see the Gullah culture. Then at sunset, you can return to where you came from, but remember what the folks at the Penn Center say, "Return home, but keep a piece of what you have seen today in your heart. And come back to see us again."

Secret Information

Location: St. Helena Island, South Carolina.
Address: Martin Luther King, Jr. Drive, P.O. Box 126, St. Helena Island, SC 29920.
Phone: 843-838-2432.
Fax: 843-838-8545.
E-mail: Penncent@hargray.com.
Hours: History and Culture Center 11 A.M. to 4 P.M. Monday through Saturday. Administration office 8:30 A.M. to 5 P.M. Monday through Friday.
Price: Admission is $4 for adults, and $2 for children up to twelve years old.
Reservations: Required for groups of 10 or more.
Credit cards: MasterCard, Visa.

TOP SECRET

Complement a visit to The Penn Center by visiting the lovely Chapel of Ease, Located in the fork in the road about a mile south of the Center. The Chapel was originally built by the planters of Saint Helena Island in the 1840's. It burned down in the 1850's, and today visitors can see the ruins. It is surrounded by three-hundred-year-old oak trees that are draped in Spanish moss, creating a favorite subject for local painters and photographers.

Sea Pines Forest Preserve

100

Wild Hilton Head

If you think the wildest thing in Hilton Head, South Carolina, has to be the pastel madras golf pants found on every manicured golf green, you've obviously been sticking to the main roads. Like everything in Hilton Head, the natural wonders are understated and inconspicuous in keeping with the strict local restrictions and codes. In fact, the prize jewel of Hilton Head's wild side is hidden behind a local school and the water treatment plant (there are other entrances, but we like this one because alligators like to hang out in the canal bordering the playing fields). It's the Sea Pines Forest Preserve and if you make it all the way to Hilton Head and don't spend an hour or two exploring there, you might as well have stayed home.

The preserve is 605 acres of forest, freshwater wetland, lakes, ponds, swamps, abandoned rice fields, and a wildflower meadow smack dab in the middle of one of the priciest plantations this side of Tara. The Charles Fraser family, who developed Sea Pines, established the preserve back in 1959 and added acreage in 1970 for wildlife habitat and outdoor recreation. Walking trails and wooden boardwalks, which follow ante-bellum rice dikes from the 1840s and logging trails from the 1950s, allow visitors to get an up close and personal view of turtles, alligators, herons, ducks, and native flora and fauna. Along the way there are wooden observation decks for viewing marshes and wildlife. (To find your way around, pick up a trail map at any preserve entrance.) Our favorite spot is the shaded deck at Rookery Point where you can sit and watch the wonders unfold across the water at Rookery Island on Lake Mary.

Rookery Island is home to a colony of snow white egrets, those willowy nesting birds that grace every golf course lagoon on the island. In spring and summer hundreds of the elegant birds return to Rookery Island to nest. The tiny island is transformed into a living snowball of sorts—all white and squawking and swaying from the

Surrounded by manicured golf courses and posh homes, the Sea Pines Forest Preserve on Hilton Head is a natural haven for egrets and other wild creatures.

motion of birds arriving and departing. If you're a bird-watcher, you could probably spend the day at Rookery Point, but even if you're the leader of a fearless family from suburbia, you'll still find yourself mesmerized by the sight. Thoughts like, *How do those birds know to come back there every year? and Why to this little island in the middle of a manmade lake?* run through your mind. Plus you'll inevitably pat yourself on the back for discovering this natural wonder less than a mile from the golf greens and beach clubs and tony shops.

Lawton Stables runs guided trail rides through the preserve and in the summer there's a tractor-pulled, narrated hayride tour, but we prefer going solo and packing a picnic to fuel our explorations. By driving through the Lawton entrance (just past the local schools) you can drive along Lawton Canal Road to the Fish Island Trail. Fish Island, which is the center point of the preserve, is the perfect picnic spot. There are picnic tables overlooking Lake Joe (the preserve's four lake names sound like a folk group—Joe, Thomas, Mary, and Chapin), restrooms, grills, a shelter, and drinking water. You can also fish in any of the stocked lakes, provided you're a Sea Pines owner, guest, or employee. Stop by the CSA Security Office on Greenwood Drive for a fishing permit if you're staying in Sea Pines. Sitting by a deep blue lake or hiking through shady woods is a nice break from the beach, even for those of us who love sun, sand, and surf.

In addition to natural wonders, the Sea Pines Forest Preserve boasts its share of local history and lore. As one tractor-hayride driver tells it, an escaped pet monkey lives in the forest and has been spotted high in the trees by more than one tourist. We're not sure if it was the monkey or the tourist who was high, but asking small children to keep an eye out for the monkey does seem to help them hike a bit further before whining. The other legends are better documented and involve the island's original settlers—nomadic Indians who lived more than four thousand years ago. These Native Americans were shellfish lovers and tossed the shells over their shoulder much like we do today with the peanut casings at a bar or a baseball game. Those shells piled up over time and today you can still see the mound created outside the Indian huts by all that shellfish shucking. It's called the Sea Pines Indian Shell Ring, and although it looks exactly like what it is—a circular mound—the fact that it has remained untouched all these years is pretty amazing—as is this entire wild slice of Hilton Head.

Secret Information

Location: Sea Pines Plantation, Hilton Head Island, South Carolina.
Address: The Sea Pines Forest Preserve and Museum Foundation, c/o CSA, Inc., 175 Greenwood Drive, Hilton Head, SC 29928.
Phone: 843-671-6486 or 843-671-6487.
Fax: 843-671-4027.
Hours: Open year-round from sunrise to sunset.
Price: $5 per car if you're not Sea Pines guests.

TOP SECRET

In addition to exploring the Sea Pines Forest Preserve, one of the best ways to reach the wild side of Hilton Head is by kayak. Since the '70s Mike Overton of Outside Hilton Head has been getting everyone from little kids to confirmed landlubbers out on the marshes to experience sea kayaking, to increase awareness of coastal ecology, and to just have the time of their lives. Outside Hilton Head has offices at Shelter Cove, South Beach, the Old Oyster Factory, and Pinckney Island Wildlife Refuge. They offer kayak rentals, lessons, guided nature tours, dolphin tours, a summer Kids Kayak Camp, plus sunrise, sunset, and birding tours. But the "can't miss" wild-side experience is the Midnight Paddle, from 11 P.M. to 1 A.M., offered only on nights with a full moon during the summer. Gliding down silent sea marshes with only the full moon to guide you is more relaxing than any day at the spa. Plus slipping into your kayak while most of the island is slipping into pajamas feels slightly illegal and very cool. For more information and a free brochure and program guide call Outside Hilton Head at 843-686-6996 or visit their Web site at www.outsidehiltonhead.com.

Index

Send Us Your Secrets

Did you discover a great lesser-known place to stay, eat, shop, or have fun during your vacation on the North Carolina or South Carolina coasts? Drop us a card or e-mail with information about it and we'll consider including it in a future edition of *100 Secrets of the Carolina Coast*. Please include your name, address, and phone number in all correspondence. Rights to all submissions immediately become the property of Media Development Group, Inc. Sorry, we cannot return submissions.

Send your secrets to:

100 Secrets of the Carolina Coast
P.O. Box 18373
Knoxville, Tennessee 37928
E-mail: Carolinas@100Secrets.com
Web site: www.100Secrets.com